D0897635

American Foreign Policy in the Congo 1960-1964

American Foreign Policy in the Congo 1960–1964

STEPHEN R. WEISSMAN

Cornell University Press
ITHACA AND LONDON

First published 1974 by Cornell University Press.
Published in the United Kingdom by Cornell University Press Ltd.,
2-4 Brook Street, London W1Y 1AA.

International Standard Book Number 0-8014-0812-1
Library of Congress Catalog Card Number 73-14064

Printed in the United States of America by Vail-Ballou Press, Inc.

Contents

Preface 7
Abbreviations 11
Introduction: The Setting 15
Congo Politics at Independence 15
Foreign Government Interests 23
American Economic Interests 28

PART I. THE ANTI-COMMUNISM OF MODERATE REPUBLICANS

I. Predispositions and First Moves 43
Deference to the Belgians: Conservative Perspectives on Africa 43
The International Communist Threat: From Chaos to Communism 52
The United Nations Umbrella 55

II. Collision with Lumumba 64
The Dispute over Katanga 66
The Overthrow of Lumumba 85

III. New Difficulties 100

PART II. THE ANTI-COMMUNISM OF LIBERAL DEMOCRATS

IV. The Kennedy Reappraisal 115
Greater Deference to African Nationalism and a Liberal Recipe for Its Development 116
Sophisticated Anti-Communism 133
The February 21 Resolution 136
The Road to Lovanium 144

V. The Battle against Katanga 152

Operation "Rumpunch" and "Round One" 153
"Round Two" 161
A Peaceful Interlude 170
"Round Three" 183
A Note on Decision-making in the Kennedy Administration 191

VI. Liberalism: The View from Leopoldville 195

The Adoula Government 200
American Influence 204

VII. From Kennedy to Johnson 211

Toward a Belgo-American Protectorate 211
The Nature of the 1964 Rebellion 214
American Perspectives on the Rebellion 222
Intervention before the Fall of Stanleyville 226
Intervention after the Fall of Stanleyville 236
The Stanleyville Airlift 246

PART III. EVALUATION

VIII. A Critique of the Basic Assumptions of American Congo Policy 257

The International Communist Threat: Moderate Republican and Liberal Democratic Versions 257
Moderate Conservatism and Liberalism in the Congo 282
An Overall Judgment 285

IX. Explanations and Conclusions 291

The Roots of American Policy 291
The Congo and U.S. Foreign Policy 299

Bibliography 304
Index 316

Preface

In this study of American foreign policy in the Congo from 1960 to 1964, I have sought to determine precisely what U.S. policies were—those pursued and those seriously considered—and on what intellectual assumptions they were based. I have inquired whether these assumptions were true, and have also tried to set forth the social, cultural, psychological, and historical factors that gave rise to them. Finally, I have discussed the ways in which the Congolese political system was affected by U.S. policies.

The introduction analyzes the Congo political situation at Independence and discusses foreign interest in Congolese politics. American economic stakes in the region are described, but their political significance is not prejudged. Parts I and II compare the policies of three American administrations in the Congo; Part III evaluates these policies. The conclusion suggests that the Congo performance was a fairly typical case of American intervention in the Third World, and of the forms it takes under different political administrations.

Sources of information for a study of recent American policy in the Congo are unusually abundant. The interests of many nations converged on the Congo; hence there is a wide range of newspaper and periodical reporting available. Many key actors in the Congo crisis have written memoirs, among whom are three African prime ministers, an American president, several top officials of the U.N. operation in the Congo, Belgian ministers of foreign and African affairs, leading State Department figures, an American and a British ambassador, European and South African mercenary leaders, plus several "inside dopesters" of varying description. Finally, of great value are the yearly volumes of documents published by the Belgian Centre de Recherche et d'Information Socio-Politiques (CRISP). These contain not only the best record of domestic forces in the Congo, but also important information (including unpublished diplomatic papers) regarding the policies of foreign powers.

In the course of my research, I personally interviewed virtually every important contributor to American Congo policy in the years 1960 to 1964, from under secretaries of state down to embassy personnel, from White House aides to State and Defense Department bureacrats, to congressmen and their staffs. The CIA's role was communicated by individuals with good "agency" contacts. Almost all of these men are no longer concerned with Congo policy; a large number have left the government. To encourage open conversation I guaranteed each interviewee anonymity (except when the same thought had been expressed in his published writings). Therefore, although it is always made clear which administration (or faction thereof) is being cited, quotations sometimes occur without specific references.

In addition to official personnel, I spoke (always confidentially) with informal government advisers, businessmen, lobbyists, reporters, and academicians.* The interviews averaged about two hours, and some went on for many hours or had to be conducted over weeks and months. The problem of faulty memory was dealt with by extensive cross-checking between interviews, and between interviews and more conventional sources.

From 1969 to 1971, I taught at the former Université Libre du Congo in Kisangani (once Stanleyville) and thus had the opportunity to talk with several important Congolese politicians and an assortment of Western observers—diplomats, businessmen, missionaries, and professors—who had "lived" the events which this book describes.

* There is also some correspondence. The author is willing to let other scholars examine his notes and written communications, provided they agree to respect the anonymity of his respondents.

Acknowledgments

I am greatly indebted to Professor Hans J. Morgenthau of the University of Chicago, who encouraged me to follow my own research interests, helped persuade some important and busy people to grant me interviews, and provided a most valuable and thorough criticism of my first draft which nevertheless left room for some honest differences of opinion. In my experience, such a happy combination of rigorous intellectual standards and open-minded tolerance is seldom encountered in academic life, though it represents the essence of good teaching. To Professor Aristide R. Zolberg, who gave me the benefit of his theoretical insights into African politics, I also want to express my gratitude.

At several stages I was fortunate in receiving comments on the manuscript by academic readers. I would particularly like to thank Catherine Hoskyns, Benoît Verhaegen, Herbert Weiss, and Crawford Young for their helpful suggestions which contributed greatly to the clarification of my own thinking. My editor at Cornell University Press helped in many ways to improve the lucidity of the text.

Preparing a manuscript for publication is probably one of the last remaining family enterprises. I owe the most to my wife, Nancy, who was deeply involved in the productive process. She discussed my ideas, encouraged my work, and furnished much wise counsel. She also shared a variety of experiences with me as the course of this research took us to Africa (for sixteen months), Europe, and parts of the United States. My son, Daniel, graciously allowed me to type while he slumbered in his crib in our cozy New York apartment. Later on, in Zaire,* he good-naturedly left me time to work—grasping the increasingly attractive opportunity to play outside with his friends and simultaneously perfect his Swahili. My father-in-law, David Schaff, provided useful comments on parts of this work and helped check out some far-off sources while I was abroad. The long-range contribution of my mother and late

* In November 1971, the Democratic Republic of the Congo was officially renamed the "Republic of Zaire."

father, Beatrice and Herman Weissman, was naturally enormous. In more immediate terms, my mother was the leading force in a floating typing pool which spanned two continents and also included my wife, myself, and various friends and acquaintances.

Finally, I am greatly indebted to hundreds of people—officials, former officials, informed individuals, my students at the National University of Zaire in Kisangani—who gave me the benefit of their knowledge and insight, and encouraged my work. I regret that circumstances are such that I cannot thank each of them individually. I hope they will find the finished product helpful in understanding what has happened, and continues to happen, in America's relations with Zaire, and with the Third World generally.

STEPHEN R. WEISSMAN

Palo Alto, California

Abbreviations

AAI	African-American Institute
ABAKO	Alliance des Bakongo
AFL-CIO	American Federation of Labor and Congress of Industrial Organizations
AID	Agency for International Development (U.S.)
AMAX	American Metal Climax, Inc.
ANACONGO	Société Congolaise pour la Production, la Manufacture et le Commerce d'Ananas
ANC	Congo National Army
APL	Armée Populaire de Libération
BALUBAKAT	Association des Baluba du Katanga
BAUXICONGO	Société de Recherches et d'Exploitation de Bauxites au Congo
BND	Bloc National Démocratique
CEGEAC	Compagnie Générale d'Automobiles et d'Aviation au Congo
CEREA	Centre de Regroupement Africain
CFL	Compagnie des Chemins de Fer du Congo Supérieur aux Grands Lacs Africains
CIA	Central Intelligence Agency
CICO	Ciments du Congo
CNL	Committee of National Liberation
COBEGA	Société pour la Fabrication au Congo de Boîtes Métalliques et de tous Articles en Tôle Émaillée
CONAKAT	Confédération des Associations Tribales du Katanga

CRISP	Centre de Recherche et d'Information Socio-Politiques
FILTISAF	Filatures et Tissages Africains
FORMINIERE	Société Internationale Forestière et Minière du Congo
GPRA	Algerian Provisional Government
HEW	Department of Health, Education, and Welfare (U.S.)
ICA	International Cooperation Administration (U.S.)
ICFTU	International Confederation of Free Trade Unions
MNC	Mouvement National Congolais
MNC-K	Mouvement National Congolais-Kalonji
MNC-L	Mouvement National Congolais-Lumumba
NATO	North Atlantic Treaty Organization
OAU	Organization of African Unity
ONUC	Opération des Nations Unies au Congo
PSA	Parti Solidaire Africain
PUNA	Parti de l'Unité Nationale
RADECO	Rassemblement des Démocrates du Congo
SOCOBANQUE	Société Congolaise de Banque
TANKS	Tanganyika Concessions, Ltd.
UNESCO	United Nations Educational, Scientific, and Cultural Organization
UNF	United Nations Force

American Foreign Policy in the Congo 1960-1964

Introduction: The Setting

On June 30, 1960, the Congo received its Independence from Belgium. It emerged as a politically fragile but internationally important state in the midst of a world diplomatic crisis. In retrospect, it was likely that the Congo would become a focus of Cold War competition.

Congo Politics at Independence

As elsewhere in Africa and among the new nations, political integration was hindered by the persistence of primordial ties.[1] Belgian "paternalism" had provided a particularly dense overlay of modern institutions: the "colonial trinity" of corporations, missions, and administration. Yet while these institutions generally undermined traditional authorities, some of which were already quite decadent, they did not produce a substitute framework for national loyalty. What they did was to accentuate ethnic and regional cleavages while giving them newer, more modern forms.[2]

This phenomenon is largely explained by the dynamism of colonial economic structures.[3] Toward 1960, the Congo had the

[1] See Aristide R. Zolberg, "The Structure of Political Conflict in the New States of Tropical Africa," *American Political Science Review*, LXII (Mar., 1968), 70–87.

[2] René Lemarchand, *Political Awakening in the Belgian Congo* (Berkeley, 1964), pp. 94–121, 285–288; Crawford Young, *Politics in the Congo: Decolonization and Independence* (Princeton, 1965), pp. 232–272.

[3] By far the best treatment of this subject is Michel Merlier, *Le Congo de la colonisation belge à l'indépendance* (Paris, 1962), pp. 107–116, 150–154, 165, 210–213, and *passim*.

largest precentage of wage earners in black Africa, and much administrative activity was devoted to the stabilization, direction, and good discipline of this labor force. At the same time, economic development took place under the auspices of export-oriented foreign trusts. This meant that productive activity was organized around a few regional "poles," which forwarded minerals and agricultural goods to world markets, and profits to Brussels and other European capitals. This form of development precluded the creation of a large interior market, with its accompanying transportation nets and mixing of ethnic groups at the scale of the whole society. Within, as well as between, regions, the interaction among European profit-makers and modernizers and favorably situated or adaptable ethnic groups superimposed socio-professional divisions on ethnic ones. These changes gave traditional conflicts a new relevance. Even more important, they brought previously isolated or fragmented groups into direct and unified contention. The first political stirrings in the Congo faithfully reflected socioeconomic competition in the cities (Bakongo vs. Bangala in Leopoldville, Lulua vs. Baluba in Lulabourg, Mongo vs. Ngombe in Coquilhatville, Lunda vs. Kasai Baluba in Elizabethville), and the particularism of well-endowed and evolved regions (Leopoldville, South Katanga).

Especially in the Congo, successful decolonization required a strong set of national political institutions. But Belgium's paternal obliviousness to the forces of change in Africa, and her peculiar political traditions, pointed in the opposite direction.[4] In former French and British Africa, an educated, urban, more nationally oriented elite seized the initiative, battled the colonial power and earned its grudging recognition, created a political machine and national alliances, and then hung on as the enlargement of the electorate produced "a general politicization of primordial ties." [5]

[4] Young, pp. 34–40, 176–178; Catherine Hoskyns, *The Congo Since Independence: January 1960–December 1961* (London, 1965), pp. 33–34.

[5] Aristide R. Zolberg, *Creating Political Order: The Party States of West Africa* (Chicago, 1966), p. 22; see also pp. 9–36.

In the Congo, the last act came first, and there was little time before June 30, 1960, for the preceding ones. The first elections were communal (1957) and territorial (1959), based on universal male suffrage. It was not until 1959 that such integrating mechanisms as parties and labor unions were permitted to form and organize relatively freely. Belgium's belated stirring, and the wall of mistrust that separated her from the Congolese political elite, resulted in a much-abbreviated transition to Independence.[6] Even the most nationally oriented politicians were compelled to rely on the pre-existing ethnic and regional associations. Lack of time also hindered the rationalization of party structures (including mechanisms for leader selection). Belgium's constitutional legacy to the Congolese was an additional force for fragmentation. There would be no provisional government to reap the rewards of power. The election system focused attention on local arenas and discouraged any nationalization of political forces.[7] The *Loi Fondamentale* set up a complicated federal system which left significant power in the hands of provincial governments, provided for a bicameral legislature and a dual executive, and forced "an already small and inexperienced political elite" to divide itself among several "different echelons of government." [8] Finally, administration (and settler) intervention in the political process, in favor of more "moderate-looking" politico-ethnic factions, was a polarizing force on both the provincial and national levels. It was an important factor, for example, in the conflict situation that led to (1) the tension between the two leading candidates for national leadership (Joseph Kasavubu and Patrice Lumumba) in the weeks preceding Independence, (2) the failure to form a compromise

[6] Herbert Weiss, *Political Protest in the Congo: The Parti Solidaire Africain During the Independence Struggle* (Princeton, 1967), pp. 9–11, 102–107; Young, pp. 157–161.

[7] Jules Gérard-Libois and Benoît Verhaegen, *Congo 1960* (Brussels, 1961), pp. 258–259; Weiss, pp. 47–49.

[8] *Ibid.*, pp. 57, 59; Gérard-Libois and Verhaegen, p. 1067. For a brief exposition of the federalist aspects, see Benoît Verhaegen, *Congo 1961* (Brussels, 1962), p. 102.

provincial government in Katanga, and (3) a state of emergency in Maniema (Kivu).[9]

Only one "national" party was therefore successful in the parliamentary election of May 1960. This was the *Mouvement National Congolais-Lumumba* (MNC-L). The MNC had been formed by the most de-tribalized, active, and politically conscious segment of the urban elite.[10] After a split between Lumumba and a more moderate faction (MNC-Kalonji), the MNC-L drew heavily upon the Batetela-Bakusu urban elite whose cultural background ("extreme fragmentation of political structures and dispersion of family clan groups") and geographical dispersion in five of the six Congo provinces made it a suitable carrier of nationalist ideas.[11] Although Lumumba was himself a Mutetela, and there was a heavy representation of Tetela in his immediate entourage, the MNC-L did not pursue a tribalist policy: its organization was both modern and national. Cadres were generally not selected on the basis of ethnic affinity or customary rank, but on grounds of competence, education, and above all fidelity to the party's rudimentary nationalist ideology and paramount leader. The MNC-L had its greatest electoral success among the Mongo cultures of the central Congo. Lacking centralized political institutions, spread out as minorities in five provinces, and largely dependent on wealth created in the backyards of other groups, the Mongo were especially open to a nationalist approach. (This does not mean that the average Mongo was less traditional or less "ethnic" than other Congolese. Rather, it was the *kind* of traditional structure he had and his geopolitical situation which predisposed him to follow modern nationalist leadership.) During the elections, Lumumba made pragmatic alliances with a number of particularist forces as well, in order to facilitate the rapid implantation of his party (Lulua in Central Kasai, little chiefs in Orientale Province, Eastern

[9] On Maniema, see Benoît Verhaegen, *Rébellions au Congo,* II (Brussels, 1969), 111–117. For the situation in Katanga, consult Jules Gérard-Libois, *Sécession au Katanga* (Brussels, 1963), pp. 64–82. The Kasavubu-Lumumba dispute is treated in Hoskyns, pp. 74–77.

[10] Weiss, p. 27.

[11] Verhaegen, *Rébellions,* II, 38–39.

Mongo customary chiefs in Kasai and Kivu).[12] In the end, the MNC-L won (with some minor allied parties) 40 out of 137 seats in the Chamber of Representatives. The remainder went to 23 ethnic and regional parties, none of which received more than 13 seats.

Lumumba was able to form the core of a governing coalition through agreements with leaders in regional parties who shared his nationalism and vaguely populist tone, such as the Parti Solidaire Africain (PSA), Centre de Regroupement Africain (CEREA), and Association des Baluba du Katanga (BALUBAKAT). But these parties were themselves beset by particularism and by the divisive temptations of a race for power in the fragmented situation which accompanied the formation of provincial and national governments.[13] Finally, Lumumba produced a sort of grand coalition. The Congo's first government was quite a patchwork: "The uneven distribution of some 22 ministerial chairs among twelve different parties was by itself a symptom of the fragility of the coalition." [14]

At the moment of Independence the shaky central power faced a number of difficult problems. First, there was the reappearance of separatist tendencies in the fiefs of the Bakongo (Leopoldville) and the Lunda-Bayeke (South Katanga). Mediation by Ghanaian and Israeli diplomats helped Lumumba toward an agreement with the Bakongo leader, Joseph Kasavubu of the ABAKO (Alliance des Bakongo) party. Kasavubu became Chief of State, but the embers of Bakongo nationalism continued to smolder.[15] A more serious situation existed in Katanga. There the provincial govern-

[12] Gérard-Libois and Verhaegen, *Congo 1960,* pp. 1072–1074; Verhaegen, *Rébellions, II,* 90–93, 158–159, 34, 38, 98–99.

[13] Gérard-Libois and Verhaegen, *Congo 1960,* p. 299; Weiss, pp. 279–281, 287–290, discusses the situation in the PSA.

[14] René Lemarchand, "How Lumumba Came to Power," in Helen Kitchen (ed.), *Footnotes to the Congo Story: An "Africa Report" Anthology* (New York, 1967), p. 16.

[15] Gérard-Libois and Verhaegen, *Congo 1960,* pp. 158–163; Hoskyns, p. 69.

ment—run by CONAKAT (Confédération des Associations Tribales du Katanga), the Lunda and Bayeke ethnic party, and backed by settlers—was threatening to secede. Katanga was "the hinge of the Congo's economy," accounting for "about one-third of all domestic production and income, between 40 and 50 percent of the foreign trade, and 40 percent of the public revenue."[16] If Katanga withdrew, the Central Government would lose the financial means of effective power.

Second, certain influential politicians were worried about "leftist" tendencies in the Lumumba cabinet and would not fail to react strongly to any moves that seemed to confirm their fears. Although Sartre's description of the MNC-L, "the Congolese *petit bourgeoisie* in the act of discovering its class ideology," is useful in view of the "integrationist" and nonradical demands of the Congolese clerks who ran the party, it does not (as Sartre himself recognizes) fully explain Lumumba's sympathy with the Ghana-Guinea brand of "left nationalism," nor his particular openness to some of the clamor from below.[17] By 1960 most "Lumumbist" leaders were criticizing the "cult" of European advisers among Congolese politicians, and seeking to create nonethnic "mass" parties along the lines of the West African experience. This was enough to impart a populist and anti-Belgian tone to much of their propaganda. Particularly during the election campaign, the MNC-L, PSA, and CEREA sections of the petty bourgeoisie seemed to draw nearer to the subelite's demands for Africanization and the masses' demands for a better life. They also became more suspicious of Belgian influences (including the Catholic church) which were supporting their "moderate" opponents.[18] Among Lumumba's ministers, Antoine Gizenga and Pierre Mulele of PSA and Anicet Kashamura and Marcel Bisukiro of CEREA appeared particularly "hard." Responding perhaps to the alienation of agricultural wage earners in their home areas, they had adopted

[16] Hoskyns, p. 15.

[17] Jean-Paul Sartre's long preface in Jean Van Lierde, *La Pensée politique de Patrice Lumumba* (Paris, 1963), pp. xvii–xx, xliii.

[18] Verhaegen, *Rébellions,* II, 94–104, 111–117; Weiss, pp. 186–250; Gérard-Libois and Verhaegen, *Congo 1960,* pp. 180–181, 346–347.

a more programmatic and demanding style than others, and had associated with some foreign leftists—mainly African left-nationalists.[19]

Opposition to these inclinations centered around several moderate personalities who were ill-suited to be mass leaders and had never fully broken the umbilical cord of Belgian tutelage. While it would be unfair to label such important figures as Jean Bolikango (the Bangala leader), Joseph Ileo, and Cyrille Adoula as "collaborationists," they were closely connected with Western religious, syndical, and political movements, benefited from Belgian support in the election campaign, and appeared to have kept up the paternal tradition of white advisers.[20] In the van of any opposition they

19 On the "left-wing" of CEREA, see Verhaegen, *Rébellions,* II, 70–75, 84; note also the statistical data on its class base in J. C. Willame, *Les Provinces du Congo: Structure et fonctionnement,* IV (Leopoldville: IRES Lovanium, 1964–1965), 113, 126–127. The PSA left faction is analyzed by Renée C. Fox, Willy de Craemer, and Jean-Marie Ribeaucourt, "The Second Independence: A Case Study of the Kwilu Rebellion in the Congo," *Comparative Studies in Society and History,* VIII (Oct., 1965), 82–93; Weiss, pp. 79–82, stresses elite syndical and political backgrounds.

The author is not suggesting that any significant class influences were independent of favorable ethnic, cultural, and historical contexts.

20 Bolikango had worked for 30 years as a monitor in Catholic schools, and had presided over several important alumni and ethnic associations in Leopoldville. His moderate approach earned him the support of the colonial Administration and the Catholic missions. In Aug. 1959, he was appointed *Commissaire Générale Adjoint d'Information,* the highest administrative post ever given to a Congolese. In June 1960, Belgian authorities considered him "too friendly" to be a viable Prime Minister.

Ileo had long-established ties with the Belgian-sponsored Christian movement. With the cooperation of Belgian Catholic advisers, he and several other leading Congolese drafted a moderate Independence plan in 1956. Later, he became a prominent official in the Catholic press. According to De Vos and Kalanda, both personal conservatism and European advisers influenced his mid-1959 split with Lumumba. Supported by the Belgian government, Ileo and Bolikango tried to organize a "rightist" front against Lumumba in May 1960.

Adoula was associated with the political and syndical branches of the Belgian Socialist Party and the American Federation of Labor and Congress of Industrial Organizations (AFL-CIO) -dominated International Confederation of Free Trade Unions (ICFTU). He joined Ileo in opposing Lumum-

might create, one would expect to see those who for personal or ethnic reasons had found it difficult to accept a Lumumba government—particularly Albert Kalonji, the Kasai Baluba leader, and Kasavubu.[21]

Third, for the subelites who constituted the subaltern cadres of the state apparatus, Independence was an occasion for the general social promotion that Belgian paternalism could never admit and for an Africanization of administration parallel to that which was taking place in the political sphere. Lumumba had some awareness of the possibility of a "revolt of the clerks" (particularly in the army), but he was also concerned lest a too rapid Africanization produce chaos and inefficiency.[22] Whatever course it followed, the Lumumba government, which desperately needed the state apparatus, was bound to be taking chances.

Lastly, the rural masses and young militants who backed the Lumumbist parties entertained an unrealistic vision of the rewards of Independence. Their coming disillusion could create disorder or, just as bad, disengagement and apathy. To counterbalance this tendency, Lumumba could rely on his nationalist charisma, his sensitivity to popular aspirations, and his good political in-

ba's leadership, probably for similar reasons. Belgian socialist and liberal milieux proposed him as a possible Prime Minister in 1960. As will be shown later, Adoula kept up his politico-syndical ties and his habit of consulting white advisers throughout his political career.

On the political views of this group, see W. J. Ganshof van der Meersch, *Fin de la souveraineté belge au Congo* (Brussels, 1963), pp. 157–59, 205–206; Gérard-Libois and Verhaegen, *Congo 1960,* pp. 276, 657–690; also see below on the Kasavubu coup. Personal background details are based on the following sources: Lemarchand, pp. 181–182, 194; B. Verhaegen, "Les Associations congolaises à Léopoldville et dans le Bas-Congo avant 1960," *Cahiers Economiques et Sociaux,* VIII (Sept., 1970), 389–416; A. Mabika Kalanda, *La Remise en question* (Brussels, 1967), pp. 20–21, 27; Pierre De Vos, *Vie et mort de Lumumba* (Paris, 1961), pp. 118–119, 138–139; "Poids socio-politique des ressortissants de l'Equateur à Kinshasa," *Courrier Africain,* No. 84, Nov. 8, 1968, *passim.*

21 On Kasavubu, see Charles-André Gilis, *Kasavubu au coeur du drame congolais* (Brussels, 1964).

22 Gérard-Libois and Verhaegen, *Congo 1960,* pp. 320–322, 346–359, 364; Hoskyns, pp. 60–62.

stincts, and on future opportunities for political education and organization.[23]

Foreign Government Interests

Western European governments were particularly concerned with events in the Congo. Belgium had an obvious interest in the security of the 100,000 Europeans in the country, since the overwhelming majority were Belgians. Many were employees of the government or the private sector who looked forward to long careers in relatively comfortable material circumstances. Others were independent businessmen and missionaries who considered themselves permanent residents. Approximately one-third of the Europeans lived in the rich mining province of Katanga.[24]

However, as Bob Dylan has pointed out,[25] the lives of nationals do not, in themselves, count for much on the chessboard of international diplomacy. Actually, most of the Belgian presence was inextricably bound up with the Belgian corporate and governmental stake in the Congo's economy. Gérard-Libois writes that,

> Société Générale de Belgique is unquestionably the most important financial group in the Congo. It is generally admitted that it controls directly or indirectly, 70% of the Congolese economy. . . . Furthermore it should be specified that its influence is practically absolute in certain mining industries (copper, cobalt, diamond, uranium) and in maritime and railroad transportation. Its mining activity is especially concentrated in Katanga and Kasai.
>
> Société Générale is equally interested in 2 firms which are active in neighboring territories of the Congo, but financially tied to Congolese companies: Tanganyika Concessions Ltd. and the Diamond Company of Angola.[26]

23 Several years later, some of Lumumba's successors who had tried unsuccessfully to lead a rural-based revolution lamented their first leader's demise: "How it is to be regretted that the foreigners did not understand P. Lumumba, for he was the only one to control the whole population." *Courrier Africain,* Feb. 18, 1967, p. 13.

24 Hoskyns, pp. 215, 34.

25 In his song, "Only Pawns in Their Game."

26 Gérard-Libois, *Sécession,* p. 107.

The veritable jewel in Société Générale's crown was Union Minière du Haut Katanga, which had "exclusive mining rights over a large area of Katanga until March 1990." It also controlled the company which refined the metals in Belgium, and "a whole range of other Katangan enterprises." [27] Union Minière's importance is shown by the following statistics. The mining industry produced 22 percent of the Congo's gross national product and 60 percent of its exports. Of this production, 75 percent came from Katanga. More than half of the total mining production, and 70 percent of Katanga's, consisted of copper—of which Union Minière had a monopoly. It was estimated that half of the Congo's budgetary receipts and the majority of its foreign exchange came from Katanga.[28]

Société Générale's empire had been built with the collaboration of the Belgian government, which traditionally provided administrative structures and military force. Even without the political influence of the most important financial group in Belgium's highly centralized economy,[29] Brussels would have had a substantial vested interest in the Congo economy. An "unofficial calculation" in 1960 indicated that a political break with the Congo would produce "a loss of about 7 percent of the total receipts in the balance of payments from the loss of the Congo export market," the "loss of about 30 percent of the overseas operations of transport and insurance firms, and the loss of about 77 million dollars in revenue from investments. In addition, it was estimated that 2 percent of the working population would be unemployed." Finally, the Belgian budget would have to decrease by "140–156 million each year" from the cost of "reintegration of approximately 10,000 administrative officers, payments on the part of the public debt guaranteed by Belgium, payments to former colonial servants now paid by the Congo, and the loss of various taxes." [30]

Clearly, any Belgian government would feel impelled to "safe-

[27] Hoskyns, pp. 17–18.

[28] *Courrier Africain,* Mar. 4, 1960, pp. 15–16.

[29] Young, pp. 17–18.

[30] Hoskyns, pp. 52–53.

guard for the long run the legal status of private enterprises in the Congo," and "to protect in the short run the industrial installations and economic infrastructure of the regions of the greatest importance from the point of view of Belgian investors (Katanga, South Kasai, Lower Congo, and Leopoldville)." [31] The Belgians did not have to be particularly humanitarian in order to protect lives; the "lives" involved were mostly part of the "infrastructure" that needed saving. (As will be shown later, a good many Belgians have lost their lives—particularly missionaries and settlers—because their government is preoccupied with the infrastructure.) If there was a break with Leopoldville, Belgium could be expected to attend to "the regions where the Belgian's interests found themselves concentrated (Katanga, South Kasai)." In pursuing its basic objectives, Belgium would have to consider the need to maintain "a certain favorable image" in the world; such an image was not simply a matter of prestige, but "a vital socioeconomic factor." [32] In this connection, one may note a certain amount of "openness" to American influence.[33]

France, West Germany, and Italy were leading consumers of Katanga copper and other minerals. They had, therefore, an understandable concern for stability on the Congo-Rhodesia Copperbelt. The British took most of their copper from the Rhodesian side, and would naturally be concerned by any threatening changes in a contiguous territory.[34] At this moment they were also sensible to

[31] Jules Gérard-Libois, *Le Rôle de la Belgique dans l'Opération des Nations Unies au Congo (1960–1964)*, Travaux Africains nos. 68–71 (Brussels, 1966), p. 58.

[32] *Ibid.*, pp. 11, 58.

[33] Gérard-Libois, *Sécession*, p. 181. See also, J. J. Servan-Schreiber, *The American Challenge* (New York, 1969), pp. 168, 44.

[34] *Christian Science Monitor*, Nov. 28, 1962, p. 3; INFORCONGO, *L'Economie du Congo Belge et du Ruanda-Urundi* (Brussels, 1958), p. 28; F. Taylor Ostrander, "The Corporate Structure of Rhodesian Copperbelt Mining Enterprise," New York, Aug. 31, 1962, p. 5 (mimeographed); Organisation de Coopération et de Développement Economiques, *L'Industrie des metaux non-ferreux* (Paris: O.C.D.E., 1967), pp. 22–27, gives recent figures.

any developments that might affect the delicate white-black balance in the Rhodesian Federation (still a British colony, but largely autonomous). Outside of the Belgians, the British had the largest investment stake in the Congo, including the great trading firm Unilever, and an important role in Union Minière through Tanganyika Concessions. Even more important, British investors were heavily engaged in Southern and Central Africa: the Congo, and particularly Katanga, appeared as the head of a gateway down which black nationalist armies might someday march. The Conservative government in England was particularly susceptible to right-wing pressure.[35]

French interests were a bit more complicated. In addition to the Katanga resources, France had to worry about the comportment of the power in Leopoldville. "Bad behavior" would threaten the French sphere of influence in the conservative, Balkanized states of ex-French equatorial Africa.[36] Above all, in the Congo, de Gaulle's diplomacy of restoring French "grandeur" required a subtle and flexible approach.

As colonial powers (the British in Central and East Africa, the French, still, in Algeria), the United Kingdom and France were also interested in preserving their liberty of action in Africa. This implied strong resistance to the new Afro-Asian nations' desire to use the United Nations as an instrument of rapid decolonization.[37] In general, Gaullist nationalism could pursue a more independent and unbending diplomacy than British conservatism, which was counting heavily on its "special relationship" with the Americans in European affairs.

For countries like Portugal—holding fast to Angola and Mozambique—the white-settler government in Rhodesia, and the Union of South Africa, the Congo was a last barrier before the onslaught of African nationalism. Even before Independence, the

[35] Hoskyns, p. 287; Gérard-Libois, *Sécession,* p. 198.

[36] Gérard-Libois, *Sécession,* pp. 170, 205; Verhaegen, *Congo 1961,* pp. 302–305.

[37] Ernest W. Lefever, *Crisis in the Congo: A United Nations Force in Action* (Washington, 1965), p. 118; Hoskyns, p. 287.

economic and political advantages of a Katanga-Rhodesian Federation were being explored in Southern Africa and, no doubt, in certain board rooms in London.[38]

The Afro-Asian nations had various objectives in the Congo, as will be seen later. But one can speak of a priority around which most were united: successful decolonization. Thus, in June 1960, the Conference of Independent African States in Addis Ababa devoted a special session to the Congo situation. "The Africans were particularly worried by the divisions among the Congolese leaders and were afraid that any breakdown in the Congo would prejudice the grant of independence in East and Central Africa." [39] As a result, warning telegrams were sent to the U.N., to the Congo, and to Belgium; and African diplomats worked to conciliate the divided Congolese leadership. Possessing little power themselves—the price of economic underdevelopment—the Afro-Asians sought to stay outside the Cold War conflict and to exploit it for their own ends. A significant stage for this diplomacy was the United Nations.[40]

Finally, without broaching here an explanation of American or Soviet objectives, it can be noted that the dispute between the great powers was very much in the background. Both the United States and the Soviet Union had been shifting more and more of their energies to fighting the Cold War in "underdeveloped" areas. As the Congo received Independence, the international atmosphere was particularly tense. In May the Paris summit conference blew up. In June anti-American riots forced President Eisenhower to cancel his trip to Japan. On July 1, a U.S. RB-47 reconnaissance plane was shot down over the Soviet Union. On the 3rd, the sugar quota for Castro's Cuba was cut from the American market. On the 9th, Premier Khrushchev warned that "Soviet artillerymen can support Cuba with rocket fire." The two superpowers would

38 Gérard-Libois, *Sécession*, pp. 196–197, 319, 53–56.

39 Paul-Henry Gendebien, *L'Intervention des Nations Unies au Congo 1960–1964* (Paris, 1967), pp. 251–252; Hoskyns, p. 84.

40 Hoskyns, p. 111.

certainly be alert to any opportunities or dangers which developed in a significant country like the Congo.

Thus, "in the event of a political crisis, considerable intervention from the outside could be expected." [41] And the political weakness of the Congo increased not only the chances for such a crisis but also the potential efficacy of foreign influence.

American Economic Interests

American officials would have to take account of any important relationships between the economy of the United States (and Western Europe insofar as her economic health was considered of material and strategic interest to the U.S.) and that of the Congo (and its neighbors). However, the significance of such economic interests for American foreign policy cannot be finally determined apart from an analysis of the assumptions, social-historical environments, and behavior of political decision makers.

(1) The Stake in Maintaining Access to Mineral Resources (especially in the Katanga-Rhodesia Copperbelt)

An access interest rather than an investment one was perhaps the most important material incentive for American involvement in the Congo. In 1959 the Congo produced 9 percent of the "Free World's" copper, 49 percent of its cobalt, 69 percent of its industrial diamonds, and 6.5 percent of its tin, as well as a number of specialized metals used in the nuclear and electrical industry.[42] Three-quarters of the mining production came from Katanga; another important area was neighboring South Kasai from which came the industrial diamonds.[43] Across Katanga's Southern frontier, the Copperbelt meandered into Northern Rhodesia, which contributed an additional 15 percent of Free World copper and 12 percent of its cobalt.[44] If geographical contiguity disposed

[41] *Ibid.*, p. 21.

[42] *Ibid.*, p. 14.

[43] *Courrier Africain,* Mar. 4, 1960, pp. 15–16. The most internationally important minerals—cobalt, copper, manganese, most of the columbium-tantalite—came from Katanga.

[44] *United Nations Statistical Yearbook 1962* (New York, 1963), pp. 152, 160.

American officials to consider the Copperbelt a unit, this was reinforced by an example of regional planning across colonial frontiers. From 1956–1960 all hydroelectric power for the Rhodesian mines came from dams in Katanga. Even after the commissioning of the Kariba Dam on the Zambezi River between Northern and Southern Rhodesia, Katanga continued to be an important source of power.[45]

The U.S. had a vested interest in the health and good functioning of mining facilities on the Katanga-Rhodesia Copperbelt. Katanga alone provided in 1960 approximately three-quarters of the cobalt imported into the U.S. and one-half of the tantalum. Both minerals had important strategic uses in aerospace production, and were mined in only small quantities in the U.S. The two sides of the Copperbelt accounted for nearly 10 percent of U.S. copper imports in the 1950's, with three-quarters of this inflow coming from Rhodesia. The U.S. imported about one-quarter of its copper needs. The strategic significance of this source of supply was even greater than the above figures suggest. The minerals requirements of the Korean War had led the U.S. government to loan $60 million to the Rhodesian copper industry, and a third of this amount had gone to the Rhodesian-Congo Power Corporation. The loans were largely repayable by deliveries of copper and cobalt to U.S. stockpiles. Outside of the Copperbelt, but not far from Katanga, were the industrial diamonds of South Kasai. These provided 80 percent of America's supply (there was no domestic production).[46] They were used to manufacture grind-

[45] Ostrander, p. 8; William J. Barber, *The Economy of Central Africa: A Case Study of Economic Development in a Dualistic Society* (London, 1961), p. 124.

[46] U.S. Bureau of Mines, *Minerals Yearbook 1960* (Washington, 1961), pp. 385–387, 395–397, 426–427, 145–153; U.S. Bureau of Census, *Statistical Abstract of the United States 1966* (Washington, 1967), p. 705; Barber, pp. 125–126.

A quarter of the cobalt was used in high-temperature, high-strength alloys for jet engines, rocket nozzles, gas turbines, and other outer-space equipment. Tantalum had high-temperature, corrosion-resistant applications in missiles, rockets, and spacecraft.

ing wheels, mining drills, and other abrasives utilized by the mining, construction, electronics, and aircraft industries.[47]

Western Europe was almost totally dependent upon Katangan and Rhodesian mines for its copper imports. This gave America an *indirect* interest in the stability of mining operations. During the summer of 1960, several U.S. business periodicals observed that any protracted closing of the Katanga mines would "seriously affect" the U.S. copper market. Shortages in Europe would raise copper prices on the London Metal Exchange, and would provoke extraordinary purchases of copper in Chile and the United States. The most immediate consequence would be a rise in prices to metal consumers. Even U.S. coppermen would not necessarily benefit from such an uncontrolled train of price rises, since consumers might begin to substitute aluminum for copper.[48] Also, Europe's industrial vitality would certainly be diminished by large price rises or serious shortages of copper. With its massive and rapidly growing investment in the North Atlantic Treaty Organization (NATO) economy, the United States had a material as well as a strategic stake in resources "essential to the industrial life of Western Europe." [49]

Although the resource stake was clearly important, it did not itself imply an ironclad preference for right-wing government in the Congo or an obsession with stability in Katanga. Presumably, mutually profitable trade relations could be worked out with leader-

[47] Pierre Gamme, *Le Diamant dans le monde* (Brussels, 1947), pp. 5, 35, 75, emphasizes the military uses of industrial diamonds. See too "How to Do Business Successfully in Africa," *Business Abroad,* XCIII (Dec., 1968), 26.

[48] National Association of Secondary Materials Industries, "Metals Report," New York, June 22 and July 13, 1960 (mimeographed); "Congo Plunges into Self-Rule," *Business Week,* June 25, 1960, pp. 102–103; *Iron Age,* Aug. 18, 1960, p. 146; Alvin W. Wolfe, "Economies in Bondage: The Mining Industry," *Africa Today,* XIV (Jan., 1967), 19.

[49] Former Secretary of State John Foster Dulles on Middle East oil's significance for U.S. policy, quoted in Walter Lafeber, *America, Russia and the Cold War 1945–1966* (New York, 1967), p. 186. On America's investment priorities in Western Europe during the 1960's, see Servan-Schreiber, pp. 35–54.

ship of various political colors. Also, temporary disruptions in Katanga would affect America less directly than Europe.

On the other hand, a compelling investment interest in the Congo or related areas might restrict the range of political alternatives that were acceptable to the U.S. government. In trying to discover the size and nature of the American business interest in Congolese political developments, the author has consulted statistical and other published data,[50] pursued personal interviews and correspondence with approximately 25 businessmen, and drawn on a restrospective analysis of the political behavior of U.S. corporations during the Congo crisis.[51]

(2) The Investment Stake—Size

American-controlled investment in sub-Saharan Africa was relatively small—less than 3 percent of the total U.S. direct investment abroad in 1960. Most important, the business was concentrated in Southern Africa, especially South Africa, the Rhodesian Federation, and Angola. This area accounted for more than half the American investments made in Africa, and an even higher percentage of the profits. Another 16 percent of American investment interests were located in Liberia, mainly in the shipping industry. The remainder was spread out in bits and pieces throughout East, West, and Central Africa, and amounted to somewhat less than U.S. direct investment in the state of Belgium. According to official and corporate sources, U.S. direct investment in the Congo totaled less than $20 million in the early sixties.[52]

[50] Aside from those cited below, the author has utilized John Sherman Porter, *Moody's Industrials Manual 1960–1964* and *Moody's Bank and Finance Manual 1960–1964* (New York, 1960–1965); also *Annual Reports* of corporations mentioned below, from 1960–1964.

[51] See below, pp. 172–177.

[52] Andrew M. Kamarck, *The Economics of African Development* (New York, 1967), pp. 264–267; F. Taylor Ostrander, "U.S. Private Investment in Africa," *Africa Report,* XIV (Jan., 1969), 38–40; U.S. Department of Commerce, *Africa: A Growth Market for U.S. Business* (Washington, 1968), pp. 10–11, 89; *Survey of Current Business,* XI (Sept., 1960), 18; "Congo Plunges into Self-Rule", pp. 102–103. The Southern Africa orienta-

Actually, the most engaged and powerful business interests in the Congo must be traced by way of nondirect U.S. investment through European companies or governments doing business in Southern Africa, including South Kasai and Katanga, as well as through those concerns having a direct stake in this area. A second category of American interests was involved both directly and indirectly in areas of the Congo other than Katanga and South Kasai, and in the black-ruled states of Independent Africa—its stake in the Congo, however, was small and largely prospective.

(3) The Investment Stake in the "Cape to Katanga" Structure —the Major U.S. Business Interest

One group of investors exploited the Southern African complex and the areas bordering it. Its main interests were in Rhodesia, Katanga, Angola, and South Africa, principally in mining but also in manufacturing. Its capital was usually tied up with that of Europeans and South Africans. Its preoccupations included: the conservation of the economic and administrative infrastructure of Katanga (and, to a lesser extent, South Kasai), the diking of the nationalist current as far to the North as possible, and the achievement of pro-business solutions in the Congo so as to reassure investors and potential investors in the white-controlled countries.[53] These cares were no doubt intensified by racial conflict in Rhodesia and the Sharpeville incident of March 1960 when 67 black demonstrators were slaughtered by the South African police. The event had precipitated a capital flight as investors anticipated bloody African reactions and damaging international boycotts.[54]

---

tion of U.S. private interests was noted in the conclusions of the "Report on the Conference on African Resources," sponsored by New York University and Africa Fair Inc., Mar. 27–29, 1961, p. 26 (mimeographed).

[53] This point was underlined in interviews with U.S. mining company representatives. In its 1960 *Annual Report,* pp. 3–4, Newmont Mining states that while it has no Congo investments, disturbances in that country have brought the safety of African investments into question and may have caused a decline in Newmont stock values.

[54] "Partners in Apartheid: United States Policy on South Africa," *Africa Today,* XI (Mar., 1964), 3–4.

American Metal Climax (AMAX) was one of the most active companies in this group. AMAX owned 50.6 percent of Rhodesian Selection Trust, which along with the Anglo-American Company controlled the Rhodesian Copperbelt. The latter two companies had approximately 7,500 European employees and their families living in six mining townships not far from the Katanga border. Both purchased hydroelectric power from a subsidiary of Union Minière in Katanga.[55] AMAX also had important investments in the copper mines of South and Southwest Africa. Newmont Mining, which was also concerned with events in the Congo, was associated with AMAX in these latter enterprises.[56]

Lazard Frères, the New York investment house, was a stockholder in Union Minière (10,000 shares valued at nearly $500,000 in 1960). Its Paris branch was one of the largest stockholders in Tanganyika Concessions (TANKS) whose major asset was a 14.5 percent holding in Union Minière and the right to a special annual royalty. TANKS, which was British-controlled, also had important interests in Rhodesia, South Africa, and Angola.[57]

The late Charles Engelhard was the single most important American businessman in Southern Africa. As the "American partner" of South African financier Harry Oppenheimer, he possessed vast holdings in the Union and Rhodesia. His financial empire extended into Katanga since he was a major investor in and director of the Anglo-American Company, which held a large block of stock in TANKS.[58]

The Ryan-Guggenheim group held one-quarter of the shares in FORMINIERE (Société Internationale Forestiè et Minière du

[55] Ostrander, "Corporate Structure."

[56] "Partners in Apartheid," pp. 5, 6, 16; *Africa Today* (Special Issue), XIII (Jan., 1966), 21.

[57] Centre de Recherche et d'Information Socio-Politiques (hereafter referred to as CRISP), *Morphologie des groupes financiers* (Brussels, 1966), pp. 180–181; Gérard-Libois, *Sécession*, pp. 111–112; Ostrander, "Corporate Structure," p. 7. Lazard Frères of New York also participated in the purchase by American stockholders of a total of 600,000 shares of TANKS in 1950. *London Times*, Nov. 3, 1950, p. 8.

[58] "The Engelhard Touch," *Forbes*, Aug. 1, 1965, pp. 21–23.

Congo) which owned the jewel diamond mines of South Kasai, and also participated in the Angola Diamond Company. Both firms were controlled by Société Générale de Belgique. Allan A. Ryan was a director of the Belgian-American Banking Corporation, Société Générale's U.S. financial subsidiary.[59] Guggenheim interests also played a major role in the Kennecott Copper Company which had some South African interests.[60]

General Motors had its sole Congo distributorship in South Katanga. A substantial part of Mobil Oil's $12,000,000 investment in service stations was located in Katanga, as was one of its three storage terminals. During 1960 the J. H. Whitney Company of New York put John van der Meersch of the American Eur-African Development Corporation on a one-year retainer. Van der Meersch was the son of the former Belgian Minister of African Affairs, and had specialized in Congo affairs for Dillon, Read and Co. before leaving that firm in 1959. He explored the possibility of American investment in Katanga in the fall of 1960 but eventually concluded that the Belgians would use their influence to defeat any offer he made.

The Dillon group's interests were more complex. In the late 1940's, Douglas Dillon's U.S. and Foreign Securities took up—together with Dillon's friends, the Rockefellers—minority interests in two Belgian Congo consumer industries. Dillon's holdings were much smaller than the Rockefellers'; their value was estimated at less than $300,000 in 1959. In April 1958, Dillon, Read managed a public offering of $15,000,000 in 5¼ percent external loan bonds of the Belgian Congo, due April 1, 1973.[61] The loan was for the Office de Cités Africains, a semipublic organization engaged in constructing workers' housing in four urban centers. A Dillon, Read representative—van der Meersch—indicated that his firm

[59] CRISP, *Morphologie,* pp. 182–184.

[60] "The Engelhard Touch," p. 23; Kwame Nkrumah, *Neocolonialism: The Last Stage of Imperialism* (New York, 1966), pp. 122–123, 151.

[61] Dillon, Read and Co., *The Belgian Congo: Fifteen Year 5¼% External Loan Bonds of 1958,* Prospectus, Apr. 15, 1958; van der Meersch's press interview is reproduced in CRISP, *Congo 1959* (Brussels, 1961), pp. 72–73.

and other "important American capital" were prepared to develop local industries for the Congo if guarantees of political stability could be obtained.[62] These interests, present and prospective, were unlike those discussed in previous paragraphs because they were not concentrated in the mining sector or in the southernmost provinces of the Congo.

But the Dillon group quickly suspended its plans for industrial development in the Congo due to the uncertainties of Independence.[63] On the other hand its stake in Southern Africa grew apace during the 1950's. Dillon, Read was one of Engelhard's investment bankers, a partner with Engelhard Hanovia in the firm managing American South African Investment (which raised $30,000,000 in the U.S. to be invested in South Africa in 1958), and was the "traditional U.S. investment banker for the South African government." At the moment of Congolese Independence, U.S. and Foreign Securities had extensive holdings of Newmont Mining and of the Newmont-AMAX subsidiaries in South and Southwest Africa.[64]

Finally, Morgan Guaranty Trust was the American bank which showed the most interest in the Congo. Its point of view was similar to that of European and American companies in the "Cape to Katanga" complex. Several factors seem relevant to an explanation of its position. First, Morgan was, in the words of another banker, "the traditional fiscal agent in the United States for the Belgian Congo government." Thus in 1959 and 1960 it was the syndicate manager and a participant in two $20,000,000 loans to the Belgian Congo, guaranteed by the Kingdom of Belgium.[65] A source close to the bank notes, "from time to time" it acted as banker to the Belgian government. In 1963 its interna-

62 "The Engelhard Touch," p. 22.

63 After Independence the loan went into default. As it had been fully subscribed, Dillon, Read's interest in its eventual repayment was purely moral and reputational. A settlement with the bondholders was reached in Feb. 1965.

64 "The Engelhard Touch," p. 22; "Partners in Apartheid," pp. 7–8; *Africa Today* (Special Issue), pp. 14, 27.

65 For details, see *Courrier Africain*, Oct. 9, 1963, p. 11.

tional subsidiary took a minority participation in the Banque du Congo, controlled by Société Générale.[66] In the light of these facts it is hardly surprising that Morgan's definition of its interests in the Congo resembled that held by its Belgian clients and partners. The bank also had substantial interests in Southern Africa. As the financial sector of the U.S. economy has been very successful in concealing its operations from the public, it is not possible to provide a full picture of the Morgan stake. However, business sources close to the company indicate that it is a "principal banker" for Newmont Mining and Kennecott Copper. Of possible significance is the strong representation of both Morgan and Guggenheim interests on the board of Kennecott. Morgan Guaranty Trust was a member of the banking consortium furnishing a revolving credit to the South African government,[67] and was one of four large banks that withdrew from a planned Africa Resources Conference when it was found that South Africa was to be excluded from the meeting.[68] Morgan's position may also have been influenced by banking and other interests in two small, conservative states bordering the Congo—Congo-Brazzaville and Gabon—and by its leading role, among American banks, in Western Europe.[69]

(4) The Investment Stake outside the Copperbelt

The second group of businessmen concerned with the Congo was less committed financially. To a large extent its interests lay in the realm of anticipated investment. Its sphere of activity was more essentially Congolese and black African. Its preferred sector was manufacturing. Insofar as this group did not altogether lose interest in the Congo, it was bound to take a position somewhat more congenial to African nationalism.

The Rockefeller brothers had a number of minority holdings in

[66] CRISP, *Morphologie,* p. 97.

[67] Christopher Hobson et. al., "Information on U.S. Involvement in South Africa," Chicago, 1965, p. 3 (mimeographed).

[68] *New York Times,* Apr. 29, 1960, p. 6; June 19, 1960, p. 2.

[69] This according to business sources. See too Victor Perlo, *The Empire of High Finance* (New York, 1957), pp. 301–302.

Belgian-controlled local industries. These included FILTISAF (a textile plant) and CEGEAC (an automobile distributor), businesses in which Douglas Dillon had lesser interests. Laurance Rockefeller also owned securities in a metal can company (COBEGA), a pineapple processor (ANACONGO), and a cement firm (CICO). In February 1959 David Rockefeller and the head of the African division of Chase Manhattan Bank visited the site of the proposed Inga Dam hydroelectric project in the Western Congo. Rockefeller observed that power development depended upon the creation of consumer industries. He then went on to Nigeria and Ghana to survey the growing operations of the Rockefeller Brothers Fund which was promoting small industries like food processing, cement, and textiles.[70] In January 1960 David Rockefeller bought shares in BAUXICONGO, a Belgian-controlled firm which was investigating the profitability of exploiting aluminum deposits north of the proposed Inga Dam. But during the next few years neither the Rockefeller family nor Chase Manhattan pursued their interests in the Inga area or in the manufacturing sector generally. "Then came Independence and a long period of uncertainty in the Congo," a Rockefeller associate explained.

The real thrust of Rockefeller interests in the Congo has not been well understood. Much attention has been paid to the 1950 purchase by David Rockefeller and the International Basic Economy Corporation of a substantial block of Tanganyika Concessions shares.[71] However, Rockefeller sources insist that these holdings were sold in the market prior to June 1960, and the political behavior of certain directors during the Congo crisis is broadly confirming.[72] Although the Chase Manhattan Bank was

[70] *New York Times,* Feb. 8, 1959, p. 4; Feb. 11, 1959, p. 57; Mar. 12, 1959, p. 42; CRISP, *Congo 1959,* p. 73. On the FILTISAF holding, see Richard Austin Smith, "The Rockefeller Brothers-II," *Fortune,* LI (Mar., 1955), 116.

[71] *London Times,* Nov. 3, 1950, p. 8. Other purchasers identified were Lazard Frères of New York and Ladenberg, Thalman and Co.

[72] See below, pp. 176–177.

expanding its South African operations in 1959 and later,[73] its directors appear to have been responding to a more complex and varied set of pressures than those of Dillon, Read or Morgan Guaranty Trust.

Reynolds Aluminum was a leader and substantial backer of the Inga Dam study group set up in the late 1950's by Société Générale. A number of studies were made of favorable sites for the establishment of an aluminum electrolysis factory in the Lower Congo, and at Independence, Reynolds was, according to company sources, "just on the point of embarking upon a large program of investment in the Congo." In July 1960, it took the controlling interest—4/9ths of the stock—in Société Aluminum and Electric International which planned to build aluminum facilities. The company "invested funds in an option to purchase a tract near Boma; however, conditions developed which made it inadvisable to proceed and this particular company was dissolved in 1968." The aforementioned conditions were primarily political. Post-Independence instability impeded external financing of the Inga Dam, which was the necessary complement to an aluminum industry. Reynolds' interest in exploiting the power resources of black Africa, and its staying power during some stormy days in Ghana, suggest a felt need to strike a modus vivendi with black nationalism.[74]

Other American investments in this group were participation in two plywood factories in the Lower Congo, an interest in oil prospecting on the West Coast (Gulf), and an IBM repair shop in Leopoldville.[75]

[73] *Africa Today* (Special Issue), pp. 12–14.

[74] J. L. Lacroix, "Inga," *Etudes Congolaises,* X (Jan., 1967), 1–17. An alternative project, the Volta Dam in Ghana, was financed by the U.S. Government and World Bank, *ibid.,* pp. 9–10; Reginald H. Green and Ann Seidman, *Unity or Poverty? The Economics of Pan-Africanism* (Baltimore, 1968), pp. 176–177.

[75] Other significant investments were Texaco (gasoline service stations and an interest in petroleum storage depots) and Bank of America (participation in SOCOBANQUE). The author has not been able to discover much about these investments, and they were not prominent politically. Eric

(5) The Commercial Trading Interest

American trade with Africa amounted to less than 4 percent of U.S. foreign commerce. Again, there was an emphasis on Southern Africa, and the Congo's own contribution was rather insignificant.[76] Although American exporters certainly wished to protect unpaid-for stocks and existing markets,[77] they were not so heavily engaged *sur place* as the investors. In the author's view their interests were not very important, and they were in any case quite diffuse. Perhaps the most notable trading interest was Farrell Lines which operated a steamer service between the Congo and other African ports. Business sources indicate that Farrell's African representative, W. C. Shields, was largely concerned with staying on the good side of any Central Government.[78]

In conclusion, the U.S. was an advanced industrial state participating in a world commodity market constructed on capitalistic lines. One feature of this world economy was a division of labor between the poor countries which furnished raw materials and the rich countries which manufactured and consumed them. A practical consequence was the U.S. economy's vested interest, both directly and indirectly, in the health and stable functioning of mining facilities in the Congo and Rhodesia—especially on the Copperbelt. But the policy implications of this interest were rather open-ended. Furthermore, the most significant American capital in Africa was concentrated in the Copperbelt and the white-ruled countries to the South. Lesser interests were concerned with the rest of the Congo and Independent Africa. Investors would

---

Johnston, a member of Bank of America's Board of Directors, did publicly endorse an "anti-Katanga" U.N. policy in 1962. See *New York Times*, Jan. 25, 1962, p. 21.

76 U.S. Department of Commerce, *Africa*, pp. 7–8, 86–88.

77 See the statement by the International Trade Relations Division of the Commerce and Industry Association of New York in *Journal of Commerce*, Aug. 17, 1960, p. 1.

78 Prudence is conveyed by the company's "Africa News Digest," New York, July 18, Aug. 11, 1960; and Apr. 30, 1961 (mimeographed).

normally favor conservative policies, but it was likely that there would be differences of approach between the two groups involved. Finally, the *political* significance of all these interests remains to be seen.

PART I

THE ANTI-COMMUNISM OF MODERATE REPUBLICANS

CHAPTER I

Predispositions and First Moves

On the eve of its Independence, American officials viewed the Congo in the light of certain broad assumptions that were to influence their interpretation of individual events and the selection of alternative policies.

Deference to the Belgians: Conservative Perspectives on Africa

After World War II and the birth of NATO, America's principal concern in Africa was for the sensibilities of its colonialist allies. President Eisenhower did little to change this policy despite the quickening pace of the Independence movement. It is true that a separate Bureau of African Affairs was created within the State Department in July 1958. But its first head, Joseph Satterthwaite, was a cautious career diplomat and "hardly a fiery exponent of African nationalist causes."[1] Moreover, some members of the Bureau felt they were up against a "stacked deck" since "no merit was seen in the Bureau at higher levels of the Department." As late as December 1960, the United States abstained from an Afro-Asian anticolonialist resolution which passed the United Nations General Assembly by a vote of 89-0, and when Guinea chose Independence outside the French community, thus earning the monumental pique of President de Gaulle, America cooperated

[1] Victor Ferkiss, *Africa's Search for Identity* (New York, 1966), pp. 298–305. Satterthwaite later rounded out his diplomatic career with a four-year stint as Ambassador to South Africa.

with French diplomatic and economic pressures by delaying recognition of the new state and refusing it economic aid.

The U.S. had been quite careful not to offend Belgium in the Belgian Congo. In 1957, according to a former government official, the State Department barred American blacks from the Congo, lest their example whet the appetite for Independence. The U.S. consul-general in Leopoldville was so cautious that in January 1960—when the Belgians announced for Independence in six months—there was almost no American intelligence on the Congo.[2] In May 1960, a handful of Congolese leaders were invited to the United States—but it was the Belgians who composed the guest list.

At the time of Independence, American officials still considered the Congo a "Belgian bailiwick." Indeed, since Belgium had the major interests in the Congo, she would take care of whatever problems developed; America's role would be largely that of an understanding friend.

Thus, U.S. aid plans for the new state were originally pushed by the American Embassy in Brussels—responding to a Belgian request for help. The proposals were worked out in close cooperation with the Belgian government. And the program was essentially one of technical assistance, designed to supplement Belgian budgetary assistance.[3]

The NATO reflex in African policy was partly the result of past estimates of Europe's strategic and politico-economic importance vis-à-vis Africa. Historical choices were institutionalized in "the senior and powerful position of the European bureau"[4] of the

[2] "In 1959 Western consulates in Leopoldville had been warned by the Belgian colonial authorities not to get on close terms with the Congolese." Ian Scott, *Tumbled House: The Congo at Independence* (London, 1959), p. 17. Scott was the British Ambassador to the Congo from 1960 to 1961.

[3] Clare Hayes Timberlake, "First Years of Independence in the Congo: Events and Issues" (unpublished Master's thesis, Department of International Affairs, George Washington University, 1963), pp. 47, 55–57.

[4] U.S. Congress, Senate, Committee on Foreign Relations, *United States in the United Nations 1960: A Turning Point,* Committee Print, 87th Congress, 1st Session, 1961, III, 29 (Senator Wayne Morse).

State Department, and in the career patterns of diplomats (bias toward European posts is indicated by the fact that in 1957 the U.S. had 256 foreign service posts in West Germany and 248 in the whole of Africa).[5] As late as February 1961, Senator Wayne Morse could write that the African Bureau "is largely staffed by persons who have spent many years on assignment in European countries and have well in mind the European point of view."[6]

The same might have been said about high officials of the Eisenhower Administration who had to deal with the Congo.[7] Secretary of State Christian Herter had been a member of the American Peace Delegation at Paris in 1919, and had subsequently worked with Herbert Hoover on the European Relief Council. As a Republican Congressman in 1947, Herter headed a committee of the House of Representatives which surveyed European relief needs and helped make the Marshall Plan respectable in Republican circles. Upon his retirement from the Foreign Service in 1961, he became cochairman of the Citizens Committee for NATO and chairman of the Atlantic Council of the United States. Under Secretary of State Douglas Dillon had begun his diplomatic career as Ambassador to France in 1953. Robert Murphy, who had just retired from the Foreign Service but was to be an influential adviser on Congo policy, had had a distinguished diplomatic career, centered almost entirely on Europe. He was also a former Ambassador to Belgium (1949–1952), and it was from that vantage point that he first came to know the Congo in depth.

The "albatross of tradition," however, cannot survive in a hostile

5 Walter Goldschmidt (ed.), *The United States and Africa* (New York, 1963), p. 275.

6 U.S. Senate, Committee on Foreign Relations, *United States in the United Nations,* III, 29.

7 Biographical information has been drawn from these sources: *Current Biography Yearook,* 1958, pp. 191–193 (Herter); *Current Biography Yearbook,* 1953, pp. 161–162 (Dillon); *Who's Who in America,* 1960–1965; John P. Muleas, "Christian Herter—Heir Unapparent," *New Republic,* Feb. 6, 1956, pp. 8–10; Christian Herter, "Problems of Foreign Aid," (speech to the Economic Club of Detroit [Michigan], Mar. 22, 1948). Other references are cited individually.

environment, and the European and Belgian claims for consideration were thus ineluctably strengthened by the political ideology of top Eisenhower officials. As "responsible conservatives," their view of the world implied sympathy for the Belgian position. For example, an absence of passion for civil rights in America was consistent with the idea of Belgian tutelage for the Congolese even after Independence. A tender regard for corporate profit-making and the benefits of social stability was consistent with the interests of Belgian investors, settlers, and civil servants in the Congo. An inclination to look at the Congo as an international business proposition—as a certain quantity of minerals that were valuable for the Western and U.S. economies and were geologically contiguous with other important deposits (Rhodesia)—raised the imperative of order in Katanga. This also coincided with Belgian, British, and French priorities in the Congo.

On this subject, President Eisenhower's memoirs are very revealing. He writes, "The determination of the peoples [in Africa] for self-rule, their own flag, and their own vote in the United Nations resembled a torrent overrunning everything in its path, including, frequently, the best interests of those concerned." Eisenhower favored European tutelage in independent Africa including the occupation by European technicians of "key positions in communications, armed services, government, and such industry as existed," and "strong economic and cultural ties with their former rulers." As for the Congo, he was aware of its administrative incapacities, tribal divisions, and fragmented politics. Perceiving "a restless and militant population in a state of gross ignorance—even by African standards," he was especially interested in close ties between the Congo and her former colonial ruler. He did not fail to remark upon "the rich province of Katanga" with "most" of the country's mineral wealth and Belgian investment; he recognized the legitimacy of Belgium's desire to "protect her interests." But "things went badly from the start" when the "radical and unstable Congolese Prime Minister, Patrice Lumumba, took the occasion [of Independence Day] to excoriate Belgium for afflicting "atrocious sufferings" on the Congolese, although he promised that the Congo would remain on friendly terms with Belgium." [8]

Within the State Department there was considerable sympathy for the views of Robert Murphy, the "grand old man of the Foreign Service." Murphy had retired in 1959 and become chairman of Corning Glass International and director of Morgan Guaranty International. But he led the U.S. delegation to Independence Day ceremonies in Leopoldville and was an influential adviser on Congo policy during 1960. As Ambassador to Belgium he had traveled in the Congo in 1951 and had become an ardent supporter of Belgian colonialism. In 1960 Murphy thought that if Independence was inevitable, it had to be worked out on a "sound basis, having in mind Belgian achievements." The Congolese were a tribal "primitive people," he felt, who had to be trained to assume responsibility. Murphy was especially impressed by the mining facilities in the Congo, particularly by their contribution to Belgium's economy, and by Union Minière's past help to the U.S. in furnishing uranium for the first atomic bombs. He was convinced of the need to safeguard mineral production for the good of both investors and natives. He was also sensitive to the fears of European residents: "My years in French North Africa had shown me how dangerous conditions could be where native races so greatly outnumbered European settlers." At the Independence celebration, Lumumba's outburst had been preceded by an exceptionally paternal speech on the part of Belgium's King Baudouin—Murphy considered it a "graceful" address.[9]

While few of the leading figures involved in Congo policy decisions expressed themselves as strongly or publicly as Murphy, most shared his basic perception.[10] As one of the foreign service

8 Dwight D. Eisenhower, *Waging Peace 1956–1961* (New York, 1965), pp. 572–576.

9 Robert Murphy, *Diplomat Among Warriors* (Garden City, N.Y., 1964), pp. 324, 328, 330–338. The first citation is from a personal interview with the author on Mar. 1, 1968.

10 For a poignant illustration from Under Secretary of State Dillon, see below, p. 76.

professionals put it: "The conservatives were more aware of tribalism and backwardness. The policy conclusions were slow independence, tutelage, schools."

An examination of top policy-makers' relations to key social and political institutions in American life helps explain their assumptions. Secretary Herter was the scion of an upper-class New England family and was listed in the Social Register. He married the granddaughter of a Standard Oil founder; in 1961 his son, Christian Herter, Jr., became a vice-president of Mobil Oil (Standard Oil of New York). After working with Herbert Hoover on European relief problems, he entered the Republican Administration in 1921 as Hoover's assistant in the Department of Commerce. At this time, Hoover was transforming the Department of Commerce from "an organization concerned primarily with domestic affairs into an agency oriented toward overseas expansion," and was "striving for an American-led community of interests with other industrial nations"—largely through economic means.[11] Subsequently, Herter became a Republican state legislator, Congressman and Governor of Massachusetts. Upon leaving the government in 1924, he bought into and edited two New England magazines. Herter's public record indicates much concern for the oil industry and for economy in government, little concern for civil rights, labor, or social legislation, and a consuming interest in American aid to the European economy. He voted against the Point-4 Program of assistance to "underdeveloped" areas.

Under Secretary Dillon was a life-long investment banker with "world-wide interests," particularly in "chemicals, metals, natural gas, oil, and public utilities." After World War II he became active in the Republican party, working with John Foster Dulles on Thomas Dewey's foreign policy positions during the 1948

[11] William Appleman Williams, "The Large Corporation and American Foreign Policy," in David Horowitz (ed.), *Corporations and the Cold War* (New York, 1969), p. 86; Williams, *The Tragedy of American Diplomacy* (Cleveland: World Publishing Company, 1959), p. 93.

presidential campaign. Following Eisenhower's victory in 1952 he was appointed Ambassador to France, then Assistant Secretary of State for Economic Affairs, a post of particular importance to the international business community. While in the State Department he retained stock in the family's Wall Street firm (Dillon, Read) and other companies.[12] He too was listed in the Social Register. President Eisenhower's affection for big business and his conservative views on civil rights are well known. One indication of his relation to the economic and political structures noted above is that both Herter and Dillon were important influences in his nomination for the presidency in 1952. Herter was co-chairman of the Eisenhower-for-President Committee in 1952; Dillon was also a leader in the "Draft Ike" movement and clashed publicly with Eisenhower's opponent, Robert Taft.

Robert Murphy's views, and similar ones prevailing in the Foreign Service, can be explained by the inclination of European-based diplomats to internalize colonialist ideology. However, it is not unimportant that Murphy gravitated toward and was selected by international business after his retirement from the Foreign Service, and that the Congo policy of Morgan Guaranty Trust was in no way different from that of Robert Murphy. Murphy's later activity on behalf of business firms displeased with President Kennedy's Congo policy[13] indicated again the crucial institutional context of his undoubtedly sincere and independently developed position.

Some individuals of lesser importance in the formulation of Congo policy may also be referred to in the same context. Thomas S. Gates, Jr., Secretary of Defense, was closely tied in with Morgan interests through his family's investment banking house in Philadelphia, Drexel and Co. This firm has been in partnership with Morgan since 1850.[14] Gates did not break his association with

12 *Washington Post,* Jan. 12, 1961, p. A-9; communications from representatives of Dillon, Read.

13 See below, pp. 173, 175.

14 E. Digby Baltzell, *Philadelphia Gentlemen: The Making of a National Upper Class* (Glencoe, Ill., 1958), pp. 38, 91.

Drexel when he became Secretary of Defense. In 1961, he became a director of Morgan Guaranty Trust Co., the most significant international banker. According to all accounts, Gates played a very minor role in the Congo crisis of 1960. But he attended some important meetings, and his inactivity may be interpreted as consent to the overall policy pursued. Ambassador to Belgium William Burden had an investment house that specialized in aircraft and resources securities. He had been an Assistant Commerce Secretary for Aviation. During his service in Brussels, he maintained directorships in two international copper firms. He vigorously pushed for U.S. aid to the Congo, and former officials state that he was "very interested" in Congo developments.

It is not excluded that conservative perspectives on the Congo may, in some cases, have been strengthened by tangible interests. Dillon was a director of U.S. and Foreign Securities; his minor interests in Belgian-controlled companies have been described above. His family firm had a moral and reputational interest in the success of its 1958 loan to the Belgian Congo. Most important, Dillon's substantial involvement in Southern Africa led toward a concern for order on the Copperbelt. As indicated earlier, American investors in Southern Africa, including Dillon's partner, Charles Engelhard, considered political stability in Katanga a vital requirement for their own operations. Murphy and Gates were connected with Morgan Guaranty Trust whose interest in a friendly atmosphere for business in the Congo, and particularly in Katanga, has been noted. Burden took a Council on Foreign Relations trip to the Inga Dam site, along with David Rockefeller and John Watts of Chase Manhattan Bank, shortly before he became Ambassador to Belgium. All three were enthusiastic about the potential of the area for resource development.[15] Even more important, Burden was a director of American Metal Climax whose Rhodesian copper interests were to make it the leading corporate defender of a conservative order in Katanga. He was also a director of Cerro de Posco, a copper firm in Peru which might be

[15] *New York Times,* Feb. 11, 1959, p. 57.

adversely affected by excessive fluctuations in international copper prices and supplies.[16]

However, "educated" by the preoccupations of dealing with an African clientele, career officers in the African Bureau generally had little feeling for African nationalism. Some may even have internalized the European point of view during previous service. Deputy Assistant Secretary James Penfield said in May 1959:

In terms of trade, administration, political and economic development, and education the European colonial or former colonial powers have contributed far more to Africa than have we. Moreover, these powers are continuing their interest and contributions, adapting them in an enlightened and sympathetic way to the rapidly changing situation. We regard this as natural, and we welcome it. We have no desire to interfere with this fruitful development of these new relationships, and in fact we are taking particular care to avoid slipping into such a position, which could only result in friction and rivalry contrary to the best interests of the new African states, of our European allies, and of ourselves.[17]

Clare Timberlake, the first U.S. Ambassador to the Congo, had been involved in African affairs during and immediately after World War II, but this was before the rise of nationalism. He was definitely sympathetic to the Belgian point of view.[18]

[16] Also, as noted previously, Christian Herter married into one of the original Standard Oil families, and his son became a Mobil Oil (Standard Oil of New York) executive in 1961. Mobil was in contact with the State Department from the beginning of the Congo crisis because of its operations in Katanga. However, it is not known whether the Secretary of State had an interest in this particular company.

[17] James K. Penfield, "The Role of the United States in Africa: Our Interests and Operations," *Department of State Bulletin,* June 8, 1959, p. 842.

[18] This is the general impression which emerges from Timberlake's written and spoken comments. His account of the events of 1960 indicates little perception of or feeling for Congolese anticolonialism. The Independence movement is portrayed against a background of external agitation, but there is no mention of the frustrations of the colonial system. He is quite content to have Belgian political advisers in high places. Indeed his only criticism

The International Communist Threat: From Chaos to Communism

American officials believed the basic premise of Cold War ideology: the threat of aggressive, monolithic international Communism (aside from Yugoslavia) led by the Soviet Union. They knew the Congo would be a valuable prize for the Communists due to its size, central location in Africa, and vast mineral wealth. They also thought that a pro-Communist Congo would jeopardize Western sources of strategic raw materials.

Most importantly, American policy-makers had some concrete ideas about *how* the Communists might take over the Congo. According to one key official, "Though there was no evidence of a strong Communist movement [in the Congo] we took it for granted that they would take advantage if turbulence developed more than we expected." Another noted, "There was a lot of thinking the Soviets would take advantage better of chaos, and not us." Eisenhower expressed the same thought in reference to Africa: "[We] could not afford to see turmoil in an area where the Communists would be only too delighted to take advantage." It was feared that instability in the Congo would be parlayed by the "Eastern bloc" into "influence," "a base," "control," and even "conversion to their ideology." These anxieties were essentially projections of past experiences in other parts of the world and the "lessons learned from them." Thus, as grounds for nervousness, policy-makers cited Soviet exploitation of chaos in Eastern Europe, Greece, Iran, Malaysia, the Philippines, and Egypt (after the Aswan Dam imbroglio) as well as recent aid programs in Guinea. Eight years later a top decision-maker recalled, "We thought then —probably falsely—the Soviets could keep control as in Eastern Europe." As a later comparison with the Kennedy Administration

---

of the Belgians is that they failed to prepare the Congolese for the responsibilities of Independence. See Timberlake, *passim.*

On Timberlake's close relationship with the Belgian Embassy, see Major-General H. T. Alexander, *African Tightrope* (New York, 1965), pp. 37–38.

will make clear, the from-chaos-to-Communism complex was rooted in the conservatives' lack of sympathy for and lack of experience in the "new nationalisms."

Such uses of history, supplemented by inexperience in Africa, could lead to the darkest imaginings. Some feared that instability in the Congo would spread beyond its borders, creating golden opportunities for the Soviet bloc. All were concerned that a Communist victory in this large, centrally located state could create a base for the subversion of Central Africa.

Fearing instability, the State Department developed a series of economic palliatives in the spring of 1960. The aforementioned technical assistance was planned by a special group of economists working out of Under Secretary Dillon's office. In early May an International Cooperation Administration (ICA) survey team was dispatched to the Congo to examine possible programs in agriculture, education, public administration, and English language training. The ICA mission in the Congo was to be the largest in Africa. To meet the Congo's budget and balance of payments deficits, the U.S. encouraged "a consortium of western nations to bail the Congo out of its immediate difficulties with prompt capital assistance." This would be convened by the International Monetary Fund immediately after Independence. The State Department favored the 5-year, 20-million-dollar loan which Belgium negotiated on the New York market to refinance part of the short-term external debt of the Congo. It supported a 40-million-dollar World Bank loan to Belgium for economic development (mainly transport development) in the Congo. And, as another kind of aid, on Independence Day Robert Murphy brought an offer of 300 scholarships.[19]

Politically, the U.S. sought stability by pressing for a government headed by Patrice Lumumba, a militant nationalist. While Lumumba's party had only a quarter of the seats in parliament, it

[19] Timberlake, pp. 41, 55–56; *Libre Belgique,* Mar. 30, 1960, p. 4; Apr. 18, 1960, p. 4; Apr. 22, 1960, p. 5; May 3, 1960, p. 5; July 2–3, 1960, p. 5. The earlier quotation from Eisenhower is in Eisenhower, p. 572.

was the strongest single party, and Lumumba was the only politician with a national organization. The American Consulate and the African Bureau respected Lumumba's political talents and thought he was the only one who could exert influence in the Congo. Their attitude resembled that reportedly held by some Belgian business interests at this time. These "argued for a strong government led by a personality who would keep order at all costs. Such a one without doubt was M. Lumumba. One might decry his use of violence; one could not deny he had authority." [20] The Consulate's efforts on behalf of Lumumba were hardly decisive; but they did irritate the Belgians who temporarily supported the candidacy of Joseph Kasavubu, until it was clear they had to settle for Lumumba. According to Resident Minister Walter Ganshof van der Meersch, named by Belgium on May 16 to supervise the transfer of power in the Congo:

> The consular agents of foreign states in Leopoldville and particularly those of signatory states of the Atlantic pact, who saw with favor in Mr. Lumumba—not without a certain *naïveté*—the strong man, the only one capable in their eyes of assuring order and exercising control tomorrow in the independent Congo, were all disturbed by the designation of Mr. Kasavubu, apparently head of the moderates, which seemed to them to reveal a change of orientation by the Belgian Government.
>
> Among them, certain let the Minister understand, not without a certain indiscretion, that there was no other card to play than the Lumumba card.
>
> The consuls of the United States and Great Britain didn't hide from Mr. Ganshof the interest they attached to the designation of Mr. Lumumba, in whom they saw the man of authority necessary for the Government of the Congo.[21]

By Independence Day, Washington had found some fuel for its anxieties. Deputy Minister Antoine Gizenga was thought to have

[20] Belgian Resident Minister Ganshof van der Meersch, quoted and translated by Hoskyns, p. 75.

[21] Ganshof van der Meersch, p. 250.

spent three months in Eastern Europe "allegedly arranging arms shipments." Lumumba's campaign funds "appeared to derive in large part from Communist and radical African sources, even though he was careful to eschew any visits to Soviet bloc countries." [22] Such incidents were minimized as unsupported rumors, or rather as minor delinquencies: e.g., Lumumba got financing from wealthy Belgian industrialists too. But the seeds of suspicion had been planted. More important were the events surrounding Independence. The Czech consul courted the new government as assiduously as the Western consuls. The Russians dispatched a twelve-man delegation to the official ceremonies, headed by the Vice-President of the Presidium of the Supreme Soviet.[23] Most disconcerting for American officials was Lumumba's attack on the Belgians in front of King Baudouin at the Independence celebration (e.g., "From today we are no longer your *Makak*" [monkeys]).[24] Lumumba apologized later, but his performance was taken as evidence of "personal instability," "erraticism," and "inexperience"—qualities which might make the Congo more vulnerable to instability and Soviet penetration.[25] Still, no one anticipated an *immediate* threat.

The United Nations Umbrella

Five days after Independence, army units in Leopoldville and Thysville mutinied. They refused to obey their Belgian officers and commenced arresting, insulting, and attacking European civilians. The root cause of the mutiny was the soldiers' demand for Africanization of the officer cadres, their feeling that Independence had passed them by, and their resentment of the new,

22 Timberlake, pp. 176, 184. Citations are from "a series of reports from the American Consulate General, and later the Embassy, at Leopoldville."

23 *Libre Belgique,* Sept. 7, 1960, p. 6; July 12, 1960, p. 5; June 30, 1960, p. 4.

24 Quoted by Colin Legum in his Forword to: Patrice Lumumba, *Congo My Country,* trans. Graham Heath (New York, 1962), p. xiv.

25 Timberlake, p. 67; Murphy, pp. 333–338; Eisenhower, p. 573.

privileged class of politicians. In fact, the army's commander, General Janssens, probably precipitated the uprising by writing on a blackboard "before Independence = after Independence."[26] The hostility toward Europeans was not murderous—no Belgian was killed at this time—but rather was an attempt to humiliate, "to show that the Congolese were masters and must be taken seriously." Lumumba finally calmed the soldiers by dismissing Janssens, allowing the few trusted Belgian officers to stay on as technical advisers, and Africanizing the command through election of officers. But hopes for a peaceful solution were dashed by mutual suspicion and lack of statesmanship. The events of the brief transition period had created much distrust between Belgians and Congolese. After the first outbreaks the Europeans panicked and began to flee the Congo—or to arm, thereby frightening the soldiers. The inexperienced and mercurial Lumumba did not realize that this was "not the moment for accusations." He made some wild charges regarding a Belgian plot behind the mutiny. These allegations frightened and angered Belgians in Leopoldville and Brussels and heightened tension in army camps throughout the country. At the same time, Belgian officers in Luluabourg and Elizabethville delayed handing over their command to Congolese, producing fresh mutinies. And the Belgian government succumbed to the habit of command by deciding on military intervention without the consent of the Congo government and without giving Lumumba another opportunity to negotiate a settlement. On the morning and evening of July 10, Belgian forces intervened in Elizabethville and Luluabourg.[27]

The first reactions of the United States government stressed Belgian responsibility for order. On July 8 the American, British,

[26] Gérard-Libois and Verhaegen, *Congo 1960,* pp. 1076–1079. The authors note that in its hostility to the politicians the army kept its *"finalité coloniale."*

[27] Hoskyns, pp. 87–97, 100–104; Young, pp. 315–321; Alan P. Merriam, *Congo: Background of Conflict* (Evanston, 1961), pp. 283–286. On the climate of mutual suspicion, see Mary C. Morgan, "Politics in the Pursuit of Power" (unpublished Honors thesis, Smith College, 1967), pp. 15–81.

and French consuls in Elizabethville made a joint plea for Belgian military intervention.[28] On July 10, Kasavubu and Lumumba consulted Ambassador Timberlake regarding outside technical aid, particularly for reorganizing the security forces. Since they had spurned Belgian help, and since Timberlake knew that the American government "was not anxious for any unilateral involvement supplanting the Belgians in a real sense," he suggested an appeal to the U.N. The Congolese leaders immediately contacted U.N. Under Secretary Ralph Bunche (who happened to be in Leopoldville to discuss a technical assistance program with the government) and made an oral request for military technical aid.[29]

The next day Secretary Herter saw "undoubted merit" in the proposal. It seemed to entail the provision of officers to the Congo National Army (ANC), a kind of collateral assistance to the Belgian troops who were now intervening in several places to restore order. State Department officials believed America would contribute to such a plan. "But they also made it clear that the United States was not seeking a leading role. Belgium, they said, must bear the main responsibility because Belgian citizens are mainly concerned and Belgians know the country best.' [30]

As the Belgian ambassador to the Congo predicted, unsolicited military intervention produced new mutinies, threatening far more lives. But there was still some hope for cooperation between the two governments. Lumumba viewed the situation at Luluabourg and gave the Belgian force permission to stay for two months.

28 *New York Times,* July 9, 1960, p. 13; July 11, 1960, p. 2. In the latter dispatch, State Department officials indicated that the consular appeal was the basis for Belgian intervention. A member of the American Consulate recalls, "Consular appeals for intervention by Belgian paratroops stationed at Kitona were quite informal and geared to the dire needs of the moment. [We] had in mind the heavy threat from the revolting 3rd Battalion to the lives of our citizens gathered within the hastily fortified perimeter of the Elizabethville High School." Letter to the author, May 26, 1970.

29 Timberlake, p. 10. Quotation is from a personal interview with the author, Sept. 1967.

30 *New York Times,* July 12, 1960, pp. 1, 12; see also *Washington Post,* July 12, 1960, p. A-5.

The Congo government was on the verge of an additional agreement with Belgium for collaboration on a country-wide basis. But on the morning of July 11, Belgian naval forces landed at Matadi, where no Europeans were in danger, killing a number of Congolese. The purpose of this unilateral action was to protect port installations. In the evening Provincial President Moise Tshombe declared Katanga independent and appealed to Belgium for recognition and assistance. Kasavubu and Lumumba flew immediately to Elizabethville but were not allowed to land at the airport, which was controlled by Belgian paratroops. The incidents at Matadi and in Katanga convinced the Congolese leaders that the Belgians "were attempting to occupy the country." The tenuous fabric of cooperation was entirely rent.[31]

At 3:30 P.M. Leopoldville time, July 12, the Cabinet met in the absence of Kasavubu and Lumumba, who were in transit at Kamina base. Present were Deputy Prime Minister Gizenga, Foreign Minister Bomboko, Defense Minister Nyembo, Belgian Ambassador van den Bosch, Belgian emissaries Ganshof and De Schryver, and—after a short time—Ambassador Timberlake with an assistant. Bomboko did most of the talking. It was clear that the latest events had compromised efforts toward collaboration between the ANC and Belgian troops. What was needed was a "foreign neutral army" to restore order. Bomboko suggested Israeli forces, but this seemed impractical. He then proposed the use of American troops. The Belgian diplomats indicated they had no objection to this course of action. Ambassador Timberlake asked for details but took no position on the matter. He did state that in his opinion the American government preferred multilateral aid and was unlikely to accept this plea while an earlier one was under consideration by the United Nations. Nevertheless, a written request for 3,000 American troops to be used in the lower Congo and Leopoldville in collaboration with the ANC was given to

[31] Hoskyns, pp. 97–100; Morgan, pp. 63–64. On the Matadi action, see Gérard-Libois and Verhaegen, *Congo 1960*, pp. 458–460; and Ganshof van der Meersch, pp. 421, 429.

Timberlake and transmitted to Washington, where it arrived at noon, Washington time, July 12.[32]

Consultations in the State Department produced a policy statement. Secretary Herter called the Summer White House in Newport to get President Eisenhower's approval, and the U.S. position was announced that afternoon by Press Secretary Hagerty:

> The United Nations has now before it an official appeal for assistance from the Congo Government, and the United States believes that any assistance to the Government of the Congo should be through the United Nations and not by any unilateral action by any one country, the United States included. . . . I think you could also add that it is the opinion of the President of the United States and the Secretary of State that such military assistance would be better for the Congo if it did not come from the United States or any of the large Western nations.

The U.S., officials added, "will extend every facility to an expeditionary force to the Congo if one is finally raised." [33]

This second encouragement of U.N. action was based on somewhat different considerations than the first. With spreading disorder and the deterioration of Congo-Belgian relations, the from-chaos-to-Communism syndrome became the urgent and central preoccupation of American policy-makers. Their principal concern was that the Soviets would offer troops or military advisers to the desperate Congo government. This, it was thought, would lead to "permanent Communist cells," a "Soviet takeover," and "turning over Central Africa to the Soviets." Another felt danger was that of chaos spreading throughout an unknown continent—with the relentless Communists waiting in the wings. Several years later the key decision-makers recalled the main options for American policy.

The U.S. could do nothing, but this implied unacceptable risks.

32 Ganshof van der Meersch, pp. 429–430, 469; *Libre Belgique,* July 13, 1960, p. 6.

33 *New York Times,* July 13, 1960, p. 13; *New York Herald Tribune,* July 13, 1960, p. 2.

Or it could agree to the Cabinet request for American troops. But this would give the Russians an excuse to offer a contingent themselves—either to the Congo government or a fraction thereof, either now or in the future. Considering Katanga's secession and the patchwork coalition government, American intervention might promote a Spanish Civil War situation with the possibility of a direct Soviet-American confrontation. Besides, the U.S. was not anxious for a heavy involvement in mid-Africa, an area outside the line of direct military responsibility and lacking substantial American investment. Nor was Congress likely to approve an expeditionary force in Africa, especially when its immediate purpose was to restore order rather than to resist Communist aggression. The last alternative was to let the U.N. stop the riot through a peace-keeping force which excluded the great powers. This seemed the most reasonable course, since it promised to block chaos and Communism at a relatively small cost to the United States. Thus the United Nations would be the "umbrella" for U.S. anti-Communist policy in the Congo.[34]

Even as Herter was conferring with Hammarskjold on means of injecting the U.N. into the situation, the U.S. underlined its fear of Soviet intervention by dispatching the aircraft carrier WASP

[34] In mid-1960 it was appropriate to consider the U.N. a satisfactory vehicle for American policy. In the Security Council, the West held four out of five permanent seats and three out of six of the elected seats. Also there was the veto. In the General Assembly the Western and Latin American states needed only 12 Afro-Asian votes for the usual two-thirds majority (less if there were abstentions), and could easily block a hostile vote. In the Secretariat a high percentage of the staff was at least basically Western in outlook. Americans, British, and Frenchmen held 49 of 102 senior positions. Hammarskjold's closest advisers were all Americans who had survived a McCarthyite purge of the Secretariat in the 1950's. These included Ralph Bunche, Under Secretary for Special Political Affairs; Andrew Cordier, Executive Assistant; and Heinz Wieschoff, Bunche's deputy and the Secretariat's African expert. See Hoskyns, p. 112; Harold Karan Jacobson, "The Changing Nations," in Roger Hilsman and Robert C. Good (eds.), *Foreign Policy in the Sixties* (Baltimore, 1965), pp. 67–89; and Conor Cruise O'Brien, *Writers and Politics* (New York, 1964), pp. 195–214.

to the Congo coast. Officially this was for possible "missions of mercy" to evacuate American civilians.[35] (These would be mainly missionaries—there were about 1,600 U.S. missionaries in the Congo in 1960.) In reality there was also a strong political motive. Eisenhower writes that while we sent no combat troops to the Congo, "we did station an attack carrier near the mouth of the Congo river." [36] In September 1960, reporter Arnold Beichman recalled, "It was made quite clear to the writer in the early stages of the Congo disorders that if Soviet troops entered any part of the country, American troops would follow. The American aircraft carrier, USS WASP, which cruised off Africa in July, carried not only supplies for any refugees that might have been embarked, it also carried strategic military supplies essential to any emergency." [37]

Washington officials felt that subsequent events confirmed the wisdom of their analysis. On July 12 Soviet Premier Khrushchev told a Moscow news conference that Belgium, with the connivance of NATO, was "sending troops to suppress the people of the Congo by force of arms" on the "pretext of alleged disorder there while in fact real order is being introduced." "The People of the Congo," he said, "want to establish genuine order, to expel colonialists . . . the colonial peoples fighting for their freedom and independence have our sympathies and our assistance." [38] On the same day, Lumumba and Kasavubu sent a new appeal to Bunche from Kasai. This was "couched in very different terms from those they had used when asking for technical assistance." [39] They accused Belgium of military aggression, of having "carefully prepared the secession of Katanga," and requested U.N. military aid "to protect the national territory of the Congo against the

[35] *Washington Post,* July 13, 1960, p. A-1; *New York Times,* July 13, 1960, p. 13.

[36] Eisenhower, p. 575.

[37] *Christian Science Monitor,* Sept. 29, 1960, p. 6.

[38] Howard M. Epstein (ed.), *Revolt in the Congo* (New York, 1964), p. 16.

[39] Hoskyns, p. 114.

present external aggression."[40] Soviet notes delivered July 13 to the U.S., Britain, France, Belgium, and West Germany reiterated earlier charges and demanded that the U.N. "put an end to the aggression" committed by Belgium in the Congo.[41] Also on July 13, Kasavubu and Lumumba returned to Leopoldville where they learned of the Cabinet's appeal for American troops the day before. They quickly sent another telegram to the U.N., making it clear that their purpose in requesting aid was to prevent aggression and "not to restore the internal situation"; that they expected a force of contingents "from neutral countries and not from the United States" and that if the United Nations did not respond without delay they would appeal to "the Bandung Treaty powers."[42] More and more it seemed that only effective action by the U.N. could prevent Communist exploitation of Lumumba's "desperate, self-contradictory, unpredictable, irrational mood."[43]

The Security Council met on the evening of July 13, and here the United States attempted to coordinate the two major themes of its policy: deference to the Belgians and fear of the chaos-to-Communism syndrome. Mongi Slim of Tunisia, unofficially representing the Afro-Asian bloc in the U.N., introduced a draft resolution. Paragraph 1 called for "Belgium to withdraw its troops." Paragraph 2 authorized Hammarskjold to provide "such military assistance as may be necessary until, through the efforts of the Congolese government with the technical assistance of the United Nations, the national security forces may be able, in the opinion of the government to fully meet their tasks." The resolution was worded so as to secure maximum approval, and a dispute arose as to whether Paragraph 1 (Belgian withdrawal) was contingent

[40] The full text of the cable (U.N. Document S/4382) appears in Ernest W. Lefever, *Uncertain Mandate: Politics of the U.N. Congo Operation* (Baltimore, 1967), pp. 224–225.

[41] Epstein, p. 16.

[42] Lefever, *Uncertain Mandate,* p. 225 (U.N. Document S/4382).

[43] Sentiment at the State Department reported by *New York Herald Tribune,* July 14, 1960, p. 1.

upon performance of Paragraph 2 (U.N. guarantee of law and order).

The Western powers on the Security Council (Britain, France, Italy, and the United States) held that it was so contingent, emphasizing the humanitarian reasons for Belgium's intervention, i.e., the inability of the Congo government to protect whites. The United States delegate, Henry Cabot Lodge, declared "no aggression has been committed." On the other hand, Tunisia, Poland, the Soviet Union, Ecuador, and Ceylon stated, or implied, that there had been an aggression and that they were on the whole inclined toward unconditional withdrawal of Belgian forces. For example, Mongi Slim noted that no deaths had occurred before the Belgian intervention, and claimed that the arrival of the Belgians had aggravated the situation. He stated that the Belgian action was a violation of the Treaty of Friendship between Belgium and the Congo and "without any doubt an aggressive act which can be justified by nothing in our opinion." He asked how innocent Congolese could be killed "in the name of humanity," and appealed for Belgian withdrawal.[44] By taking the stand it did, the United States indicated that *its anti-Communist policy in the Congo would be pursued through cooperation with its European allies, particularly Belgium.* It was considered too dangerous to let the Belgians solve the Congo problem alone; but every effort would be made to protect Belgian interests, the more so as these were basically the interests of America's European allies in Africa: European lives, property, and spheres of influence.

44 Tilden LeMelle, "Role of Large and Small Powers in the Congo Crisis" (typewritten paper), discusses the various positions. Excerpts from Lodge's speech appear in *Department of State Bulletin,* Aug. 1, 1960, pp. 159–162.

CHAPTER II

Collision with Lumumba

"The failure of the U.N. to dislodge Tshombe and the Belgians as quickly as Lumumba desired led the Congo premier to call on the Soviet Bloc for assistance and thus to provide the entering wedge for Soviet penetration."

—Department of State, Report from U.S. Embassy in Leopoldville, September 5, 1960.[1]

The consistency of the American position (conservative deference to Belgium and anti-Communism) was rapidly brought into question. While a United Nations Force (UNF) was being organized and deployed, Belgian troops continued to intervene in the Congo. Against the background of previous events, these interventions "convinced Kasavubu and Lumumba that Belgium was taking control and that the whole independence of the Congo was threatened." [2] On July 14, they asked Khrushchev to "watch hourly over the development of the situation" as "we may have to ask for the Soviet Union's intervention should the Western camp not stop its aggression." Khrushchev's return cable pledged "resolute measures" if the West didn't stop its "criminal actions." [3] On July 15, Lumumba made a long speech in the Congo Chamber in which he criticized the U.S. for supporting the Belgian interpretation of the Security Council resolution; at the same time the Congo Senate passed—unanimously—a resolution calling for immediate withdrawal of Belgian troops.[4] Two days later Lumumba and Kasavubu gave the U.N. an ultimatum: if Belgian troops were not out of the

[1] Timberlake, p. 88. [2] Hoskyns, p. 128. [3] Epstein, p. 17.
[4] Hoskyns, p. 129.

Congo in 72 hours they would appeal for Soviet forces. By July 20 some Belgian troops had left Leopoldville and been replaced by U.N. troops. But the Congo Cabinet was not satisfied with a partial withdrawal and threatened to call in Soviet or Afro-Asian troops unless the U.N. took decisive action. In the Security Council the Soviet delegate stated that if aggression continued, more active measures would have to be taken both by the U.N. and by "peace-loving States which are in sympathy with the Congo's cause." [5]

Washington reacted stiffly to threats of Soviet military intervention. Actually, Khrushchev was thought to be bluffing; he could not defy so blatantly a U.N. force that was backed not only by the West but also by the Afro-Asians. State Department officials said they were more concerned that the Soviets would "provide the Congolese with advisers, technicians and credits" to further their "penetration of the African continent." [6] Still, the problem of Belgian withdrawal was not invested with any added urgency. In the Security Council, Lodge expressed confidence in the pace of retreat. He pointed out that some Belgians had already left and that the Belgian government had promised to take back the others when order was re-established.[7] In the end, the weight of official criticism fell on Lumumba, whose "peremptory demands" and flirtations with the Russians bolstered earlier impressions of his volatility and dangerous opportunism.[8]

The fear spawned by Lumumba's early moves was somewhat lessened by his trip to the United States in late July. In Washington, Lumumba declared he was satisfied with the most recent U.N. resolution, announced an economic agreement with a group of Wall Street financiers, requested U.S. public and private aid (and at one point U.S. troops), and stressed his policy of neutrality. His performance at State Department meetings did not purge him of suspicion; many found him "untrustworthy" ("He never looked you in the eye," explained a top official), "slippery," and "oppor-

[5] Epstein, p 17. [6] *New York Times,* July 21, 1960, p. 1.

[7] *Department of State Bulletin,* Aug. 8, 1960, pp. 221–222.

[8] *New York Times,* July 21, 1960, p. 1; *Time,* Aug. 8, 1960, p. 29.

tunistic." But most were impressed by his "brilliance," "articulateness," and controlled passion. (Herter is said to have remarked, "He's crazy all right—crazy like a fox.") He was accepted as a "genuine nationalist," and one participant recalls him "making a fairly good impression in his talk with the Secretary." American policy-makers felt that with the U.N. providing security and technical assistance, the Lumumba government would be able to withstand Communist pressures.[9] Until such time as Katanga became the central issue, American diplomats were not averse to "working with" the Lumumba government.

The Dispute over Katanga

By August 7, Belgian troops had departed from five of the Congo's six provinces, and a week later they began to withdraw from Katanga. The problem of Katanga's secession now rose to the fore and increased the tension between the two strands of American policy: conservative deference to the Belgians and hard-line anti-Communism. Eventually the U.S. Central Intelligence Agency (CIA) took up the task of resolving the tension.

Locally, Katangan secession was based on a late marriage of convenience between two very different groupings. The Lunda and Bayeke of South Katanga's cities and mining centers were concerned about economic and political competition from socially ascendant "strangers"—particularly the Baluba from Kasai. In organizing to counter this threat, and to secure its position in the period of decolonialization, the Lunda-Bayeke modern elite relied heavily on strong customary structures which had weathered the colonial period. The power of these structures is indicated by the fact that the first President of the modern political association, CONAKAT, was Godefroid Munongo, a civil servant and member of the royal house of the Bayeke, and the second President was Moise Tshombe, a wholesale merchant and the son-in-law of the paramount chief of the Lunda. The customary authorities seem to

[9] On the positive reactions to Lumumba, see *Christian Science Monitor,* July 28, 1960, p. 1; *Time,* Aug. 8, 1960, pp. 29–30.

have been worried that the transition to Independence, with its introduction of democratic participation, would undermine their legitimacy. Traditional influence in CONAKAT was also the result of the paternal economic and social regime in the copper mines, which had retarded the growth of modern, nationalist ideas among the Lunda and Bayeke workers.

CONAKAT's parochialism and traditionalism were well suited to the political objectives of Katanga's white settlers, who were principally independent businessmen and professionals and comprised about one-third of all white settlers in the Belgian Congo. Concentrated in the mining cities of the South and well organized, they exerted considerable influence in the larger European community of company personnel and colonial agents. The settlers had long resisted the central authorities whom they accused of neglecting their economic interests (not always the same as those of the trusts) and opening the door to various liberalizing influences which, they felt, menaced their social position. The autonomist impulse was heightened by the prospect of Independence, since the centralizing threat was now that of a black nationalist government in Leopoldville. In addition, the settlers had for some time been tempted by the great wealth of Katanga and by the proximate example of white rule in Rhodesia.

When it became clear that white reaction alone could not prevent Belgium from transferring power to African nationalists, the settler organizations sought an alliance with local Africans. CONAKAT's aspirations for leadership on the Copperbelt and wish for preservation of traditional structures were consistent with the settlers' theses of autonomy, loose federalism based on a recognition of each region's economic contribution, resistance to modern nationalism, and cooperation with Belgium. However, the political education of CONAKAT was by no means left to chance. The party's adoption of settler ideology occurred in direct relation to the political force, and to the financial and technical assistance brought to it by the Europeans. By mid-1959, only eight months after its formation, CONAKAT accepted the affiliation of the main settler group and gave it a monopoly of European recruitment and organization. The Europeans' influence was further reinforced by the withdrawal of the Katanaga Baluba organization (BALUBAKAT) from CONAKAT in late 1959. The BALUBAKAT dominated the Northern half of the province. It was disturbed by the continuing anti-Kasai Baluba orientation of CONAKAT, and feared that separatism could become a device for the installation of an anti-Baluba regime. In addition, customary authority structures had been weakened, in some cases, among the Katanga Baluba, producing a modern elite which was at least more open to nationalist currents and a volatile mass with a history of anticolonial resistance.

It is, therefore, not surprising that the BALUBAKAT leaders resented the depth of European influence in CONAKAT. By Independence Day, then, the original political division in the Southern cities (strangers vs. authentic Katanganese) had been supplanted by a province-wide conflict between the CONAKAT in the South (honeycombed with settler and conservative European influence) and the BALUBAKAT in the North (which attracted more liberal European advisers whose inclinations were antitrust and anticlerical). Both groups looked to the outside for decisive assistance, the BALUBAKAT to the Central Government and its supporters, the CONAKAT to Belgium and its European allies and to the interested regimes of Southern Africa.[10]

At the very moment in which the Lumumba government lost control of its army and administration, Belgian assistance enabled Katanga to secede from the faltering new State. Before the mutiny, Brussels had supported a united Congo under the provisional federalist constitution. Belgian force and diplomacy put down two CONAKAT secession plots in 1960.[11] However, the collapse of the *Force Publique* (Congo Colonial Army), the attacks on Euro-

[10] Gérard-Libois, *Sécession,* pp. 7–76; Crawford Young, "The Politics of Separatism: Katanga 1960–1963," in Gwendolyn M. Carter (ed.), *Politics in Africa: 7 Cases* (New York, 1966), pp. 167–188.

On the political history of North Katanga, see Merlier, pp. 247, 312; and J. C. Willame, *Les Provinces du Congo,* I, 115–116.

[11] Gérard-Libois, *Sécession,* pp. 72–82.

peans, and the Lumumba government's strong nationalist reactions destroyed a certain image of Independence that was at the heart of Belgium's support for Congo unity,

This image was that of a country endowed with immense natural resources, which would accede peacefully to independence, without breaking with the colonial power; this country would doubtless dispose of all keys to its sovereignty but because of objective requirements its administration and army—the instruments of its unity—would for a long time depend on European cadres promoted to the rank of technical advisors, while the private enterprises would pursue their economic and social action and the missions would benefit from a statute of subsidized liberty, guaranteeing their development and socioreligious influence.[12]

Now Belgium hoped that Katanga, which had the most important investments and a third of the European population, could be insulated from the disorder and militant nationalism sweeping other provinces. Rapidly, a new image of Independence took form in government and business circles: friendly Katanga would be built up as a strong counterweight to the Lumumbist center, and would serve as a pole around which the Congo could eventually be reorganized on confederal lines. It is noteworthy that even at the moment of maximum shock and desperation, most Belgian leaders did not envision a *permanent* secession. Such an extreme alternative would have endangered Belgian interests in other parts of the Congo and unnecessarily antagonized Afro-Asian opinion, which neither Belgium nor her partners in the Atlantic Alliance could wholly ignore. Thus Belgium never gave Tshombe formal recognition.[13]

Given the economic importance of the province and its place in the emerging Belgian strategy, Belgian forces in Katanga had

[12] Gérard-Libois, *Le Rôle,* p. 10.

[13] *Ibid.,* pp. 8, 11–12; Gérard-Libois, *Sécession,* pp. 134–136. Belgian Prime Minister Pierre Wigny stated the arguments against an internationally organized and permanent secession in a note sent to other Western powers July 10 and 11. Gérard-Libois and Verhaegen, *Congo 1960,* p. 721.

different orders from those in the rest of the Congo. Their role went well beyond the protection of Belgian nationals. They disarmed and expelled all members of the army who were loyal to the Central Government, "irrespective of whether the soldiers were really in a state of mutiny and threatening lives and property or were only, as was frequently the case, hostile to the provincial government." [14]

In August, as U.N. troops began to replace the Belgians in Katanga, hundreds of Belgian officers were seconded to the Katanga gendarmerie, and raced to create a military backing for Tshombe. These cadres were by no means "mercenaries" since they continued to take orders from the Belgian Ministry of Defense. Starting from scratch with the "debris" of the Katanga *Force Publique*—no more than 200 men—they organized and officered a main force consisting largely of 1,500 Lunda and Yeke volunteers. They also "advised" auxiliary forces of traditional warriors led by their chiefs and of settlers grouped in European *"corps de volontaires."* These groups were equipped from old *Force Publique* stocks transferred from the Kamina military base in Kasai and from material captured during the recent Belgian interventions. All Belgian air elements from colonial days were transferred to Katanga; these included more than a dozen aircraft. Belgium's Sabena airlines flew in arms, including one notable delivery of 7–9 tons in early September. The remnants of the colonial *Surêté,* operating out of neighboring Congo-Brazzaville and certain provinces, supplied a constant stream of military-political information. In these ways, Belgium moved directly to meet the twofold military threat to Katanga: from the Central Government and from the Baluba rebellion which had begun in August.[15]

On the civilian side, a Belgian "technical mission" was set up

[14] Hoskyns, p. 142.

[15] Gérard-Libois, *Sécession,* pp. 138–139, 177–178. On the status of the Belgian officers, see the statement of their Commandant (Guy Weber), quoted in "Les Mercenaires dans l'histoire du Congo (1960–1967)," *Courrier Africain,* Nos. 74–75, Feb. 26, 1968, p. 6n.

under Count Harold d'Aspremont-Lynden, former *chef de cabinet adjoint* of Prime Minister Eyskens. This was the "real command post for Katanga." Lynden ordered Belgian civil servants to remain at their posts in Katanga; "Elsewhere in the Congo they were told that their security would no longer be assured and that they were free to return to Belgium, where places in the metropolitan public service were promised." Furthermore, Lynden attended Katanga Cabinet meetings, met with military chiefs, advised private parties on their legal obligations, and arranged material, technical, and financial assistance with Brussels.[16]

In addition to local Europeans, a number of Belgians who depended on Brussels now moved into the CONAKAT ministries as *chefs de cabinet* and advisers. As for the private sector, itself a major influence on Belgian policy, it furnished Katanga with the taxes, royalties, dividends, and foreign exchange that would normally belong to the Central Government. The collaboration of the Belgian business structure with Katanga secession was later illustrated by its production of tanks, bombs, explosives, armored trucks, air strips, and its provision of demolition squads for the Katanga Ministry of Defense.[17]

On the diplomatic level, Belgium first sought to delay U.N. entrance into Katanga. Afterwards, when U.N. intervention appeared inevitable, she tried to ensure that it would not influence the "internal" dispute between Lumumba and Tshombe.[18] From July 26th, Belgian agents in Brazzaville and the Congo had instructions to encourage "any rallying of other provinces of the Congo to Katanga . . . of course with discretion." [19] In the fol-

16 Gérard-Libois, *Sécession,* p. 129; Young, "The Politics of Separatism," in Carter, p. 183.

On Oct. 11 a Belgian representative in Elizabethville wrote, "The Belgian cadres are an essential and decisive element in the maintenance of order in Katanga. . . . Their withdrawal would in 24 hours result in the collapse of the gendarmerie and would be followed shortly thereafter by the collapse of the Tshombe government." Gérard-Libois, *Sécession,* p. 154.

17 *Ibid.,* pp. 130–131, 140–141, 246.

18 *Ibid.,* pp. 137–138; Hoskyns, pp. 159–160.

19 Gérard-Libois and Verhaegen, *Congo 1960,* pp. 744–745.

lowing weeks, these agents encouraged a secessionist movement in Equateur, furnished limited financial and military aid for a Baluba "Mining State" in South Kasai, and subsidized a new ABAKO campaign for autonomy in Leopoldville.[20]

From the start, Katanga received help from a number of other powers. Important in its own right, this assistance would, at a later moment, give the CONAKAT-settler alliance increased leverage on Belgian policy. As explained above, British and French interests in Africa were roughly similar to those of Belgium. In different ways—France by boycott, Britain by critical participation—they proceeded to influence U.N. decisions in favor of Belgian policy in Katanga. Their position was also felt in the capitals of former French Africa and in the Central African Federation.[21] In Paris, certain members of the de Gaulle government favored a more direct approach, perhaps even a partial supplanting of Belgian influence in Elizabethville. As a result, French authorities permitted the recruitment of mercenaries and the sale of jet aircraft for Katanga in 1960 and 1961. Additional encouragement was provided through diplomatic contacts, mostly via secret services.[22]

Congo-Brazzaville, in the person of President Fulbert "Abbé" Youlou, offered assistance which "if not the most effective and the most disinterested [was] at least the most constant and spectac-

[20] On Equateur, see *ibid.*, pp. 979–982. For South Kasai, see *ibid.*, p. 809; Gérard-Libois, *Sécession,* p. 143 (The parallel role of Société Générale and its satellite, FORMINIÈRE, appears in Gérard-Libois and Verhaegen, *Congo 1960,* pp. 801, 1032). Belgian activity in Brazzaville, including support for ABAKO, is discussed in *ibid.*, p. 687; Gérard-Libois, *Le Rôle,* p. 14; and Hoskyns, p. 187.

[21] Gérard-Libois observes that in "all probability" the authorities of Malagasy expelled a Belgian adviser of President Kasavubu during a conference at Tananarive on the recommendation of the French. Tshombe's European advisers were permitted to stay. Note too the role of French political-commercial circles in the creation of an air route from Brazzaville to Elizabethville. Gérard-Libois, *Sécession,* pp. 170, 201. On British-Rhodesian relations, see Sir Roy Welensky, *Welensky's 4,000 Days* (New York, 1964), pp. 213–264.

[22] Verhaegen, *Congo 1961,* pp. 303–305; Gérard-Libois, *Sécession,* pp. 187–191, 198, 204–205; Hoskyns, pp. 287, 385–387.

ular." [23] Some of Youlou's long-run objectives were similar to those of the French: to prevent development of a strong, nationalist Congo and to use Katanga's wealth in the framework of an association of economic cooperation in Central Africa. (That his principal advisers happened to be French nationals may not have been foreign to his point of view, or to the zeal with which he pursued these goals. In this regard, one must also take account of such short-term ends as the financing of his political apparatus and of the proposed Kouilou Dam, the keystone of his economic policy.) Congo-Brazzaville became Tshombe's window on Congo developments, and provided a safe meeting ground for negotiations with Congolese and foreign representatives. It was also a center for the re-export of war materials to Elizabethville.[24]

The most stable support for secession came from the colonial and settler governments of Southern Africa. Sir Roy Welensky, Prime Minister of the Central African Federation, had raised the possibility of Katanga's joining the Rhodesias as early as March 1960. Rhodesia and Angola furnished essential routes for the export of Katanga's mineral production, and for the importation of civilian goods, military equipment and white mercenaries. These last were sent up from Rhodesia and South Africa by Katanga recruiters beginning in late 1960. Portuguese Angola, Rhodesia, and South Africa supplied aircraft. The Angolan port of Lobito became a key point of transshipment for European and African exports bound for Katanga. In times of trouble, Rhodesia was to provide safe refuge for Katangan leaders and their European cohorts; it also guaranteed the security of Katangan installations near the Rhodesian frontier.[25]

The Lumumba government was strongly opposed to the emerging power complex in Katanga. Militantly nationalist, its foremost concern was to bring Katanga back under the authority of the

[23] Verhaegen, *Congo 1961*, p. 301.

[24] *Ibid.*, pp. 301–303; Hoskyns, pp. 187, 288; Gerard-Libois, *Sécession*, p. 198.

[25] *Ibid.*, pp. 53–56, 196–197.

Central Government. Secessionist movements in other provinces, partly stimulated by Belgium, imparted added urgency to this task. It seemed that the Central Government's authority was swiftly disintegrating. In its foreign policy, the Congo demanded first an immediate U.N. move into Katanga, and, next, that the weight of the UNF be used to end Katanga's secession. Presenting evidence that the Belgian government was actively encouraging secession, the Congo government made numerous demands for action by the U.N., such as a request for disarmament of Belgians in the service of "rebellious provincial authorities," confiscation of all arms and ammunition distributed in Katanga, the sending of African and Congolese troops to Katanga, and consultation with the Central Government and an Afro-Asian advisory committee in interpreting the various Security Council resolutions on the Congo. If the U.N. were not sufficiently responsive, the Congo warned that it was ready to seek the assistance of others, particularly in the militarily crucial area of long-range transportation.[26]

The American position was—essentially—support of Belgian policy. While the U.S. favored U.N. entry into Katanga (in accord with its overall support of the U.N. operation), it acquiesced in the various delays. Most important, it held "that the United Nations cannot be drawn into the political struggle between Prime Minister Lumumba and Provincial President Tshombe,"[27] this being a purely internal dispute. In personal interviews with the author, former Eisenhower officials were quite candid about the rationale of American policy. First, there was the NATO reflex: other (colonialist) allies were supporting Belgium. Still, as one official remarked, "we were not under the gun of the Belgians" if it ap-

[26] Hoskyns, pp. 151, 160–161, 165–180, 189–194; Colin Legum, *Congo Disaster* (Baltimore, 1961), pp. 125–142; Legum, Forword, in Lumumba, p. xvii.

Lumumba's request to the Soviet Union for long-range transportation (Aug. 15, 1960) is reproduced in P. Houart, *La Pénétration communiste au Congo* (Brussels, 1960), Appendix VI.

[27] Henry Cabot Lodge at the Security Council meeting of Aug. 8, quoted in *Department of State Bulletin,* Sept. 5, 1960, p. 384.

peared that an alternative policy was in the interests of the "free world." This brings up the second, and possibly most significant, consideration of the policy-makers: Katanga was an "isle of stability" in the center of a "parlous" situation. Tshombe had a "reasonable attitude toward Belgians and whites," while Lumumba frightened away thousands of Belgians, producing economic and administrative "chaos." The question was not simply order or chaos, however. Many foreign diplomats argued that "the secession of Katanga was actually preventing a settlement between United Nations, Belgian, and Congolese troops and so contributing to disorder in the rest of the Congo." [28] But American officials now preferred the conservative order of a Tshombe to an extension of the rough and tumble militant, nationalist order of a Lumumba. Tshombe accepted white tutelage, protected white lives, property, and resources, and demanded a political autonomy which seemed appropriate in "tribal" Africa. It is noteworthy that Robert Murphy, the archexpositor of conservative colonialist ideology, was consulted by senior U.S. administration officials on Katanga, and there seems to have been a real meeting of the minds.

Two other considerations were of lesser importance. Some thought that if the Communists gained control of the Central Government through the undependable Lumumba, then Katanga could be held via the pro-Western Tshombe. Yet at this time the Communist threat was quite remote. And one may ask whether a decision to disarm the Communists by working with Tshombe rather than Lumumba does not reflect the aforementioned conservative bias in American policy. Finally, some officials admit they were not informed of the extent of Belgian assistance to Tshombe. Incomplete intelligence from the embassies in Leopoldville and Brussels apparently left the impression that Katangan secession was largely a tribal phenomenon, abetted by *local* European interests. However, the policy-makers minimize the influence of these factual distortions, and stress the basic strategic and ideological assumptions discussed above. In short, America's policy of anti-Communism in

[28] Hoskyns, p. 130.

the Congo was qualified and even shaped by her deference to Belgian policy—a deference which was in part the customary nod to NATO partners and in part the conservative ideology of the Eisenhower Administration.

There were some differences within the State Department over the Katanga secession. Thus, the African Bureau held that the Congo was economically unviable without Katanga's revenues and, further, considered support for Tshombe a political anachronism in the Year of African Independence. In the first weeks of July, a representative of American Metal Climax contacted Satterthwaite and Penfield of the Bureau of African Affairs to urge that Katanga be supported as a barrier to chaos on the Rhodesian Copperbelt.[29] The representative indicated that he was dismayed by their "instinctive" preference for "large units in Africa." Still, the Africanists were neither willing nor powerful enough to suggest an activist policy. For the most part, they merely sought to hedge U.S. backing of Belgium enough to make it "palatable" to the Africans. On the other side, the European Bureau's recommendations received a friendly hearing in the upper reaches of the State Department. For example, an officer of the African Bureau recalled Under Secretary Dillon's position as "Don't close the door on Katanga," and understood Dillon to be concerned for stability on the rich Copperbelt. Another participant in policy discussions also recalls Dillon's open-mindedness on the Katanga gambit. Finally, a member of a special interdepartmental task force on the Congo, which provided "continuous education of the many high officials who were able only temporarily to deal with decision-making during the crisis," writes,

There were, basically, only two points of view about the Congo, and in that respect the Congo crisis was perhaps not different from many others. There were the people who looked for clear-cut solutions and

[29] In addition to its concern for stability on the Copperbelt, the company was worried by its European and American cadres' fearful reactions to the influx of thousands of white refugees from Katanga at the time of the mutiny.

a consistent policy stand, and those who felt that one should work for a compromise of varying interests and "keep the options open." Naturally, representatives of the European Bureau were adherents of the latter school of thought.[30]

The United Nations was the transmission belt for American policy. As Ernest Lefever has pointed out, the Security Council and the Secretary-General were "sustained and guided, formally and informally, by a moderately stable coalition of states which stood behind the peace-keeping effort throughout its four years. The most important member was the United States, without whose political, financial, and logistical support the UNF would have collapsed."[31] On Katanga, the other members of the Security Council were deeply divided. The Europeans supported Tshombe; the Soviet bloc backed Lumumba; and the Afro-Asians were divided between moderate and militant opponents of secession. Hammarskjold sympathized with the European view,[32] but "he knew that the real decisions in international politics were made by states, particularly the Big Powers. He knew that the office of Secretary-

30 Letter to the author, Mar. 20, 1970.

31 Lefever, *Uncertain Mandate,* p. 30. In 1960 the U.S. paid nearly half the costs of the U.N. Force in the Congo. It paid its assessment of $16.2 million and voluntarily contributed another $3.9 million. The U.S., as well as Britain, Canada, and the Soviet Union, waived nearly the entire U.N. debt for the airlift—which came to $10.3 million for the Americans and $2.4 million for the others.

32 Hammarskjold told the Security Council that the dispute between the Central Government and the provincial authorities was an internal affair "which did not have its root in the Belgian attitude." As O'Brien points out, "Nobody who followed the news . . . could remain in doubt about the seriousness of the Belgian involvement or about the fact that Tshombe and the Belgian commander were working in close concert. . . . Hammarskjold did, I think, share the very widespread and sometimes unconscious European assumption that order in Africa is primarily a matter of safeguarding European lives and property." Conor Cruise O'Brien, "The United Nations and the Congo," *Studies on the Left,* VI (May–June, 1966), 7–8.

Even the moderate Mongi Slim of Tunisia produced evidence before the Security Council that Belgium was actively encouraging secession. Hoskyns, p. 168.

General was essentially an instrument, not an actor." [33] United States support shifted the political balance in favor of the Europeans. Hoskyns suggests that the United Nations might have pursued a moderate policy of acting "much earlier to prevent the build up of a new gendarmerie [in Katanga]" and using "its presence in Katanga to open negotiations between Tshombe and the Central Government." She also thinks that Hammarskjold possessed enough independent leverage to have put this through on his own initiative ("He would have had the full backing of the Afro-Asians, and though both the Soviet Union and the Western powers might, for different reasons, have disapproved, it would have been hard for them in these conditions to use the veto.") [34] How much more influence and leverage was possessed by the Americans!

Lumumba's reactions to U.S. and U.N. policy led the State Department to conclude that the chaos-to-Communism syndrome was working itself out with Hegelian splendor.

In their Washington discussions neither Lumumba nor the State Department seems to have raised the Katanga question. Both sides were anxious to avoid conflict. And the general problem of troop withdrawals was still dominant. But the underlying tension erupted as Lumumba boarded a plane to Canada. The previous day he had received a telegram from Gizenga reporting a battle between Belgian paratroops and loyal ANC at Kolwezi barracks in Katanga. There was "an exaggerated account of the number of Congolese dead." [35] In an airport statement Lumumba abandoned his studied moderation, charging that "the whole of Africa" was "threatened by Belgium." [36] Under Secretary Dillon was disturbed by the vehemence of his statement and its "Communist phraseology," so he answered back "more frankly than usual."

U.N. hesitation in entering Katanga (Bunche had exaggerated the resistance Katanga could offer to a non-negotiated entry) resulted in threats by the Lumumba government to rely on (1) its own forces and (2) African assistance, especially from radical

[33] Lefever, *Uncertain Mandate,* p. 28.
[34] Hoskyns, p. 180.
[35] *Ibid.,* p. 157.
[36] Epstein, p. 20.

African countries which the State Department considered "pro-Soviet." [37] The situation became more serious when the first U.N. troops flew into Elizabethville on August 13. Lumumba thought that the modalities of entrance and its declared purposes favored Katanga secession. On August 15, after an exchange of five letters in one day, relations between Hammarskjold and Lumumba broke down entirely. Three days later Congolese soldiers attacked and beat eight Canadian soldiers of the U.N. force at Leopoldville airport. "The assault . . . was attributed to the Lumumba government's encouragement of popular fears that white U.N. [38] troops were Belgian agents, seeking to reimpose colonial rule." The whole U.N. operation seemed threatened by Lumumba. Meanwhile the Russians were issuing statement after statement backing Lumumba, including one which demanded that "troops of other countries" be sent to the Congo if the U.N. failed to "cut short the occupation of Katanga" or failed to arrest separatist leaders who were "at the bidding of foreign powers." [39] An August 5, a Soviet boat left for the Congo laden with food, medicine, trucks, and technicians.[40]

The spectre of chaos and its scavenger, Communism, haunted the State Department. On August 19, James Reston reported:

> The outbreak of racism, tribalism and primitivism in the Congo has sent a shiver through this Government. There have been a series of urgent and private meetings here all last week leading to a very simple but hard conclusion, namely, that unless the irresponsible Congo

[37] For example, when Nkrumah's deep anticolonialism prompted him to denounce Western policy in the Congo as "imperialist intrigue" (in Sept.), Herter responded that Nkrumah had marked himself as "very definitely leaning toward the Soviet bloc." Veron McKay, *Africa in World Politics* (New York, 1963), p. 345. Timberlake, pp. 94–96, expressed a similar view regarding both Ghana and Guinea. Arthur M. Schlesinger, Jr., *A Thousand Days* (New York, 1967), p. 524, notes that, "by 1960 Washington had consigned Guinea to the Communist bloc."

On Bunche's overestimation of Katangan forces, see Hoskyns, pp. 162–164.

[38] Epstein, p. 34.

[39] Statement of Aug. 16, issued by Tass; quoted in *ibid.*, p. 31.

[40] *Libre Belgique*, Aug. 5, 1960, p. 5.

"Government" of Patrice Lumumba is contained, the future of the U.N. and of the whole of Africa will be seriously affected.

The "stakes were high" because we were relying on U.N. technicians and security forces to ease "the convulsive development of Central Africa" and "serve as an important buffer between the hostile great powers in Africa." But Lumumba's defiance of the U.N. with "Soviet diplomatic support" would be a precedent favoring chaos and its exploitation by international Communism.[41]

At the end of August the State Department regarded the situation as critical. Every move of Lumumba's seemed to encourage disorder and set the stage for Communist or left-neutralist intervention.[42] He urged a U.N. withdrawal from the Congo soon after the Belgian troops' departure because the U.N.'s "white troops" hoped to "substitute United Nations colonialism for Belgian colonialism."[43] He requisitioned Sabena airplanes for an invasion of South Kasai (and, ultimately, Katanga), and convened a Pan-African conference to obtain support and material assistance. He appeared to be postponing "reasonable administration" by his attacks on the U.N. and the Belgians. His very personality seemed to be disintegrating under the burden of so many difficult problems in so short a time ("weeks of crisis [which] would have tested the wisest and most experienced of statesmen").[44] Colin Legum has written of this period:

He lived in a perpetual frenzy. In a single day he wrote three consecutive protests to Mr. Hammarskjold. When he was excited his mind seemed to retreat behind an impenetrable glass wall; nothing could get through to him at all. It was unnerving. Incessantly, he would repeat his own arguments. . . . He was kept going through his own restless energy, fortified by drink and hemp-smoking.[45]

Ambassador Timberlake thought him mentally incompetent, a paranoiac.[46] Gradually, the Soviets and their friends were seen to

[41] *New York Times,* Aug. 19, 1960, p. 22.

[42] Timberlake, pp. 91, 94–95, 104.

[43] Epstein, p. 31.

[44] Legum in Lumumba, p. xxviii.

[45] *Ibid.*

[46] Quoted to this effect in Morgan, p. 159. See also Timberlake, p. 96.

be cashing in on chaos and on the good will they had carefully created. The Soviet chargé, André Fomin, was reported to have assisted in the formulation of Lumumba's legal case against the U.N.[47] On August 22, Lumumba visited the Soviet Ambassador for two hours. By the 24th, at least five Soviet correspondents had arrived in Leopoldville, "an impressive contingent by Soviet standards," including the foreign editor of *Pravda.* On the 26th "a major Soviet delegation led by G. K. Zhukov, long a close confidant of Khrushchev's and head of the State Committee for Cultural Relations with Foreign Countries, arrived . . . for talks with Premier Lumumba. . . . According to Tass, Zhukov discussed cultural and educational cooperation and offered places in Soviet institutions to 150 Congolese students."[48] *Washington Post* reporter Russell Warren Howe wrote that "authoritative sources" had confirmed offers of arms and vehicles to Lumumba by Egypt and Guinea. Already there were an estimated 125 Soviet bloc technicians in Leopoldville with more expected shortly.[49] In the words of Ambassador Timberlake,

> The rapid arrival of Soviet and Czech technicians in the Congo in July and August under the Lumumba regime indicated that the Soviet Bloc was prepared to move quickly and on a substantial scale to take advantage of the unforeseen opening.[50]

The connection between Lumumba's policies and Communist designs was made more explicit—hence more frightening—by a series of dispatches from the Embassy in Leopoldville. These reported Lumumba "under strong leftist influence," due to his "increasing reliance on Marxist (or 'Communist') advisers." (American diplomats used terms like "dangerous radical," "Marxist," "strong leftist," and "Communist" interchangeably since the first

[47] *New York Times,* Aug. 17, 1960, p. 1 (citing "2 Western delegations" at the U.N. as the source); also Aug. 20, 1960, p. 6.

[48] Helmut Sonnenfeldt, "The Soviet Union and China: Where They Stood in 1960," in Kitchen, p. 30. See also *Libre Belgique,* Aug. 29, 1960, p. 4; *Washington Post,* Aug. 28, 1960, p. A-5.

[49] *Washington Post,* Aug. 30, 1960, p. A-7, and Aug. 31, 1960, p. A-4.

[50] Timberlake, p. 138.

three were considered "very susceptible to Communist policies and suggestions" and even possible "agents.")[51] The key counselors were said to be: (1) Serge Michel, a Polish-born Frenchman who had been "lent" to Lumumba by the rebel Algerian Provisional Government (GPRA) as his press secretary, and who arrived in Leopoldville August 9;[52] according to Hoskyns, Michel was "certainly a Marxist" but "was by no means an uncritical supporter of the Soviet Union and had, for example, protested openly and publicly about the suppression of the Hungarian revolt in 1956";[53] (2) Mme. Andrée Blouin, a mulatto from ex-French Equatorial Africa, who was Lumumba's chief of protocol and "one of his most influential advisers"; she was also said to have political influence over Minister of Information Kashamura and Deputy Minister Gizenga (the latter reportedly shared her bed); the American Ambassador referred to her as "a confirmed Marxist" and Gizenga's "Communist confidante";[54] as will be shown later, these descriptions were highly inaccurate;[55] and (3) a small number of Belgians (possibly three) who held minor posts in the Central Government and were of lesser importance—they were said to be Communists or fellow-travelers or simply left-leaning.[56]

Increasingly the Lumumba government's actions were traced to a conspiracy within the Prime Minister's entourage. Timberlake came to consider the antiwhite, inflammatory Kashamura radio "virtually a Communist mouthpiece." He also thought one could discern a hidden purpose in Lumumba's attacks on the U.N. and the Belgians:

[51] *Ibid.*, pp. 104, 184–185, 65, 175.

[52] Michel was called "Red lining" by *Time*, Aug. 29, 1960, p. 20; "left wing," "Marxist extremist," and "Communist" by the *New York Times*, Aug. 20, p. 6; Sept. 4, p. 3; Sept. 7, p. 40; and "Communist" by the *Washington Post*, Sept. 11, p. A-29. On his political background, see Hoskyns, p. 188.

[53] *Ibid.*, p. 189.

[54] Timberlake, pp. 176, 65.

[55] See below, pp. 259–261.

[56] *New York Times*, Sept. 7, 1960, p. 40. James Reston notes three Belgians—two Communists and a "fellow traveler"—who officials indicated "were working closely with Lumumba."

> Many responsible Congolese came to the conclusion that Lumumba was trying to force all remaining Europeans out so that he would have the excuse to invite a mass influx of Bloc technicians.[57]

Embassy officials blamed Mme. Blouin for their growing lack of access to Lumumba and members of his government. There were press reports that Serge Michel had drafted (along with Soviet chargé Fomin) Lumumba's arguments against Hammarskjold.[58]

By August 29, American policy-makers were convinced that the chaos-to-Communism syndrome was on the verge of fulfillment. "Western diplomats" in Leopoldville gave out that the Congo was "sliding slowly but surely into the Communist bloc." *Washington Post* correspondent Lynn Heinzerling relayed the basis for this judgment. First, there was "the fevered activity of Communist bloc nations here," including the arrival of the Soviet cultural mission and the editor from *Pravda*. Second, he reported:

> Premier Lumumba's startling changes of position, his open challenge to the United States and Secretary-General Dag Hammarskjold, his constant agitation of the largely illiterate Congolese can be explained in no other way, veteran observers say.
>
> Lumumba begins to act more and more as if he were being propelled by someone with vastly more political experience and subtlety than he has ever been able to acquire.[59]

From Washington, Neal Stanford wrote in the *Christian Science Monitor:*

> News from the Congo has official Washington worried. Why? Time seems to be running out in the which the United Nations can bring law and order to the Congo.
>
> Not only is the Soviet Union moving in and beginning to all but run the Lumumba government, but Premier Patrice Lumumba is thwarting U.N. policy and action and aiding Moscow—though perhaps without realizing it—in penetrating and establishing a foothold in Central Africa.

57 Timberlake, pp. 66, 99. 58 *New York Times,* Aug. 20, 1960, p. 6.
59 *Washington Post,* Aug. 28, 1960, p. A-5.

According to some estimates, the United Nations has only two or three weeks in which to restore law and order to see a Communist takeover—however gradual in the Congo.

Judging from past events, something like the following scenario was in prospect:

(a) All white troops would be forced out.

(b) The Ghanaian and Guinean contingents of the U.N. force would remain.

(c) In time these would be made subservient to Lumumba and "an arm of his apparent program to make himself authoritarian ruler of the Congo."

(d) "Along with this would go consolidation of Communist control of Mr. Lumumba's regime"; already there were 125 or more Communist technical "advisers," and an increasing number of "Communist-trained Africans" were moving into positions of power.[60]

The *New York Times* noted "fresh reports of 'Communist,' 'left wing,' and 'anti-Western' influence in the Congo government greater than heretofore indicated by officials."

These reports, based on "first-hand observations by an acknowledged specialist," included the warning that unless the United Nations succeeded in pacifying the Congo in the next two weeks, outside Communist domination of the area was almost certain.[61]

On August 30, a squadron of Ilyushins put down at Stanleyville airport to help airlift troops for the Kasai-Katanga invasion. On September 1, Secretary Herter expressed the basic analysis (and predetermining perspective?) of American officialdom:

The Soviet Union has sought to complicate rather than assist U.N. efforts to aid the Congo Republic to get on its feet. The collapse of order is the purpose of Soviet policy—a collapse which is a condition precedent to their hoped-for new order of Communist control.[62]

60 *Christian Science Monitor,* Aug. 30, 1960, p. 1.

61 *New York Times,* Aug. 30, 1960, p. 2.

62 *Washington Post,* Sept. 2, 1960, p. A-12. Speaking to the same audience as Herter—the American Bar Association banquet—presidential candidate

The Overthrow of Lumumba

Under the circumstances the U.S. and U.N. searched "for a means of ousting Mr. Lumumba, swinging the independent African nations into support of a new anti-Communist government, and subsequent disarmament of the disruptive *Force Publique.*" [63]

Lumumba's patchwork coalition of July buckled under the cumulative impact of crisis after crisis. Weakness in the Central Government stimulated various politico-ethnic forces, including Kasavubu's ABAKO party, to demand a more federal constitution. Administrative and economic breakdowns displeased the trade unions. Lumumba's flirtation with the Soviets alienated important Catholic politicians and threatened to disturb the political balance by bolstering Lumumba's personal position. And many Congolese politicians were worried about the Prime Minister's increasing authoritarianism, a product of the emergencies, the aforementioned centrifugal forces, and the absolute self-confidence of Patrice Lumumba. All these factors seem to have moved Kasavubu, whose disquiet was more and more apparent. In addition, the opposition in parliament was laying plans for the censure of certain "hard" ministers, such as Gizenga, Kashamura, and Mpolo.[64]

A motion of censure was to be offered September 8th, to be followed by resignations of ABAKO and PUNA (Parti de l'Unité Nationale) ministers and popular demonstrations. If all this came

---

Adlai Stevenson presented a similar view. He said, "Many sections of the globe are returning to the chaos from which Western rule briefly rescued them," and added, "in chaos, the Communists are better manipulators than we are." He drew consolation that upsets like the Congo might be beneficial in showing America new dangers and opportunities. *New York Times,* Sept. 2, 1960, p. 2.

63 *Wall Street Journal,* Sept. 6, 1960, p. 1 (The search reportedly consumed "many days."). See also *Christian Science Monitor,* Aug. 30, 1960, p. 1 (quoted below, p. 87).

64 Gérard-Libois and Verhaegen, *Congo 1960,* pp. 658–704; Hoskyns, pp. 198–199. For American appreciation of the internal situation, see *Christian Science Monitor,* Aug. 26, 1960, p. 1.

off, Lumumba would be forced to change the composition of his government or risk his own defeat.[65]

From Brazzaville, Belgian agents and French advisers of Abbé Youlou were heavily engaged in the anti-Lumumba activity. Following Belgium's policy of provoking centrifugal tendencies in the provinces and encouraging their rallying to Katanga, they supported the ABAKO, MNC-K, and PUNA opposition groups, and enabled them to send delegations to Katanga. Albert Kalonji took frequent trips to Brazzaville, while his lieutenant, Joseph Ngalula, organized the State of South Kasai.[66]

On the American side, the CIA seems to have been particularly active. The "CIA dispersed its agents to learn Congolese politics from the bush on up, to recruit likely leaders and to finance their bids for power." [67] At the end of August reports from Washington suggested that the American government was encouraging Lumumba's domestic opponents, directly and through the U.N. "A new act in the Congo is, according to authoritative reports, ready for mounting. When the curtain rises this time—reportedly a matter of days or weeks at most—it is doubtful that Patrice Lumumba will have star billing," wrote Arnold Beichman in the *Christian Science Monitor.* Officials expressed hope that the parliament would remove Lumumba from the premiership. They had rather specific ideas about the succession: Lumumba's place "will be taken by a form of 'collective leadership' from the Congo's six provinces. Given time and adequate economic and technical support, the Congo could become a nation. . . ." [68]

Neal Stanford's dispatch from Washington on August 29th reflected a growing activism in American diplomacy:

> The widely held feeling here is that the U.N. has to act much more firmly and vigorously in the immediate future, or the Congo goes

[65] Gérard-Libois and Verhaegen, *Congo 1960,* pp. 689–690.

[66] *Ibid.,* pp. 687–688; Gérard-Libois, *Le Rôle,* p. 14; G. Heinz and H. Donnay, *Lumumba Patrice: Les cinquantes derniers jours de sa vie* (Brussels, 1966), pp. 27–28.

[67] *New York Times,* Apr. 26, 1966, p. 1. From a series on the CIA based on several months of research.

[68] *Christian Science Monitor,* Aug. 26, 1960, p. 1.

down the drain as a free and independent country and becomes in time a Soviet satellite and Communist appendage.

If Lumumba ordered the U.N. out, "some officials" urged "defying and perhaps displacing Mr. Lumumba." If Lumumba ignored a parliamentary censure, "the United Nations would have stronger ground for declaring Lumumba no longer the legitimate ruler of the country. Then it might be possible to reorganize the country under the more moderate President Kasavubu and others." A federation of provinces was suggested, because it would "deflate the power and authority" of Lumumba.[69]

U.N. policy resembled, and partly reflected, that of the United States. Top U.N. officials considered Lumumba "a potential dictator bent on wrecking our operations";[70] and their most important supporter—the U.S.—was pressing for "vigorous and drastic action."[71] On August 28th the Secretary-General told the U.N. Consultative Committee:[72] "Certain people currently consider—or want to consider—the U.N. force as a hostile element. As long as this continues, nothing will be accomplished. You do not ask for help to obtain a scapegoat and someone to knock around. It is there that the fundamental change must come."[73]

According to P. H. Gendebien, who later interviewed the personalities in question,

During the month of August the Secretariat took discreet soundings in view of seeing whether a new more moderate political line would be possible in the central government. Young university students who were finishing their studies in Belgium were approached. An assistant of the Secretary-General, Mr. Wieschoff, received Mr. Cardoso and

69 *Ibid.,* Aug. 30, 1960, p. 1.

70 Major General Carl Von Horn, *Soldiering for Peace* (New York, 1967), p. 195.

71 *Christian Science Monitor,* Aug. 30, 1960, p. 1; see also *Libre Belgique,* Sept. 2, 1960, p. 5.

72 This advisory committee on the Congo was created in August. It consisted of representatives of those countries which had troops in the Congo. After formulating basic policy for the U.N. operation, the members of the "Congo Club" (Hammarskjold, Bunche, Wieschoff) discussed it with this largely Afro-Asian group. Hoskyns, p. 183.

73 Gendebien, pp. 64–65.

Mr. Lihau in New York and charged them with spreading the idea of a reconciliation between Leopoldville and Elizabethville. Another university student, who was also [to become] part of the College of Commissioners, mentions contacts at Geneva during August. All the same, there was no question at this time of Colonel Mobutu.[74]

The rapid influx of Soviet equipment in the first days of September pointed to a quick move against Lumumba. Kasavubu was particularly worried and decided to employ Article 22 of the *Loi Fondomentale,* which gave the Head of State the right to dismiss the Prime Minister and his cabinet. The President was disturbed by massacres in South Kasai on the part of poorly organized, undisciplined government troops. He was also afraid that Soviet intervention would upset the balance of power between himself and Lumumba.

Foreign influences undoubtedly contributed to Kasavubu's decision. Several reports agree that French emissaries from Youlou's entourage played a role at this time. These included Croquez, Kasavubu's former lawyer, and Jayle, a close friend and political adviser of the President. Belgian advisers (Van Bilsen, Denis) helped Kasavubu with the legal arguments, the drafting of a statement, and the marshaling of U.N. support.[75] A Western diplomat with long experience in the Congo (but not involved at this moment) affirms that the Kasavubu move was a "Western coup" and adds that Foreign Minister Bomboko was "paid" at this time. Bomboko was one of two ministers who countersigned Kasavubu's revocation of Lumumba. Justin Bomboko's benefactor may have been a Belgian official—such is the content of an alleged confession contained in a book by a former colleague.[76] Or the money may have come from the American Embassy, as the aforemen-

[74] *Ibid.,* p. 74.

[75] Gérard-Libois and Verhaegen, *Congo 1960,* pp. 689–690, 818, 825, 834; Hoskyns, pp. 198–199; Heinz and Donnay, p. 28. Van Bilsen's role was clarified by Professor Benoît Verhaegen of Lovanium University; see also below, p. 90.

[76] Cléophas Kamitatu, *La Grande Mystification du Congo-Kinshasa* (Paris, 1971), p. 66.

tioned diplomatic source believes. In any case, the Americans were also supporting the coup.

According to Andrew Tully the CIA had let "it be rumored that if President Kasavubu was uncertain about his constitutional powers there were American 'officials' who would be glad to offer him counsel." Wanting "support in strong quarters," Kasavubu "sat at the feet of the CIA men, who reminded him that it was within his realm of responsibility to depose Lumumba and form a new government." [77]

Tully's account draws credence from the fact that his description of *other* CIA activities at this time has been confirmed by authoritative sources (see below). In Leopoldville much of the diplomatic colony believed that Kasavubu obtained the blessing of the American Ambassador before he acted.[78] This seems probable in the light of (1) America's energetic policy from the end of August, (2) Timberlake's reputation for "activism," (3) the opinion of American and foreign diplomats that there was no contradiction between CIA and Embassy policy at this time, and (4) Kasavubu's consultation with other important foreigners (e.g., Andrew Cordier of the U.N.) [79] before he made his move. At the moment of the coup, Washington's private comment was, "It's about time." [80] The American role seems to have consisted largely of advice and promises of support. It has been supposed that Western intelligence agencies were not involved in the actual engineering of the takeover. The absence of simple precautions such as placing guards at Lumumba's residence and the radio station suggested a homemade operation.[81] However, the aforementioned Western diplomat warns that just because a coup

[77] Andrew Tully, *C.I.A.—The Inside Story* (New York, 1962), p. 221.

[78] Conor Cruise O'Brien, *To Katanga and Back* (New York, 1962), p. 93; Von Horn, p. 208. O'Brien maintains this was "generally believed"; Von Horn that it was "possible but not likely."

[79] See below, pp. 90–91.

[80] *New York Times,* Sept. 6, 1960, p. 22, notes: "The State Department has considered him to be slipping steadily, and has thought him to be under Soviet control."

[81] Eisenhower, p. 575; Hoskyns, p. 200.

appears poorly organized doesn't mean that Western services are not involved.

Evidence of U.N. complicity in the Kasavubu coup appears overwhelming. In New York, some U.N. diplomats expected an attempt to remove Lumumba several days in advance and let it be known that "few tears would be shed here if the effort were to succeed." [82] In Leopoldville "there is no doubt at all that senior ONUC [Opération des Nations Unies du Congo] officials knew several days beforehand what Kasavubu intended and that most of them hoped fervently that he would succeed." [83] According to a high-ranking member of the American Embassy in 1960, U.N. diplomats "encouraged the replacement" of Lumumba. Cordier himself has written that Kasavubu consulted him about the coup over the weekend of September 4 (the President acted on the evening of September 5), and that afterward he was convinced of "the likelihood of a major crisis" and began to "plan our resources for safeguarding law and order." [84] One may suspect, then, that Cordier did not place the power and prestige of the U.N. force behind the idea of peaceful reconciliation in his conversations with Kasavubu.

This interpretation is strengthened by two additional facts. Right before the coup, Kasavubu dispatched an adviser (A. J. Van Bilsen) who asked Cordier to arrest Lumumba. Cordier would not go that far, but it seems significant that Kasavubu thought he

[82] *Christian Science Monitor,* Sept. 1, 1960, p. 4.

[83] Hoskyns, p. 201. That they passed this information on to Hammarskjold is confirmed by Brian Urquhart, *Hammarskjold* (London, 1973), pp. 440–441. In addition to external political pressures and legal mandates, top U.N. officials were surely influenced by historically and culturally formed ideas of what was right. Hammarskjold's closest associates on the Congo question were Americans who had the approval of the State Department. O'Brien, *To Katanga and Back,* pp. 53–58; *Writers and Politics,* pp. 208–212.

[84] Andrew W. Cordier, "Challenge in the Congo," *Think,* XXXI (July–Aug., 1965), 27. The former British Ambassador to the Congo recalls that, "at one time" Kasavubu sent for Cordier to "ask him how a *coup d'état* should be organized." Scott, p. 79.

might. At the same time, Cordier agreed to provide a guard for Kasavubu's residence and to consider a U.N. takeover of the airport and radio station (which would hamper Lumumba in rallying his supporters). This was hardly the way to discourage Kasavubu.[85]

At 8:15 P.M., September 5, Kasavubu announced the dismissal of Lumumba and named Joseph Ileo, a Catholic federalist, as his successor. Von Horn describes the reaction among U.N. officials at the Hotel Royal:

> Looking around the room where we gathered about Uncle Andy [Cordier], it was impossible not to detect an atmosphere of relief, almost of satisfaction.[86]

It appears unlikely that Kasavubu would have gone ahead without outside support. He consulted the American and U.N. officials frequently in the days before the coup. By Von Horn's account, he even hesitated at the last minute because Cordier would not arrest Lumumba.[87] Kasavubu's requests to the U.N. show that he was aware of its military and political importance in a situation of civil conflict. In his speech removing Lumumba he called on the U.N. force to assume responsibility for "peace and order" in the Congo.[88]

Within hours Cordier, having received wide latitude from Hammarskjold to act in the emergency, decided to close the airports (except to U.N. traffic) in order to prevent Russian planes from airlifting Lumumbist soldiers to Leopoldville. According to a member of the American Embassy, Cordier consulted Ambassador Timberlake before taking this step. The next day he closed the radio station, since Lumumba's "highly charged emotional appeals inciting the people were on the verge of producing a totally uncontrollable situation." (Kasavubu had free access to Radio Congo

85 Hoskyns, p. 200. *Time,* Sept. 19, 1960, p. 28, reported that Kasavubu had the "tacit consent" of U.N. officials in Leopoldville.

86 Von Horn, p. 208.

87 *Ibid.,* p. 207. Kasavubu said he might alter the timing of the coup but reserved the right to call on the U.N. for protection.

88 Gérard-Libois and Verhaegen, *Congo 1960,* pp. 818–819.

in neighboring Brazzaville, however.)[89] While these actions hurt Lumumba—probably decisively[90]—there was considerable justification for them under the U.N.'s mandate to preserve "law and order." At the same time, the U.N. had no mandate to interfere in internal affairs and was "under a strong obligation to do everything possible to try to ensure that the existing balance of power was not upset by their actions."[91] In this wider context the U.N. was clearly prejudiced against Lumumba. The airport ban was applied indiscriminately to military and nonmilitary movements, preventing such important Lumumbists as Cléophas Kamitatu and General Victor Lundula from returning to the capital and marshaling support.[92] Two Belgian planes supporting Katanga military operations against Baluba rebels were permitted to take off from Elizabethville September 8th "without however provoking anything other than formal protests on the part of the U.N."[93] No effort was made to keep Kasavubu from using Radio Brazzaville. The Secretary-General quickly endorsed the legality of Kasavubu's action, although the legal situation was complex and controversial.[94] Presumably this was the reason for an alleged incident in which Ileo was allowed to fly to the provinces to test out support for his proposed government.[95] Most important, the U.N. gave no support to efforts at negotiations being carried on by the Congolese parliament, African diplomats in Leopoldville, and one of its own civil servants.

These efforts resulted in significant progress, including a tentative accord between Kasavubu and Lumumba. Hoskyns concludes the peacemakers were "very nearly successful" and "it is possible

[89] Cordier, p. 28. On the latitude given to Cordier, see Urquhart, pp. 441, 445.

[90] Hoskyns, p. 223. Similar judgments are expressed in Lefever, *Uncertain Mandate,* p. 48; and O'Brien, *To Katanga and Back,* p. 94.

[91] Hoskyns, p. 223.

[92] *Ibid.,* p. 204.

[93] Gérard-Libois, *Le Rôle,* p. 15.

[94] Hoskyns, pp. 208–210.

[95] *Libre Belgique,* Sept. 10–11, 1960, p. 3. Cf., however, Urquhart, p. 477n, which denies this event occurred.

that a strong U.N. initiative . . . might just have made the difference."[96]

All this may appear surprising in view of Kasavubu's rather precipitate action of September 5th. However, according to Hoskyns:

> [Kasavubu] did not intend to exclude either Lumumba or the Lumumbists permanently from power. He was fully aware that they represented far too large a section of the population for government to be possible without them. His intention was to pull Lumumba up short and show him that the country would not stand for authoritarian methods in a time of crisis. If Lumumba accepted this he was quite prepared to open negotiations with him and perhaps even include him in the next Government.[97]

Why then did the conciliation effort ultimately fail? Kasavubu was to some extent influenced by the situation in Katanga. He

[96] Hoskyns, p. 224. There are different versions of the accord. Ghanaian sources report that African diplomats got the two principals together behind proposals for closer cooperation between Head of State and Head of Government. Kasavubu would have consented verbally, but subsequently refused to sign a joint communiqué. *Ibid.*, pp. 219–222; Kwame Nkrumah, *Challenge of the Congo* (New York, 1967), pp. 58–61. Two authors write of a successful negotiation by Jean David, a U.N. official. However, they provide few details of the substance. Gendebien, p. 79; Kamitatu, p. 68. David himself claimed to have seen Kasavubu's signature on a written accord. *Libre Belgique,* Sept. 21, 1960, p. 6. At the time, Joseph Kasongo, President of the National Assembly, stated that Kasavubu and Lumumba had signed a protocol of the parliamentary conciliation committee, which was based on a purge of right- and left-wing bitter-enders. "Compte Rendu de la réunion tenue au Cabinet de Monsieur Finant, Président du Gouvernement Provincial, le 24 septembre 1960," Archives de la Province Orientale, Kisangani (mimeographed; copy of document in author's possession); Gérard-Libois and Verhaegen, *Congo 1960,* pp. 849, 864. *Ibid.*, pp. 866–867, reproduces an alleged 10-point agreement dealing with executive collaboration and also foreseeing "a new cabinet." According to "certain people," the plan would have been signed by the two principals.

These accounts suggest there might have been two or more accords negotiated by different groups. More important, they provide strong support for Hoskyns' conclusion that Kasavubu and Lumumba were willing to go far toward each other's position in order to achieve a compromise.

[97] Hoskyns, pp. 199–200.

wanted to negotiate an end to the secession, and Tshombe was saying that "negotiations were unthinkable if Lumumba had any place in the government." On the other hand, "there is no doubt" that "strong counterpressure was being exerted by various outside advisers" on Kasavubu. These included emissaries from Youlou, the Belgians (at this time promises of aid were given to Ileo),[98] the U.N., and the U.S.

The United Nations' attitude was indicated by its reaction to one of its officials' participation in the negotiations. Jean David, a Haitian in the U.N. Civilian Operation, had been working on a plan to "delimit the functions of Head of State and Prime Minister" as early as August. During the crisis, he "suggested that this project should be continued and used as a basis for reconciliation." When his superiors disapproved, he went ahead on his own. However, "his actions were considered embarrassing and soon afterwards he was sent out of Leopoldville." [99]

From "Congolese sources well situated to be informed," Charles Howard learned that the CIA and the American Embassy played an important role in the failure of the projected accord. A telephone call was said to have prevented Kasavubu from going to the radio to read the agreement. At the moment of the call, the American and British Ambassadors, the chief of the U.N. Civilian Operation, and Colonel Joseph Mobutu (who had just taken power in a coup) were assembled together in a meeting.[100] P. H. Gendebien reports an interview in February 1965 with a high Congolese official "who spoke to us in the same sense." [101] The author has received a similar account from one of the leading parliamentarians

98 *Ibid.*, pp. 222, 221; Gérard-Libois, *Le Rôle,* p. 14. Some idea of the Belgians' advice at this time is given by the following message from the Foreign Ministry in Brussels to its representatives in Brazzaville Sept. 10: "The constituted authorities have the duty to put Lumumba where he can do no harm." Heinz and Donnay, p. 31.

99 Hoskyns, p. 221; see also above, p. 93, n. 96.

100 Charles P. Howard, "Katanga and the Congo Betrayal," *Freedomways,* II (Spring, 1962), 146.

101 Gendebien, p. 79.

of the time, a moderate Lumumbist. The source of his information is said to be a Congolese participant in the crucial meeting. A Belgian professor who was acquainted with Jean David remembers that he blamed the failure of negotiations on "American advisers." Luis Lopez Alvarez, a Spanish friend of Lumumba, wrote that the Prime Minister also accused the American Ambassador of subverting reconciliation.[102] Embassy officials have only said that they did not encourage attempts to reconcile Kasavubu and Lumumba. Even such a negative role might have been enough to dissuade the U.N.—which controlled decisive military and financial means—from taking a positive stand.

The Americans had not, however, waited until this late date (September 17th) before moving to secure their gains. Several days earlier they had become concerned that Kasavubu and Ileo were losing the initiative. Lumumba was showing his old ability to control parliament, and Ileo was afraid to submit his proposed government for legislative approval.[103] The Embassy quickly concluded that Ileo was a "bad executive" and "ineffectual." The details of what happened next are classified, and American officials are reluctant to divulge them. But the main point—that the CIA was heavily involved in the emergence of Col. Joseph Mobutu and his College of Commissioners—has been confirmed by a former official of the American Embassy who observed the events in question. Further substantiation was provided by two former government officials who spoke directly with the CIA-station Chief in Leopoldville, Lawrence Devlin. A knowledgeable Western diplomat adds, "Mobutu and Bomboko were paid by the CIA around this time."

But who was Joseph Mobutu? He had been a clerk in the *Force Publique* before becoming a journalist and a member of

[102] Luis Lopez Alvarez, *Lumumba ou L'Afrique Frustrée* (Paris, 1964), pp. 116–117.

[103] Hoskyns, pp. 203–206; *Wall Street Journal*, Sept. 13, 1960, pp. 1, 17, reports anxiety over the "slow-moving Kasavubu" and the "pacifistic" Ileo, and "uncertainty" over their ability to "hold together" the Congo. A Belgian friend of Ileo recalls that he was also quite ill at the time.

Lumumba's party.[104] He was one of four MNC-L state secretaries in the Lumumba government. After having helped calm the Thysville garrison during the mutiny, Mobutu was appointed chief of staff of the Army. Later, he spent four days in his home region of Equateur mollifying the soldiers and supervising the election of African officers. In August and September he "established a certain authority" over the officers and soldiers in Leopoldville, particularly those who came from Equateur. U.N. officials who were engaged in reorganizing the Army, especially General Kettani of Morocco, "seem to have felt that Mobutu was the kind of officer round whom the new army could be organized." The young colonel increasingly depended upon the U.N. for the professional and financial ingredients of his power. Indeed, Mobutu referred to Kettani as "my military adviser and my best friend." Thus, on September 10, when the U.N. paid the troops in Leopoldville, "It was apparently agreed that Mobutu should be allowed to claim the credit for this payment, in the hope that it would help to build up his authority and increase the hold which he had on his men." Since the U.N. was paying the troops to keep them from interfering in the struggle between Lumumba and Kasavubu, it was clearly expected that Mobutu would also remain neutral. As the U.N.'s desire to neutralize the army was bound to a most un-neutral political policy being pursued by the U.N. and the Western powers, it is not surprising that Lumumba regarded Mobutu's action as a betrayal.[105]

Concerning the CIA role in the "Mobutu coup" of September 14th, the following account has been pieced together from various unofficial sources. "Devlin was with the American Embassy in Brussels in the period immediately prior to Congolese independence and got to know Mobutu there during the year in which he had a fellowship with Inforcongo" (1959–1960).[106] As the Congo be-

[104] Had he also been an agent of the Belgian Sûreté? This charge is made by Kamitatu, p. 37; and De Vos, *Vie et mort,* pp. 85–87.

[105] Hoskyns, pp. 29, 77, 90, 125, 102, 211–213, 222.

[106] Letter to the author from a reporter who has talked with Devlin's diplomatic colleagues and journalists in Leopoldville during this period,

came a Cold War battleground, a modest CIA office "bloomed into a virtual embassy and miniature war department." The CIA "soon found Joseph Mobutu, Victor Nendaka, and Albert Ndele. Their eventual emergence as President of the country, Minister of Transport, and head of the national bank, respectively, proved tribute to the Americans' judgment and tactics." [107]

"Like his soldiers [Mobutu] grew angry at Lumumba's whimsical use of the military, disgusted at the Lumumba-provoked civil war in the interior. Mobutu became a frequent visitor to the U.S. Embassy and held long talks with officials there." [108] When "it was obvious that the indolent Kasavubu was no match for Lumumba," the CIA "had the man to take charge in Kasavubu's name." [109] Colonel Sinclair, the military attaché at the British Embassy, "who had particularly close contacts with the ANC, admits he knew several days in advance that something of this kind was being planned." [110] On the evening of September 14th, Mobutu

---

January 3, 1968. If Mobutu was a Belgian informer, as some have charged (see above, p. 96, n. 104), this would help explain his fateful encounter with the CIA.

[107] *New York Times,* Apr. 26, 1966, p. 30. "In Sept. 1960, Devlin was in Leopoldville for the CIA and strongly urged that Mobutu was the man to back." (Letter to the author from a reporter, cited in previous note.) Nendaka was actually appointed head of the *Sûreté* after Lumumba's dismissal, a position of power which he continued to hold under succeeding regimes. Hoskyns, p. 502. It was only in 1966, and symptomatic of flagging influence, that he became Minister of Transport.

[108] *Time,* Sept. 26, 1960, p. 31. The article continues: "Colonel Mobutu left no doubt about which side of the Cold War he had joined. 'Russia sent us vehicles, planes and seven technicians who were with me in Camp Leopold,' he declared. 'Ten days ago I discovered that these technicians were Russian officers disguised as civilians. They had brought with them tons of pamphlets and posters which they had distributed through camp without my or my government's approval. I have expelled them all.' An observer from the U.S. Embassy whispered, 'Well, I'll be damned!' "

[109] Tully, p. 222. "Many of the correspondents who were reporting the Congo in 1960 believe or strongly suspect . . . the Central Intelligence Agency and Mobutu were working hand-in-glove." Stephen S. Kaplan, "Images of the Congo" (unpublished Ph.D. dissertation, University of Chicago, 1968), p. 148.

[110] Hoskyns, p. 215.

announced his "peaceful revolution" to "neutralize" the strife-ridden Central Government. The politicians would have until December 31 to compose their differences; in the meantime, a group of Congolese graduates and students would exercise power. A little later, at a press conference, Mobutu warned that the army wanted all Russian, Czech, and "other Socialist" personnel expelled from the country.[111] Ambassador Timberlake reportedly commented, "I have always been accredited to President Kasavubu and that has not changed. But now we will have some one at government level to deal with." [112]

Did the U.N. play a direct role in the Mobutu coup? At the time, some European newspapers discerned a "discreet but capital" intervention by Kettani.[113] The U.N.'s action in letting Mobutu claim credit for the troop payment on September 10th could not fail to arouse suspicion. At least it seems clear that Kettani and other U.N. officials knew about the coup in advance [114] and did not take steps to preserve "law and order" this time. The unorthodox notion of a government of university students and graduates may also reflect U.N. influence. As noted earlier, this idea was explored in August by the U.N. Secretariat which had already contacted several of the future Commissioners.

The composition of Mobutu's emerging regime, its first moves, and its international backing all worked in favor of an alliance with Kasavubu against Lumumba. Yet for about two weeks, Mobutu stuck with his idea of a temporary "neutralization" of the two main combatants. But "outside pressure" played an important role in changing his mind. Mobutu himself called attention to such influences on the part of Kettani and the Moroccan government.[115] Gérard-Libois reveals that Belgian agents in Brazzaville and Leopoldville were disturbed by Mobutu's hesitation, and that "be-

[111] Gérard-Libois and Verhaegen, *Congo 1960,* p. 869.

[112] Said "with a straight face," according to Tully, p. 222.

[113] *Libre Belgique,* Sept. 17–18, 1960, p. 4. Two French and one Spanish dailies appearing in Morocco were suspended by the Moroccan Ministry of Information for reporting Kettani's role in the coup.

[114] Hoskyns, p. 215.

[115] *Ibid.,* p. 222.

tween the 20th and 30th of September all the Belgian influence in Leopoldville is applied (often spontaneously) to influence Colonel Mobutu, the President, and certain commissioners." [116] Given their interest in the situation, it is not excluded that the Belgians were also proponents of the Mobutu coup—such was the impression of "some of the American officials serving with ONUC" who "considered that both the CIA and Belgium had a hand in Mobutu's actions." [117]

[116] Gérard-Libois, *Le Rôle,* p. 16.

[117] Hoskyns, p. 215. Heinz and Donnay, p. 34, who had access to certain Belgian diplomatic records of this period, write of Mobutu's "contacts with Western representatives before the coup."

CHAPTER III

New Difficulties

The environment for American policy changed as a result of the September coups. In the Congo it was no longer a question of manipulating battling politicians to get rid of an unfriendly government. The problem now was to create enduring influence through a stable and effective pro-Western regime. Here the Kasavubu-Mobutu-Commissioners alliance had several outstanding disadvantages:

> Of the personalities involved, only Kasavubu and Bomboko were elected politicians and the support which they had was extremely localized. The rest were technicians rather than politicians and had little or no contact with or support from the mass of the people. Thus since the regime could not depend on the political element to maintain contact between the provinces and the centre, it could only hope to function adequately if the army was able to enforce effective discipline throughout the country as a whole and if the administrative links could be restored. In fact the army itself was a source of indiscipline and the commissioners had neither the means nor the personnel to make the administration effective outside Leopoldville. The situation was made even more anomalous by the fact that although politicians had been neutralized in the centre, elected Governments and Assemblies continued to function in the provinces. In addition, neither Kasavubu, Mobutu, nor any of the commissioners had the personality to make himself a figure-head or to provide a focal point round which the unity of the nation could be re-established. One of the most serious results of this situation was that the Leopoldville regime could do nothing either by force or persuasion to convince the Katanga authorities that they would be better advised to negotiate their re-entry

into the Congo rather than to continue to consolidate their attempt at secession.[1]

The situation at the United Nations had also become more difficult. Earlier the Afro-Asians had been dissatisfied with Hammarskjold's caution on the Katanga issue. But militants and moderates alike had supported him against Soviet and Congolese criticism, hoping that the U.N. would yet achieve successful decolonization and Cold War prophylaxis in the Congo. Now the Afro-Asians made it clear to Hammarskjold that their support was conditional upon "the ending of the vendetta against Lumumba, the refusal of any kind of recognition to Mobutu, and a real effort to encourage political reconciliation and to prevent Belgian military assistance from bolstering the Katanga regime." They were deeply disturbed by the advent of a military solution (the militants because they sympathized with Lumumba's hot-blooded nationalism, the moderates because they preferred legality and political settlement). And the Congo's embroilment in East-West rivalry was seen as a further demonstration of the need to exclude outside meddlers, the most prominent of whom was now Belgium.[2] The Afro-Asians had significant leverage on Hammarskjold, especially if they could maintain a semblance of unity. Not only did they control a large bloc of votes in the General Assembly; they also supplied the vast majority of troops for ONUC.[3]

Independently, the attitude of the Secretariat was changing too. U.N. officials in Leopoldville were disappointed by the political weakness and disorder of the new regime. They began "to think in terms of a return to a Kasavubu-Lumumba alliance and the withdrawal of the army from power." With the Russians now excluded, Lumumba "seemed much less of a danger, and in retrospect even his methods of government seemed to have something to recommend them." In addition, Hammarskjold's representatives were now reporting the full extent of the "Belgian factor" in Katanga. This "convinced United Nations officials that further action must be

[1] Hoskyns, p. 245. [2] *Ibid.*, pp. 234–236, 247, 256–258.
[3] Lefever, *Uncertain Mandate*, p. 131.

taken." Changes were "undoubtedly encouraged" by Rajeshwar Dayal, an Indian diplomat who had replaced Cordier as head of ONUC.[4]

The above factors conjoined to produce a new U.N. policy in the Fall of 1960. Hammarskjold asked Brussels to "withdraw all military, paramilitary, or civilian personnel which it had placed at the disposal of the authorities in the Congo," and channel all assistance through the U.N. This rather sweeping request was aimed at Belgian support of separatism in Katanga and South Kasai, and at Belgian advisers in Leopoldville who were said to be preventing a "return to constitutional government." The Secretariat also decided to "only recognize institutions and actions in accordance with the *Loi Fondamentale.*" Hence the College of Commissioners was refused recognition, and its attempts to arrest Lumumba were thwarted on the ground that he possessed parliamentary immunity. Dayal expressed the basic analysis in a report to the General Assembly on November 2:

> At the heart of the present confusion and disintegration in the Congo is the complete lack of progress in the way of a political settlement.
>
> In the confusion which prevails the only two institutions whose foundations still stand, are the office of the Chief of State and the parliament; if the minimum conditions of noninterference and security mentioned earlier could be established, it would open the way to the leaders of the country to seek peaceful political solutions through the medium of these two institutions.[5]

The direction of American policy was not altered by these developments. In the first place, it continued to be solicitous of Belgian interests. With Lumumba out—but still a threat—Brussels hedged its bets, supporting both Leopoldville and Elizabethville.

[4] Hoskyns, pp. 297–298.

[5] United Nations Security Council, *Official Records, Supplement for Oct., Nov., Dec., 1960,* S/4557-B, pp. 44–47; S/4557, Nov. 2, 1960, pp. 7–34. See also King Gordon, *The United Nations in the Congo: A Quest for Peace* (New York, 1962), pp. 79–82.

(The dichotomy was reduced by Mobutu's attempts to conciliate Tshombe.) U.S. policy was consistent with this objective. On the one hand, Ambassador Timberlake flew to Elizabethville to persuade Tshombe to accept Mobutu's olive branch.[6] On the other, Katanga was allowed to set up a miniature embassy on Fifth Avenue in New York City. Katanga Information Services was run by Michel Struelens who entered the U.S. as a foreign journalist. Struelens published a bulletin, *Katanga Calling,* rounded up "a network of sympathizers on whom he could draw if any crisis arose," [7] and arranged for Tshombe to visit Washington and meet State Department officials; however, Tshombe backed out at the last minute. Struelens had established a cordial relationship with the American government. He realized that he could not hope for direct encouragement of the Katanga cause, but he was pleased that the Americans were not interested in a quick decision.

At the United Nations the U.S. resisted Hammarskjold and Dayal's attempts to "fully circumscribe the Belgian factor [in the Congo] and *eliminate* it." [8] While rejecting some of Belgium's diatribes against the U.N., the State Department endorsed her overall behavior. Dayal's criticisms were countered by an official communiqué expressing "every confidence in the good faith of Belgium in its desire to be of assistance in the Congo," and declaring that "we are therefore unable to accept the implication to the contrary contained in various parts of this report." Even in private, officials would concede only that some individual Belgians might have exceeded their authority.[9]

The American position precluded a firm U.N. approach to Belgian influence in the Congo. With its European and Latin-American allies, the United States had enough voting strength to defeat an unfriendly resolution in the General Assembly (where a two-thirds vote was necessary). Furthermore, the flexibility of the

[6] *Libre Belgique,* Nov. 19–20, 1960, p. 5. [7] Hoskyns, p. 288.

[8] Hammarskjold, quoted in Lefever, *Uncertain Mandate,* p. 138.

[9] *New York Times,* Nov. 5, 1960, pp. 1, 6. American officials at the U.N. were concerned with Hammarskjold's initiatives "at the expense of the Atlantic Alliance." *Libre Belgique,* Nov. 5–6, 1960, p. 7.

Secretariat was limited by the fact that America was carrying nearly half the financial burden of ONUC. Hammarskjold was frequently reminded of this by the American government.[10]

Fearing the chaos-to-Communism syndrome (and insensitive to Afro-Asian criticism) the U.S. opposed reconciliation with Lumumba. Practically, this implied the postponement of representative and legal government, since Lumumba would be a powerful force in any such government. The American Ambassador considered him "undoubtedly the most effective political organizer and rabble-rouser in the country" and believed that his return to power was "more than likely" if he could rejoin his supporters in Stanleyville.[11] Therefore the U.S. strongly defended the Kasavubu-Mobutu-Commissioners triumvirate, its own illegitimate progeny, as it were.

When the General Assembly called on the Afro-Asians to use their good offices in an attempt to help the Congolese settle their political differences (September 20), the U.S. rightly detected a threat to the status quo. Ambassador to the U.N., James J. Wadsworth, warned:

> We must guard carefully against introducing ourselves any complicating elements into the Congo. The timing and nature of any such efforts, as well as the willingness of those concerned to accept them, should be carefully considered before they are initiated.[12]

Dayal's suggestion that the Congolese parliament help solve the political crisis provoked "one of the infrequent instances when the United States has gone on record as openly critical of U.N. activities or reports." [13] A State Department communiqué stressed parliament's inability to act "because of existing conditions" and indicated the U.S. would only accept a return to parliamentary government "under the nominee of President Kasavubu for Pre-

[10] See below, pp. 105, 111.

[11] Timberlake, pp. 184, 128.

[12] *Department of State Bulletin,* Oct. 10, 1960, p. 587.

[13] *New York Times,* Nov. 5, 1960, p. 1; *Christian Science Monitor,* Nov. 7, 1960, p. 1.

mier" (i.e., under Ileo, not Lumumba).[14] In conversations with the author, American policy-makers said they opposed the re-convening of parliament because a nose count of legislators and Lumumba's renowned oratory heralded a Lumumba victory. As John Hightower explained in a background story at the time: "But the dominant United States' view now is that at present return of parliament would almost certainly mean the restoration of Mr. Lumumba to the premiership." So America backed "a strong executive in the Congo rather than trying to work hastily with a timid and unstable legislative group." [15]

Charles Bohlen, the State Department's top Soviet expert, was now directing U.S. policy at the U.N. He and Wadsworth proceeded to "infuriate" Hammarskjold with their "peremptory demands" for support of Kasavubu-Mobutu and "pointed reminders" that the U.S. was footing the bills.[16]

At the same time the African Bureau and the American Embassy were looking for a *political* alternative to Lumumba once things calmed down and the parliamentary situation became more malleable. They soon came up with Cyrille Adoula, a nationalist who had broken with Lumumba over the latter's dictatorial tactics and had become one of his most influential opponents in the summer of 1960. Adoula had been a labor leader and appears to have been promoted by the AFL-CIO which knew him through the International Confederation of Free Trade Unions (ICFTU).[17]

[14] *New York Times,* Nov. 5, 1960, p. 6.

[15] *Washington Star,* Nov. 6, 1960, p. A-15. In press interviews, officials stressed the possibility of intimidation and violence by Lumumbists. *New York Times,* Nov. 14, 1960, p. 9; *New York Herald Tribune,* Nov. 5, 1960, p. 1. But in conversations with the author, Lumumba's eloquence and political ability were emphasized.

[16] Joseph P. Lash, *Dag Hammarskjold: Custodian of the Brushfire Peace* (Garden City, N.Y., 1961), pp. 247–248.

[17] When asked for comment on this report by an official of the African Bureau, an AFL-CIO international affairs official replied, "I think you should know that Adoula was first a trade unionist. . . . Therefore, our relationships with Adoula go back to the days when he was General Secretary of one of the leading unions in the Congo. Our relationship with him

Timberlake's portrait of Adoula is quite revealing:

[Adoula is] an intelligent and well-balanced moderate whose chief interest had been in organizing an independent African labor movement. A forceful and articulate spokesman for the Congo, Adoula is strongly anti-Communist. He has talked openly with the American Embassy in Leopoldville, which long considered him one of the best prospects for top leadership in the Congo. He is one of the few leading Congolese who does not depend considerably on foreign advisers.[18]

Dismayed by the Dayal Report and by militant Afro-Asian moves to seat a Lumumba delegation at the U.N., the Americans encouraged Kasavubu to fly to New York and demand recognition for his own representatives. However, the General Assembly was not interested in reaching a decision at this point and thereby prejudicing the work of conciliation. It voted 48-30-18 to adjourn debate *sine die*. This seems to have been a relatively free and unpressured vote. The U.S. now mobilized the pro-Western majority on the Credentials Committee to pass a resolution recommending that the General Assembly seat Kasavubu's delegation.

According to Afro-Asian sources, the United States used every possible pressure to get this decision, and in the period between the adoption of the resolution in the Committee and discussion in the General Assembly lobbying was intense.

In the Assembly on November 18 the Ghanaian representative proposed that this debate should also be adjourned for the same reasons that had been accepted on November 9. But this time the motion lost by 51-36-11.

As soon as the vote had been taken there were accusations of lobby pressure and "arm twisting" and it is undeniable that the majority of

---

was continued over the years even when he became Prime Minister." Letter to the author, July 1, 1970.

[18] Timberlake, p. 174. Adoula, who represented Kasavubu-Mobutu at the U.N. in October, was *the* American candidate for future leadership by late Autumn. In early December, he was introduced to Edward Kennedy who was in Leopoldville on behalf of his brother, the president-elect.

countries which changed their votes were those susceptible to pressure from the countries of the Western alliance.

The converts included: Chile, El Salvador, Peru, Senegal, Chad, Austria, Bolivia, Brazil, Cyprus, Denmark, Greece, Haiti, Honduras, Iceland, Israel, Japan, Norway, Thailand, and Uruguay. The Dominican Republic and Ecuador, absent for the first vote, now appeared in order to oppose the motion. After this, the vote to seat Kasavubu's delegation (53-24-19) was almost anticlimactic. The American majority was swelled by assiduous lobbying and by the fact that some Afro-Asian delegates now abstained because they did not wish to appear to be taking sides between Kasavubu and Lumumba.[19]

Partly because of this result, Lumumba abandoned his U.N.-guarded residence and set out for Stanleyville. He was soon arrested by Mobutu's troops.[20] Hammarskjold immediately appealed to Kasavubu for due process of law, reminding him of Lumumba's parliamentary immunity.[21] Now Washington gave out that Lumumba's detention provided Kasavubu-Mobutu with a "good chance for effective government." [22] In the U.N., Ambassador Wadsworth defended the arrest, saying that only "the Congolese people and government" could determine the fallen premier's legal status.[23] The U.S. seemed relieved that Lumumba had been captured alive, since "he would be a less significant rallying symbol for pro-Communist opposition than if he had been killed." [24] Again it is

19 Hoskyns, pp. 259–265. See too n. 25, p. 108, below. In all the votes the new African states of the French Community gave overwhelming support to the Western position, diluting the strength of Afro-Asian moderates and militants.

20 *Ibid.*, p. 266; Heinz and Donnay, pp. 16–21.

21 Gérard-Libois and Verhaegen, *Congo 1960*, pp. 1059–1060.

22 *New York Times*, Dec. 5, 1960, p. 4.

23 *Department of State Bulletin*, Jan. 9, 1961, p. 52. Urquhart, p. 484, discloses that Hammarskjold protested to the U.S. and British missions in New York the failure of Western embassies in Leopoldville to exercise a moderating influence on the regime regarding its treatment of Lumumba.

24 *New York Times*, Dec. 5, 1960, p. 4; Tully, p. 224, suggests the CIA was reluctant to have Lumumba arrested at first, fearing Mobutu would have a tendency to "shoot first," producing a "phony martyrdom."

clear that the U.N. would have taken a different view of internal Congolese politics if not for the American position. The votes surrounding the seating of Kasavubu showed that most delegates preferred a political solution and that the United States was the decisive force in delaying it. Conor Cruise O'Brien has discussed the mechanics:

I was a member of my own country's delegation to the Assembly during these proceedings, and that delegation was one of those subjected to "arm-twisting" with, in the end, a measure of success (shift noted by Miss Hoskyns from a vote against seating the Kasavubu delegation to an abstention). This shift was brought about, not by any change in appreciation of the merits of the case, but by the conviction brought home that the United States was determined to have its way on this matter and that, for a variety of good and sufficient reasons, it would not be wise to persist in opposing the clearly determined and maintained policy of the Government of the United States. My country (Ireland) was one with a relatively independent voting record, was not dependent on United States military or technical aid, nor were American corporations in a position to determine its policy. Most countries outside the Communist bloc are more open to United States pressure than that, and shifting United Nations voting patterns cannot be adequately understood without a consistent unsentimental awareness of this basic set of factors.[25]

Finally, the Americans tried to furnish the wherewithal to keep their Congolese clients in power. In October the Commissioners began using a $5 million gift made through the U.N. to finance certain essential imports. (This contribution was stipulated in an August 23 agreement with the Lumumba government and the U.N., but the U.S. did not turn over the money until after the Kasavubu coup.)[26] In November, eleven of Mobutu's officers arrived in Washington to visit the Pentagon and Army training camps.[27] Meanwhile, the CIA spent considerable sums on the Congo's political elite. American officials admit that the CIA

25 O'Brien, "The United Nations and the Congo," pp. 13–14.

26 *Department of State Bulletin,* Oct. 3, 1960, p. 530; Timberlake, p. 152.

27 *New York Times,* Nov. 2, 1960, p. 12.

was "passing money" around at this time. A Belgian adviser to one of the most illustrious payees provides further confirmation. The author has also interviewed some American missionaries who were close to the U.S. Embassy during this period. They cheerfully maintain that the political leadership—Mobutu, Bomboko, Adoula, and Sûreté Chief Victor Nendaka—was "bought . . . millions were spent." The missionaries consider themselves personal friends of these individuals.[28]

A more or less compact vehicle for CIA and American influence was beginning to emerge. This was the informal "Binza group," named after the Leopoldville suburb in which members resided. The most important participants were Mobutu, Nendaka, Foreign Minister Bomboko, Assistant Commissioner of the Interior Damien Kandolo, and Vice-President and Commissioner for Finance Albert Ndele.[29] CIA-man Devlin's means of influencing this group went beyond mere bribery, according to a Belgian diplomat who observed the phenomenon at close range. Especially in the beginning, the anti-Lumumbist leaders were inexperienced and mistrustful. Truly "men alone," they needed the political advice that Devlin could provide. Unlike many Americans in the Congo, Devlin spoke excellent French, his wife being a Frenchwoman born in Algeria. Finally, in their weakness the "Binza boys" had to depend on powerful outside support, largely American, in order to build up their position.

How successful was American policy in late 1960 in terms of its overall objectives? How well did the policy-makers fare in a new and less favorable environment? They managed to buttress a polit-

28 *Christian Science Monitor,* Dec. 9, 1960, p. 1, reported it "generally accepted as fact" that Communist and Western money was "buying up" Congo legislators, the competition having the effect of bidding up the representatives' prices. Hoskyns observes: "By all accounts Mobutu had a considerable amount of money at his disposal and he was, for example, able to win the support of the officers in Luluabourg partly by guaranteeing the pay of the troops. . . ." Hoskyns, p. 243.

29 Based on interviews with several U.S. and foreign diplomats. Cf. a written account by Kamitatu, pp. 97–98, who was later in a position to observe the group directly as Minister of the Interior.

ically weak pro-Western government. In fact, they probably kept it in power. Most students of this period believe that outside encouragement and financial support prevented a more realistic sorting out of Congo politics,[30] i.e., a government based on *internal* political forces. The United States also helped neutralize pressure on Katanga and opposition to the return of Belgian technicians (including political advisers). Still, it was unable to build a secure dike against any anti-Belgian, Communist-supported government in the Congo. By December, Gizenga headed a rival regime in Stanleyville which "despite its recent formation and lack of organization could certainly count on a wider support than either Leopoldville or Katanga."[31] Lumumbist separatism attracted the same international backing as Lumumba had, although this consisted mainly of financial support and did not yet include diplomatic recognition.[32] In January, the American Embassy was disturbed by Stanleyville's military expansion and Mobutu's "disappointing" return "probes."[33] Throughout the Congo, Lumumba's followers took heart, and there were rumors of a pro-Lumumba coup in Leopoldville—resulting in Lumumba's transfer to Elizabethville. Noting these developments, the State Department voiced apprehension that "forces hostile to the West" were about to take over the Congo through civil war.[34]

Meanwhile, America was discovering that its power in the U.N. was not sufficient to its purposes. Washington could veto the new directions proposed by Hammarskjold and most Afro-Asians. It could even get a voting majority on the key issue of whether to take up the credentials dispute. But in December, the West could not get the necessary two-thirds majority in the Assembly to endorse its Congo policy.[35] Furthermore, Lumumba's arrest and

[30] Hoskyns, pp. 237–246.

[31] *Ibid.*, p. 292.

[32] Timberlake, pp. 118–125, refers to the "merest trickle" of supplies from outside, and concludes that "outside support of Gizenga proved to be of little practical use but did help to preserve him in office and give him hope and finances." See also Hoskyns, p. 292, and below, pp. 272–273.

[33] Timberlake, pp. 129–130.

[34] *New York Times*, Jan. 18, 1961, p. 2.

[35] Deadlock in the Security Council threw the issue into the Assembly. The U.S. and Britain offered a resolution calling on Hammarskjold to

U.N. inaction caused six of the eighteen nations contributing to the U.N. Force to order—or threaten to order—the withdrawal of their contingents.[36] This all occurred at a time when the Central Government needed more international support than ever. As a result, American representatives at the U.N. became increasingly blatant in their tactics. Wadsworth insisted on the withdrawal of Dayal and strong action against the Gizengists.[37] Hammarskjold's lack of cooperation led to a story in the *New York Times* saying Washington was "uneasy" over the U.N. performance, Hammarskjold was "under pressure" from "hostile forces," and "our money" was subsidizing ONUC.[38] But a high-pressure campaign was no substitute for the missing political support. On the eve of the Kennedy Administration, outgoing Secretary of State Herter had to apologize to Hammarskjold for American "un-diplomacy." [39]

---

continue to discharge his mandate, and to pursue his "vigorous" efforts to bar foreign personnel. It also stressed the observance of human rights. The resolution failed to obtain the necessary majority by one vote (43-22-32). On the other hand, an eight-power resolution proposed by the militant Afro-Asians was defeated 42-28-27. However, members of the moderate group either approved or abstained. As in November, the conservative French African states voted basically with the West.

36 Epstein, pp. 65, 76. Ceylon delayed her order, but Yugoslavia, Guinea, Morocco, the United Arab Republic, and Indonesia persisted.

37 Lash, p. 256.

38 *New York Times,* Jan. 18, 1961, p. 1.

39 Lash, p. 256.

PART II

THE ANTI-COMMUNISM OF LIBERAL DEMOCRATS

CHAPTER IV

The Kennedy Reappraisal

In early 1961 certain objectively viewed realities would have forced any Administration to reconsider its Congo policy. The Lumumbist resurgence, crystallized by the Stanleyville regime, coincided with new signs of deterioration in Leopoldville. If military failure had undermined the Central Government's prestige, economic woes now threatened to do it in entirely. Without the export revenues from the provinces in opposition, urban unemployment soared to an estimated 70 percent.[1] At the United Nations, Afro-Asian dissatisfaction with Hammarskjold's performance was jelling. Both moderates (through the U.N. Conciliation Commission) and militants (through the Casablanca Conference) demanded a new mandate. It was widely rumored that when the Secretariat approached India for combat troops to replace those being withdrawn, "the Indian government had replied that it was not willing to contribute a new contingent under the existing mandate." [2] There was some danger then that the whole U.N. operation might suddenly unravel. The growing "constituency" of the African and U.N. Bureaus (sixteen African countries entered the United Nations in the Fall of 1960) was less and less manageable.

It was also clear that the nature and extent of any policy change would reflect the thinking of the new Democratic Administration, whose outlook on African affairs diverged considerably from that of its Republican predecessor.

1 Timberlake, pp. 141–159; *Christian Science Monitor,* Feb. 20, 1961, p. 1; Hoskyns, pp. 277–279.

2 Hoskyns, p. 310; see also *Christian Science Monitor,* Feb. 2, 1961, p. 2.

Greater Deference to African Nationalism and a Liberal Recipe for Its Development

Arthur Schlesinger, Jr., has counted 479 references to Africa in the index of John Kennedy's 1960 campaign speeches. His basic theme was: "We have lost ground in Africa because we have neglected the needs and aspirations of the African people." [3] In a major address shortly before the election, Kennedy warned of rising Soviet influence in Africa and castigated the Republicans for yielding to French pressure in Guinea, leaving President Touré no recourse but to seek aid from the Communists. He offered a six-point program for American policy at the heart of which stood this notion:

> We must ally ourselves with the rising sea of nationalism in Africa. The desire to be free—of all foreign tutelage—the desire for self-determination is the most powerful force in the modern world. It has destroyed old empires, created new nations and redrawn the maps of Asia, the Middle East and Africa. America must be on the side of the right of man to govern himself because that is one of our historical principles, because the final victory of nationalism is inevitable and because nationalism is the force which disposes of sufficient power and determination to threaten the integrity of the communist empire itself.[4]

Other proposals envisaged a multinational development fund, more American scholarships for African students, expansion of the surplus food program, use of the U.N. to show Africa that the U.S. did not want to involve it in the Cold War, and the elimination of racial discrimination at home to win the respect of blacks abroad. Over the summer, "when students in Kenya who had scholarships in American universities could not meet their travel fares and the Eisenhower Administration declined to do anything about them, Kennedy arranged through the Kennedy Foundation to bring them over on a well-publicized airlift." [5]

[3] Schlesinger, p. 511.
[4] *Libre Belgique*, Oct. 14, 1960, p. 4.
[5] Schlesinger, pp. 511–512.

Kennedy's view of Africa represented in part the culmination of a series of personal experiences. His childhood was filled with tales of Ireland's long struggle for independence. His trips to Indochina, and then Algeria, had introduced him to colonial decay in its contemporary forms, and convinced him that the French were driving true nationalists into the hands of the Communists.[6] On his way to the presidency, he was chairman of the African Subcommittee of the Senate Foreign Relations Committee, a post which did not keep him terribly busy (there were three meetings in two years),[7] but helped demonstrate his liberalism to party skeptics. In the 1960 election, an emphasis on Africa seemed not only intrinsically right but "good politics" in the strategically important black precincts.[8]

Yet it is unlikely that Kennedy would have translated his personal experience into a political program without the encouragement—and speechwriting—of a group of influential liberals. In the fifties this group dominated the Foreign Policy Committee of the Democratic Advisory Council and publicized a distinctively liberal approach to the underdeveloped world. In 1960 they joined the Kennnedy campaign. Afterwards they became part of the new Administration and influenced the development of an African policy.

The key figures included Chester Bowles (Under Secretary of State), Adlai Stevenson (Ambassador to the United Nations), G. Mennen Williams (Assistant Secretary of State for African Affairs), and Harlan Cleveland (Assistant Secretary of State for International Organization Affairs).[9]

Rejecting Europeanism, tutelage, and the politics of "business-as-usual," they substituted a conception of the world-wide mission of American liberalism.[10] Positing a basic similarity between the

6 *Ibid.*, pp. 509–510. 7 McKay, p. 348.

8 This pragmatic element was noted by several people who were involved in the Kennedy campaign.

9 All but Cleveland had been on the Democratic Advisory Council.

10 This paragraph is based on the following sources: Chester Bowles, *The Conscience of a Liberal: Selected Writings and Speeches* (New York,

aspirations of inhabitants of underdeveloped countries and those of the domestic liberal constituency ("revolution of rising expectations") they sought an Africa free of the curse of racial discrimination, raising living standards through economic modernization and industrialization, adapting and perfecting representative political institutions. To accomplish these ends, they favored an informal alliance with African nationalism—at the expense, inevitably, of the NATO tutors and white corporate colonialism which bolstered Tshombe and dominated Southern Africa. American economic power, both public and private, would fuel the new arrangement (hopefully in tandem with enlightened Europeans). Lest it be supposed that the liberal Messianists were prepared to aid all African nationalists, it should be added that they preferred to channel their money through structures whose efficacy had been validated by American or Western experience. Thus, reaffirming their belief in human equality in settler areas, they advocated "collaboration" between white economic power and blacks to avoid racial conflict, and suggested programs to educate the blacks for increased responsibility. In the economic sphere, they plumped for agricultural research, education, and extension programs, a form of economic development which preserved "considerable freedom of economic choices," and the Western model of "modern industrial democracy" with its "regulated competition and bargaining," employee welfare, and "good return" to the public purse. They put forth the virtues of an economic association with the West which would open new markets for both sides, attract private and public capital to Africa, and happily preserve the Western stake in raw

1962), esp. pp. 24–31, 52–55, 61–73, 177–180; *Africa's Challenge to America* (Los Angeles, 1956); *Ambassador's Report* (New York, 1954), *passim; Tomorrow Without Fear* (New York, 1946). Adlai E. Stevenson, "The New Africa," *Harper's*, CCXX (May, 1960), 48–54; Harlan Cleveland, "Memo for the New Secretary of State," *New York Times Magazine*, Dec. 11, 1960, pp. 11 ff.; and "The Capacities of the United Nations," in Francis O. Wilcox and H. Field Havilland, Jr. (eds.), *The United States and the United Nations* (Baltimore, 1961), pp. 137–146; and "The Theory and Practice of Foreign Aid," (paper prepared for the Special Studies Project of the Rockefeller Brothers Fund, Syracuse, Maxwell School, 1956).

materials. They pointed out the economic and political benefits of regional and federalist approaches "based on our own experience." Grandly, they spurned dogmatism on the question of political forms, but they expected "free institutions," "the spirit of liberal democracy," the Locke and Jeffersonian tradition of compromise" and "checks and balances" to emerge from the process of non-Statist economic development.

Characteristically, liberals favored a strong United Nations. With large numbers of new nations arriving in the General Assembly, this interest tended to merge with the liberal vision of the "Third World." As Bowles put it,

> The Cold War conflict is paralleled by a growing partnership between the United States and the peoples of Asia, Africa, and Latin America. It is this evolving world which helps shape the United Nations and which, increasingly, may be shaped by it.[11]

Cleveland pointed out the value of U.N. coordination of increased multinational development aid.[12]

To a considerable degree, the Messianic impulse appeared as independent of material, and even strategic, calculations. For example, the youthful Chester Bowles had been "tremendously excited" by Woodrow Wilson's campaign for the League of Nations. This had led to spirited arguments with his father, "a high-tariff Republican of the old New England school," and a consuming ambition to enter the State Department. Two months after Pearl Harbor, from the humble vantage point of the Connecticut State Rationing Commission, he recommended a strong anticolonial policy in Asia:

> To transform Asian indifference into a crusading fight to achieve freedom from all foreign rule, I proposed a far-reaching workable charter of liberty for all Asian nations.[13]

In January 1947, with official attention concentrated on European developments, Bowles declared

[11] Bowles, *Conscience*, p. 59. [12] Cleveland, "Theory," p. 58.
[13] Bowles, *Ambassador's Report*, pp. 4, 5, 39.

If the American people will support the investment of 2 percent of our total income each year for the next twenty years in the development of less fortunate countries, we may change the tide of history.[14]

Proposing a kind of Marshall Plan for the entire world, replete with regional economic authorities like the Tennessee Valley Authority, Bowles justified it as "living proof our our American system not only to provide a high standard of living for ourselves, but to help others get a start toward a more prosperous life with greater measures of dignity." [15] A recurrent theme of Bowles' prolific pen was America's responsibility, as the world's greatest economic power, to help create a peaceful and democratic world. In a 1946 pamphlet, *Tomorrow Without Fear,* he argued that planned prosperity in the U.S., plus American loans, would "provide the markets as well as the goods which other nations require." In turn, this would lay the foundation for a durable peace. ("If all nations are forced to compete more bitterly for shrinking world markets, then war itself becomes finally unavoidable"), and would favor the spread of democracy (the "impoverished" were "rarely" for democracy).[16] In article after article, Bowles repeated the key point, that the objectives of Asians, Africans, and Latin Americans "are easy for us Americans to understand and to accept: freedom from colonial rule; human dignity for all, regardless of race, creed or color; and expanding economic opportunities." [17] The hortatory tone was equally prominent in the more elegant prose of Adlai Stevenson. Stevenson considered Africa "a continent almost entirely opened up and developed by Westerners in the last century." It seemed like a good place to disprove "the Communist claim that free institutions and free enterprise, whatever their fate around the North Atlantic, are irrelevant to man's destiny anywhere else." America had a moral obligation to redeem the errors of the Old World in Africa:

To finish the work well which the West has begun demands more effort and more help and generosity than have yet been given. But to

[14] Bowles, *Conscience,* pp. 7–9.

[15] *Ibid.*

[16] Bowles, *Tomorrow,* pp. 2, 62.

[17] Bowles, *Conscience,* p. 28.

finish it badly would mean that Western man, coming to the most innocent of all continents, would have achieved nothing there, but the destruction of the old gods and the frustration of the new.

Such an indictment of the efficacy of our civilization would imperil every confident claim on our part to be the wave of the future. And so we must see that more than economic interests, more than social influence, more than the political balance, are at stake in Africa. What is being tested is, in the last analysis, the moral capacities of our society.[18]

In a paper for the Rockefeller Brothers Fund (1956), Harlan Cleveland sought "a new rationale" for economic aid to undeveloped countries "which is neither straight anti-Communism nor straight humanitarianism." The rapprochement was facilitated by his adoption, as a starting proposition, of the fundamental liberal premise: there was a "triple revolution" of rising expectations, resentment at inequality, and national self-assertion going on in the "new societies" of Asia and Africa. Hence, it was necessary to fight Communist infiltration through an alternative model of rapid development, the liberal model:

The Asian and African leaders are beginning to see the true choice in these terms; they can pursue their economic development by maintaining considerable freedom of economic choices by their own people and importing a significant part of their investment capital from the outside, or they can adopt the Soviet idea of autarchic development by rigid state control of economic choices which makes it possible for a nation to squeeze its needed industrial capital out of its own domestic production, especially out of its farmers. One formula makes it possible to maintain a degree of freedom in political and economic choices by individuals.

Summing up his synthesis, Cleveland permitted himself this quotation from the Lebanese diplomat Charles Malik:

18 Stevenson, pp. 48, 54. Some of the limitations of his view are suggested by his hope that "the lot of the new African nations might resemble that of Puerto Rico with its assured entry to a large consumer market" (Europe in the African case) rather than "Haiti or the Central American Republics" which went "from colonial status to the risk of anarchy and stagnation." *Ibid.*, pp. 50–51.

"The cultural line of battle today lies between the Christian-European civilization and the unholy alliance of its internal rebels with those outside."[19]

G. Mennen Williams' appointment as Assistant Secretary of State for African Affairs was based on his civil rights' zeal and President Kennedy's desire to reward not only his black constituency but also one of his earliest political supporters. According to a source close to the negotiations between Kennedy and Williams, the Michigan governor "had a lot of ideas in the field of education and welfare and preferred [the Health, Education, and Welfare (HEW)] Department." However, he was the beneficiary of an estate that held a major block of stock in the Mennen Company, manufacturers of pharmaceuticals and toiletries, and subject to regulation by that Department. When this was pointed out as a possible source of a conflict of interest, "Kennedy asked Williams to consider the African position, in view of the remarkable record Williams had made with Negro Americans." Williams was greatly attracted to the idea and quickly came to have such a high regard for it that he discouraged efforts "to explore the possibility of removing the sources of the HEW conflict."[20]

Some liberal policy-makers also advanced material arguments for liberal interventionism. In *Africa's Challenge to America* (1956) Bowles emphasized the contribution of African raw materials to the American economy:

> During the past twenty years, the United States industrial machine has consumed more raw materials than in all of our previous existence. Already we're importing half of all our industrial raw material requirements.

[19] Cleveland, "Theory," p. 11.

[20] Letter to the author, June 30, 1970. Cf. Schlesinger, p. 127, which explains Williams' failure to get the HEW appointment this way: "As for Williams, who had long been under attack for supposed prodigality as governor of Michigan [Kennedy said] 'there were just too many difficulties. . . . I just don't think he is the man to go before this Congress and request big spending bills for education and medical care.' " For an idea of Williams' New Dealish approach to African economic development, see "Report of the Conference on Economic Resources," p. 66.

By 1970 our present consumption will have doubled, our own resources will have further diminished, and we will be competing with other nations now in the process of rapid expansion. If we should be denied access to the raw materials of Asia, we should be seriously handicapped, but we could still maintain our economic growth. But if we were also cut off from the apparently limitless natural resources of Africa, we would face formidable difficulties within a decade even though the resources of Canada and of South America remained available to us.

Continued access to these resources was said to be endangered by the Republican Administration's inability to anticipate political changes in Africa. A "mutually profitable economic association" with the emerging nations, and the frustration of Soviet designs for an alternative arrangement, depended upon the abandonment of America's procolonial, pro-NATO, and military-oriented policy:

If the simmering South African volcano should erupt or the tricky balance of forces in the Congo break down, our position in the nuclear jet age could be mortally threatened. If practical American policy is to extend beyond the arrival of the next shipload of cobalt, columbite or pitchblende from Africa, such factors must be taken into account.[21]

Stevenson too noted America's "direct economic interests" in Africa's raw materials and her markets' "rising value." [22] The latter consideration loomed large in Bowles' pamphlet, *Tomorrow Without Fear,* written in a moment of widespread fear among business and government leaders that the American economy could not survive the transition to peace without an increase in domestic planning and an expansion of overseas markets for goods and idle capital.[23]

The dependence of the interlinked economies of America and Western Europe on African mineral imports undoubtedly worked in favor of an interventionist policy. The Western stake might be jeopardized by any severe breakdown of order, by hostile nation-

21 Bowles, *Africa,* pp. 52–54, 56, 100.
22 Stevenson, p. 53.
23 Bowles, *Tomorrow,* pp. 62, 85; Lafeber, pp. 6–9.

alism, and by Soviet penetration. Still, a straight economic self-interest analysis does not seem to provide an adequate understanding of liberal interventionism in Africa. In the first place, material considerations did not rank very high in the overall liberal outlook; and both the genealogy of the evolving program and the way it tended to outdo a merely calculating rationality indicated a certain liberty from marketplace compulsions. Then, it was the fundamental liberal perception and positive valuation of the "triple revolution" in underdeveloped lands, and not just the resources themselves, that implied a turn toward support of African nationalism. Lastly, more than any other form of politics, diplomacy requires the rational ordering of priorities. Even the most powerful nation cannot accomplish all its objectives, given the scale and complexity of the international order. The liberal Africanists themselves recognized that industrialized Western Europe's economic and strategic importance to the U.S. was greater than that of Africa. Therefore, the roots of the liberal decision to oppose European policies in Africa, a decision which nowhere provoked more bitterness than in the Congo, cannot be found in any balance-sheet of resources, markets, and investments. Ironically, the liberals were the most zealous proponents of expanded economic relations with black Africa and received the *least* support from the business community and its representatives in government. The conservatives had their investments in white Africa and Europe; by definition, they rejected liberal perspectives and crusading zeal.

Again, the social and political affiliations of the Africanists help account for their particular vision.[24] They were all upper-class liberals with a marked vocation for "public service" rather than

[24] Materials used in the following analysis include: *Current Biography Yearbook,* 1963, pp. 104–106 (Cleveland). *Ibid.,* pp. 466–669 (Williams). *Current Biography Yearbook,* 1961, pp. 440–442 (Stevenson). *Who's Who in America,* 1960–1964. Kenneth S. Davis, *The Politics of Honor: A Biography of Adlai E. Stevenson* (New York, 1967). Other sources are cited individually.

business careers.[25] They had received their political baptism as handmaids of the "Roosevelt Revolution" and would spend much of their lives managing and rationalizing the post New-Deal accommodation between corporate privilege and the claims of the less-advantaged (including racial minorities). After World War II, Bowles, Stevenson, and Williams immersed themselves in the grass-roots liberalism of Northern Democratic politics, and became governors of urban states. Cleveland became editor and publisher of the *Reporter,* an important liberal periodical. Except for Williams, all had extensive experience in foreign affairs, particularly in areas which might be expected to attract liberal New Dealers.

Bowles was an American delegate to the first United Nations Educational, Scientific and Cultural Organization (UNESCO) conference in Paris 1945, then chairman of the national convention of UNESCO in the United States. In 1947–1948 he served as special assistant to Trygve Lie, the Secretary-General of the U.N., working in the U.S. and Europe as international chairman of the

[25] In two cases liberalism was entwined with deep religious feelings. Cleveland was a prominent Episcopalian whose father had been a minister. He believed that "progress is natural and good and practicable." He was particularly interested in the concept of Christian service in international relations. Christianity, he wrote, "ought to help Americans to escape the narrowness of being an American." He often spoke of the need for an "ethic for mutual involvement." *Current Biography Yearbook,* 1963, pp. 104–106. Williams came from a "devoutly Episcopalian" family. During the 1960 presidential campaign, John Kennedy received the following analysis of the connection between Williams' religious beliefs and his political positions: "Every one seems agreed that Williams is a man of strong convictions. He takes himself very seriously and believes that he is an instrument of God's will in furthering liberal, humanitarian causes. He is a devout Episcopalian and will show moving pictures of his trip to the Holy Land at the drop of a hat. Williams apparently sees himself as having been tapped to put the Sermon on the Mount into governmental practice. This is not a pose but reflects a sincere, if unusual conviction. I must go into this in some detail because I think that any approach to him which overlooks this strong religious drive—which is completely intermeshed with his personal ambition—will miss the mark." *Current Biography Yearbook,* 1963, pp. 466–469; The long quotation is from Theodore White, *The Making of the President 1960* (New York, 1962), pp. 161–162.

U.N. Appeal for Children. Subsequently, he helped formulate Washington's Point-4 program of technical aid to underdeveloped countries. From 1951 to 1953 Bowles was Ambassador to India and Nepal. Returned to private life by the new Republican Administration, he became a world traveler and a prolific commentator on the subject of developing continents.

Stevenson had played an important role in the founding of the United Nations, and was a U.S. delegate to the U.N. in 1946 and 1947. Between presidential campaigns and conventions he traveled extensively in the Third World, including two trips to Africa in 1955 and 1957. Stevenson's world-wide prestige and interest in Africa led to a number of close relationships with businessmen investing in Africa, particularly *liberal* businessmen. These political and legal contacts may have in turn spurred his own interest in African policy. Thus, he was a close friend of Harold R. Hochschild, chairman of American Metal Climax, who helped plan Stevenson's first trip to Africa. Hochschild was described by an associate as a "liberal of strong convictions" who later became involved in the Negotiations Now movement to end the war in Vietnam. The Hochschild family was one of the largest contributors to Stevenson's 1956 presidential campaign.[26] Stevenson considered AMAX's successful effort to break the color bar in white Rhodesian labor unions a model of enlightened capitalism.[27] In the Congo, however, AMAX's interest—order on the Copperbelt—diverged from its owners' heartfelt liberalism. In this case, the Hochschilds consulted their pocketbook. Although he discussed the Copperbelt dilemma with Harold Hochschild, Stevenson stayed on the liberal course.

As a private lawyer, Adlai Stevenson represented Reynolds Metals Co. which valued him for his "entree to the ruling powers of Jamaica and the rising young nations of Africa." [28] The

[26] *Congressional Quarterly Almanac,* 1957 (Washington: Congressional Quarterly Service, 1958), pp. 209, 219, 228.

[27] Stevenson, p. 50. For a contrasting view, stressing the token results of the company's effort, see Barber, p. 31.

[28] Davis, p. 362.

company's President, J. Louis Reynolds, gave $6,000 to national and local Democratic candidates in the 1956 election.[29] It will be recalled that Reynolds Aluminum had a direct interest in Congo political developments, an interest which was not particularly favored by Katanga secession. Stevenson also represented Leon Tempelsman and Son, another family-owned, liberal corporation with interests in Africa. The Tempelsmans had long been active in New York Democratic politics, particularly in the Eleanor Roosevelt-Herbert Lehman reform group. A close associate described Maurice Tempelsman as "among the kingpins" of state politics, "an important Democratic contributor," and a "personal friend" of Stevenson and President Kennedy. According to several business sources, Tempelsman was interested in getting a foothold in the minerals development of the Congo. His principal business was industrial diamonds, of which the Congo happened to be the largest producer. Beginning with diamond trading, the firm had branched out into manufacturing (especially tools and other machine products for the mining, construction, electronics, and aircraft industries) and mining. Much of this integrated operation was based on the control of sources of industrial diamonds. These came from Ghana, Guinea, Sierra Leone, and Latin America. During the early sixties, Tempelsman appears to have taken advantage of Belgium's compromised relation with Katanga to win a position of influence in the Central Government. Maurice Tempelsman quickly became friends with General Mobutu, Foreign Minister Bomboko, and future Prime Minister Adoula. He offered technical assistance to the Congo government in reorganizing the marketing of Congo diamonds. The diamonds came from Kasai, which had been wracked by tribal and political strife, where the marketing system, operated by an affiliate of Société Générale, had completely broken down. Most of the diamonds were being sold illegally by national and international entrepreneurs through Congo-Brazzaville. With no diamond mines, this

29 *New York Times,* Feb. 3, 1957, pp. 52–53; *Congressional Quarterly Almanac,* 1957, p. 210.

happy little republic became the world's largest diamond exporter, while the Congo government received virtually no revenue from these escaping resources. In reorganizing the marketing system, Tempelsman helped the Central Government play a larger role at the expense of the Belgian company. During the Johnson Administration Tempelsman arranged a long-planned barter deal wherein the Congo swapped excess industrial diamonds, needed in the U.S. strategic materials stockpile, for surplus wheat and gem stones which the American government did not need. In 1967 he promoted a consortium which totally displaced the Belgian marketing interests in favor of the Congo government and a new combine of mainly British and French capital. Having carved out a strong position of influence in the Congo, Tempelsman received a larger allocation of diamond production from the Central Selling Organization in London (the Oppenheimer-controlled world sales monopoly which even markets Soviet production). Tempelsman supported the liberal Africanists' policy—out of liberalism and "superior local information" according to his associates—but perhaps more essentially because of his need to delicately maneuver Congolese nationalism in order to weaken Belgian control of diamonds without putting into question the foreign capitalist order itself. One American banker acquainted with Tempelsman's bold and somewhat unorthodox ploy remarked acidly that "political upheavals, such as those which occurred in the Congo, often open up business opportunities which otherwise might have remained closed." Interestingly, the pattern of Tempelsman's opportunism persists in contemporary Congo politics, as does his association with Stevenson's law firm and with prominent Democratic figures.[30]

[30] Information on the Tempelsman business was provided by both private businessmen and diplomats. Some idea of the firm's operations is conveyed in "How to Do Business Successfully in Africa," *Business Abroad.* In 1966 Tempelsman recommended Theodore Sorenson, of Stevenson's former law firm, as the Congo government's counsel in the dispute between Union Minière and the Mobutu government. He also nearly succeeded in having Robert McNamara, now President of the World Bank, named as a mediator. In 1967–1969, Tempelsman put together a minerals development con-

Stevenson's ties to these liberal family corporations with interests in the Congo may partly represent the mutual gravitation of liberals in politics and business. It has also been shown that Stevenson's business supporters had divergent interests and policies in the Congo, so an interest-based interpretation of Stevenson's policy is not readily apparent. Nonetheless, it is probable that Stevenson's overall concern for Africa was promoted by his business connections; and it is not at all excluded that these interests influenced, in some measure, Stevenson's Congo policy.

Cleveland's experience was in the various economic aid organizations which arose after World War II. He had worked as a United Nations Relief and Rehabilitation Assistance official in England and Italy and as an aid administrator in Europe, China, and Southeast Asia. In 1950 he had invented the phrase, "revolution of rising expectations." As an analyst for the Rockefeller Brothers Fund and later as Dean of the Maxwell School of Public Administration at Syracuse University, he advanced programs for increased economic and administrative aid to undeveloped countries and a larger role for the U.N. in coordinating this aid.[31]

In sum, the views of liberal Africanists were largely derived from their social-political affiliations and their career experiences

---

sortium including also Standard Oil of Indiana, Mitsui Industries, Anglo-American Co., and a French government corporation, whose existence is said to have made Union Minière more reasonable in the compensation (for nationalization) negotiations of 1969. Recently, this consortium received a large copper concession in Katanga; see *East African Standard,* Sept. 21, 1970, p. 2.

31 Cleveland may be regarded as an ideologist of the foreign aid bureaucracy. For example, in "Memo," p. 11, he announced exuberantly that "we have recently passed from the era of foreign relations to the era of foreign operations. Nowadays 'international relations' consist mostly of the thousand and one ways in which whole societies get deeply involved in each others' affairs." For the more than one billion inhabitants of "undeveloped countries . . . we need to build the kinds of strength concentrated at the 'point of sale' in each emerging nation that can most directly be converted into government institutions staffed with people who know, or at least are trying to learn, how to govern."

in "the new nationalisms." In fact, it seems likely that the decision to concentrate on the problems of underdeveloped countries was the result of the policy-makers' liberal inclinations.

Within the Kennedy Administration a certain political logic promoted these ideas. Bowles, Williams, and Stevenson were important political figures with large liberal constituencies. Such men would be less cautious, and more difficult to "coordinate" with variant interests, than career officers like Joseph Satterthwaite. And while Bowles lasted less than a year as the No. 2 man in the State Department, he managed to clog the African policy machine with a goodly number of sympathizers.[32] Harlan Cleveland headed the U.N. Bureau. Wayne Fredericks was plucked from the Ford Foundation to be Deputy Assistant Secretary for African Affairs, violating the tradition that the foreign service filled such posts. Fredericks had previously worked for Kellogg Company in Southern Africa and for the Defense Department (1951–1954). Two former officials of the Defense and State Department declared that he was also "an old CIA man." [Fredericks, who is currently directing Africa programs for the Ford Foundation, refused to confirm this information.] A determined opponent of apartheid and related settler policies, he was concerned about racial tension in Africa and the rising "line of confrontation" between white-dominated regimes in the south and black ones in the north. In Katanga he saw a "small European-interest group" contributing to a destructive racism in Africa. If this continued, he feared that moderate nationalists with visions of racial harmony, such as Kenneth Kaunda and Julius Nyerere, might be overwhelmed.

Fredericks' appointment had been pushed by Williams. The Kellogg Company's home base was Battle Creek, Michigan, and Fredericks was already on close terms with Michigan Democratic party leaders in the late fifties. Strongly opposed to the Republican Administration's foreign policy, Fredericks contemplated running for Congress in the Third District (then heavily Republican). After a sobering discussion with State Democratic Chairman Neil Staebler, Fredericks realized that his point of view was "too far

[32] Schlesinger, p. 146.

ahead of his time" in the Third District, and at the same time Staebler became thoroughly acquainted with Fredericks' experience and outlook. When Williams was appointed, Staebler suggested Fredericks for "some position in the Department," and then at Williams' request brought them together at Staebler's home. Williams was so deeply impressed that he immediately set the machinery in motion to make Fredericks his deputy. Both men were strongly committed to the idea of government action to help blacks achieve equality, at home and abroad. As explained by an associate: "To this view of things, Williams brings a religious approach of brotherhood and Fredericks a parallel social or anthropological approach on the ridiculousness of color differentiation." [33]

Another Bowles' selection was Edmund Gullion for Ambassador to the Congo. He was a "professional" who had displayed a prescient anticolonialism in an earlier assignment. As counselor of the American legation in Saigon during the first Indochina war he argued "that the French could not organize successful resistance on the basis of either military plans calling for conventional assault or of political plans retaining Indochina as part of France." [34] Gullion also had the advantage of the President's confidence. An old friend and trusted adviser, he had worked with Kennedy on his Indochina speeches.[35]

If a good part of the Kennedy Administration favored a new priority for African relations, and a New Deal for Africa, there were some who were quite skeptical. For one thing, it took several months for the new Administration to purge itself of the Eisenhower influence. Fredericks did not replace Penfield until May 12, and Timberlake stayed on into the middle of June. Then the senior European Bureau of the State Department institutionalized the Western allies' interest in keeping the American role down. It had the backing of important members of the "Foreign Policy Establish-

[33] Letter to the author, June 30, 1970. [34] Schlesinger, p. 300.

[35] Theodore C. Sorenson, *Kennedy* (New York, 1965), p. 66; see also Schlesinger, p. 301.

ment," men such as Robert Murphy who had access to high officials through personal relationships.[36] After November 26, 1961, the No. 2 and No. 3 posts in the State Department were held by men who had serious reservations about "those passionate missionary types" revamping African policy.

George Ball, who replaced Bowles as Under Secretary, had just arrived in the upper class when the New Deal appeared. (His father rose from a $65-a-week salesman to the vice-presidency of Standard Oil.) He seemed less touched by the New Deal than upper-class liberals with established wealth and sentiments of *noblesse oblige*. Short stints in the Farm Credit Administration and the Treasury Department left him with a yearning for private law practice. "It [the New Deal] didn't seem real," he explains. A friend comments, "I think that George wanted to make money." [37] His career was largely in the private sector, first as a tax lawyer for corporations and then as a leading international lawyer representing the European Economic Community, the European Coal and Steel Community, the *Patronat* (French manufacturers), Venezuelan oil interests, Cuban sugar-mill owners and cane growers, etc. However, he was a Democrat and active in the presidential campaigns of his former law partner, Adlai Stevenson. As a noncrusading liberal, he lent his legal and other talents to nations which had already "developed." "[Jean] Monnet's man in Washington, it was Ball's responsibility to maneuver the U.S. government into positions favorable to the various initiatives being taken in the postwar decade toward European unity." [38] He was "one of the very few Americans" involved in drafting the Schuman Plan for a European Steel and Coal Community and worked with Monnet on plans for a Common Market. Ball's law firm had

[36] A favorite setting for these informal influences was the Metropolitan Club in Washington.

[37] Joseph Kraft, "George Ball—An Operator on the Potomac Comes to the East River," *New York Times Magazine,* July 21, 1968, p. 54. Some of the biographical information in this paragraph is derived from *Current Biography Yearbook,* 1962, pp. 23–25; and *Washington Post,* Jan. 2, 1961, p. A-2.

[38] Kraft, p. 55.

offices in Paris and Brussels.[39] Ball thought the "industrial heartland of Europe"—and its unification—should have top priority at the State Department. He was inclined to favor European spheres of influence in Africa (hopefully a single unified sphere) where American investments and strategic interests were minimal.[40]

The new Under Secretary for Political Affairs was George McGhee. A Texas oilman who had gotten rich with his father-in-law's backing, McGhee had some sympathy for the "international business structure" in Africa. A Democrat, he served President Truman as director of Greek-Turkish Aid, Ambassador to Turkey, and Assistant Secretary for Near East, South Asia, and Africa. In the latter post he encouraged university programs on Africa and better training for U.S. diplomatic and consular officers there. But —as all concerned were wont to do in 1950—he conceived of Africa as an appendage of Europe and a contributor to the restoration of a sound European economy. This vision persisted. McGhee was an old colleague of Dean Rusk, and his advice carried weight with the Secretary.[41]

If the President was inclined toward the "Africanists," there remained the question of how far he would go at the expense of European relations or domestic political standing. Kennedy was not, after all, a particularly passionate liberal (this was perhaps the secret of his charm). He seems to have accepted the Bowles' line on Africa mainly for pragmatic reasons, i.e., to counter Soviet influence.

Sophisticated Anti-Communism

Like its predecessor, the Kennedy Administration had a dualistic or "bipolar" perspective on international politics. The Presi-

39 *Ibid.*

40 These views are elaborated in George W. Ball, *The Discipline of Power* (Boston, 1968), esp. Chapters II and XI.

41 A short biography appeared in the *New York Times,* Nov. 13, 1962, p. 19. McKay, pp. 279–280, 289, gives McGhee's early statements on Africa. The close tie with Rusk is noted by Schlesinger, p. 145; and Sorenson, p. 289.

dent and his advisers read Khrushchev's January 6 (1961) speech as a virtual declaration of war by the Soviet bloc in the Third World. The enemy's means were new and subtle—support for "national-liberation wars," economic, political, and ideological struggles—but his ends were the same as always. "We must never be lulled," the President said in his first State of the Union message, "into believing that either power [Russia or China] has yielded its ambitions for world domination—ambitions which they forcefully restated only a short time ago. On the contrary, our task is to convince them that aggression and subversion will not be profitable routes to pursue these ends." [42] (No hint of any "polycentrism" here!) When, in February 1961, Harlan Cleveland and four ex-governors (Bowles, Stevenson, Williams, and Averell Harriman) gathered to consider the next steps in the Congo, they started by rehearsing the rationale for U.S. policy. Of utmost importance was the "U.S. interest to frustrate active efforts by the Soviets in the fall of 1960." In later months, when these same officials had to bring the Congo problem to the President, he would often remind them of "what you said the first time: If the U.N. wasn't in, there'd be a Soviet-American confrontation in one form or another." [43] This estimate of Soviet intentions was also supported by historical analogy. Where the Eisenhower men had recalled Czechoslovakia and Greece, New Frontiersmen worried about "another Laos" or "another Cuba."

The Congo's importance—its size, location, and wealth—was fully appreciated. Even George Ball who "cannot see how we would be endangered by a Communist regime in Mali or Brazzaville or Burundi" withdraws before such a prospect in Angola or Mozambique, those "extensive and strategically important territories lying at the heart of Africa." [44] Furthermore, President Kennedy formalized a tendency in American foreign policy to invest *every* Communist gain with an unbearable significance. At Vienna

[42] Schlesinger, p. 284. For the evaluation of the Jan. 6 speech, see *ibid.*, pp. 282–284.

[43] Kennedy's view also appears in *ibid.*, p. 530; and Sorenson, p. 63.

[44] Ball, pp. 233–235, 251.

he told Khrushchev that there was a delicate balance in world politics:

> The issue was the disruption of the existing equilibrium of power . . . social changes must take place peacefully and must not involve the prestige or commitments of America and Russia or upset the balance of world power. . . . The entry of additional nations into the communist camp, the loss of Taiwan—such developments would alter the equilibrium.[45]

Yet the old notion that the Communists were Supermen in chaotic situations was challenged. With their sympathy for and experience in the new nationalisms the liberals knew that turbulence was often the inevitable by-product of indigenous progress.[46] They were less apt to seek out Communist conspiracies when unpleasant things were said about the West. Thus in 1958 Senator Kennedy, though fervently anti-Communist, had warned against "the illusion prevalent in North American discussions that all Latin-American agitation is Communist-inspired—that every anti-American voice is the voice of Moscow—and that most citizens of Latin America share our dedication to an anti-Communist crusade to save what we call free enterprise." [47]

The Democratic Administration was impressed by the strength of those indigenous forces which were not vehicles of Soviet influence. Hence it was willing, *where necessary,* to countenance coalition governments in the expectation that the "neutralists" and "conservatives" would keep the "pro-Communists" in line. This was the case in Laos and Indonesia.[48] Even the "pro-Communists"

[45] Schlesinger, pp. 338–339. Kennedy's "intense desire to avoid giving the impression of weakness" is analyzed by George Kateb, "Kennedy as Statesman," *Commentary,* XLI (June, 1966), 54–60.

[46] For example, see Bowles, *Conscience,* pp. 52–55.

[47] Schlesinger, p. 181.

[48] The clearest explanations of why these coalitions were acceptable are in Roger Hilsman, *To Move a Nation: The Politics of Foreign Policy in the Administration of John F. Kennedy* (Garden City, 1967), pp. 152–154 (Laos), 369–370, 400–402, 409 (Indonesia); and Schlesinger, pp. 305–318 (Laos).

were now referred to as "allied with the Communists" or "influenced" by them rather than "Communist controlled" or "converts to their ideology." In certain carefully certified cases it was thought that a Communist-leaning neutralist might be capable of redemption (e.g., Touré or Nkrumah). But this was a highly selective and touchy process—as Cheddi Jagan and Nkrumah would discover.[49] And no one thought that a Lumumba or a Gizenga was strong enough—or inevitable enough—to make such an effort worthwhile. These views encountered less opposition within the Administration than the pro-Africa line. This was because there were fewer institutional interests involved, and because a *liberal* "Europeanist" like Ball was likely to endorse liberal positions.

The February 21 Resolution

The new Administration was immediately seized with the Congo problem. A meeting of the Security Council had been called for February 1. The key question was whether the U.S. and the Afro-Asians could come to an agreement. If this were accomplished, the Western allies and the Soviet Union were unlikely to veto the resulting resolution. In the absence of an accord, the U.N. Force would continue to disintegrate and might have to withdraw in the near future.

Overhanging the discussions in the State Department toward the

[49] Jagan failed interviews on "Meet the Press" and with the President. The State Department, in a reversal of policy, came to support his opponent, Forbes Burnham, for Prime Minister of British Guiana. Jagan seemed, "though perhaps not a disciplined Communist," a person with "that kind of deep pro-Communist emotion which only sustained experience with Communism could cure, and the United States could not afford the Sekou Touré therapy when it involved a quasi-Communist regime on the mainland of Latin America." *Ibid.*, pp. 710–713. Nkrumah's anti-Western statements and personal dictatorship disturbed the Administration. He almost lost the American-financed Volta Dam and was finally cut off from further long-term credits. *Ibid.*, pp. 527–529. Sekou Touré's salvageability had to be verified personally by four prominent Americans: Harriman, Robert Kennedy, William Attwood (Ambassador to Guinea), and the President. *Ibid.*, pp. 523–525; William Attwood, *The Reds and the Blacks* (New York, 1967), Chapters ii and iii.

end of January was the very real possibility that Lumumba was already dead, murdered in Elizabethville. Rumors to this effect began to spread in Leopoldville within a few days of his transfer on January 17th. Among the sources appear to have been two government ministers who accompanied Lumumba and his collaborators in Elizabethville.[50] According to American officials, Ambassador Timberlake "believed" Lumumba was dead, but "some recommendations" assumed he was still alive. It seems that even Timberlake was probably less than certain of Lumumba's death when he returned to Washington at the end of the month.[51]

Available information indicates the U.S. was not *directly* responsible for the murder of Lumumba, although one can never wholly exclude a hidden CIA "success." As mentioned previously, Tully's CIA informants stressed that they did not want Lumumba killed lest he become a "martyr." [52] The very thorough study of Heinz and Donnay concludes that European advisers played an important role in Lumumba's transfer to Katanga by the Central Government—but does not accuse the Americans. The authors present evidence that the State Department tried, too late, to prevent Lumumba's death:

> Lumumba and his companions died during the night of January 17–18. On the afternoon of January 18, in Washington, the American Under Secretary of State for Africa [sic] calls in one of the representatives of Belgium to tell him of his concern on the subject of the transfer and treatment reserved to the prisoners. He insists that P. Lumumba not be "liquidated," nor submitted to bad treatment: these would have the effect of attracting new sympathy in his favor in the moderate African countries.[53]

[50] Heinz and Donnay, p. 172; see also pp. 166, 175.

[51] *Ibid.*, p. 172, shows that a Belgian adviser to the Congo *Sûreté* retained some doubts as late as Jan. 27.

[52] Significantly, Mobutu's actions up to the transfer were consistent with this CIA position. *Ibid.*, pp. 31–39, 57.

[53] *Ibid.*, p. 171.

This moving scene of pragmatic humanitarianism notwithstanding, American officials in January 1961 do not seem to have taken much precaution to save Lumumba's skin. Given the CIA's close relationship with top Congolese leaders and their Belgian advisers, the U.S. Embassy must have known of the governmental decision to transfer Lumumba. It must have learned that Bakwanga and Elizabethville were the most likely destinations. It surely knew that the President of South Kasai and the Interior Minister of Katanga had threatened to murder Lumumba if he ever fell into their hands.[54] Finally, embassy officials knew that the Belgians in Brussels and Leopoldville were not in full control of the regimes in Bakwanga and Elizabethville. Yet during the four or five days when Lumumba's fate was being determined, there is no sign that the Americans were trying to assure his safety.[55] In this context the tardy intervention of the African Bureau looks like a mere afterthought.

It may be that in the rush to move Lumumba and thereby counter an immediate political threat the security of the West's Congolese protégés outweighed *and pushed aside* any other consideration. Perhaps it is in this light that one must read a remark made by a Belgian official who worked closely with the CIA's Larry Devlin: "Lumumba's death really cemented the relationship between Devlin and the Binza boys. It added an important psychological factor. Now they had a skeleton in the cupboard."

Deliberations in Washington concerning the upcoming Security Council meeting on the Congo revealed two distinct approaches within the Administration.[56] The Stevenson-Bowles-Williams group advocated a "neutral" Congo. They proposed a coalition government to absorb Lumumba (or the Lumumbists) "just as the Germans later neutralized Franz Joseph Strauss by including him in

[54] *Ibid.*, pp. 80, 117–118.

[55] In Dec. 1960 Lumumba was severely mistreated by Mobutu's paracommandos in prison. Again, it is clear that Western agents were aware of the situation but little action was taken. *Ibid.*, pp. 69–72.

[56] The following account is based on interviews with the principals as well as the sources cited below.

the cabinet." Naturally this required the release of political prisoners. On the military plane, they suggested that the big powers stop helping the various factions and that the U.N. proceed to disarm Congolese soldiers. Once these arrangements were in place, parliament could be reconvened. The latest nose count from the Embassy's political section indicated that Lumumba had already lost his narrow parliamentary majority. As for Katanga, this group was willing to move a considerable distance toward the Afro-Asian position.

The other side was led by carry-overs from the Eisenhower Administration who claimed the wisdom of experience. They received some support from the European Bureau and the Pentagon, and their principal spokesman was Ambassador Timberlake. They urged strong support for the "pro-Western" Central Government. They considered a coalition government a prelude to a Lumumba (Lumumbist?) takeover and feared his old sway over parliament. Without a satisfactory political settlement they were not particularly eager for a military stand-down, especially one which was being pushed by unreliable Afro-Asians. The point was made that the Congolese Army (Leopoldville branch) would never accept disarmament. This group hoped the Congo could be reorganized into a "loose federation of tribal or power factions," as "it was not felt realistic . . . to insist upon a completely democratic government at this time." [57] Since a strong Katanga was the best argument for such a federation, it should not be weakened by a hasty dismissal of the Belgians; nor should U.S.-European relations be needlessly bruised.

A tentative compromise was worked out for preliminary negotiations at the U.N. The plan was based on the first group's proposals but modified them in two ways. First, the military measures would precede the political settlement, presumably to enhance stability and moderation. And there was apparently some hedging on just when Lumumba would be released—before or after a new government was in place and parliament had reconvened. Sec-

[57] *Christian Science Monitor,* Feb. 13, 1961, p. 1.

ondly, the withdrawal of Belgian advisers was not mentioned. The American position seems to have been that this should be a last step after the others had assured stability.[58]

While Stevenson sounded out the Soviets and Afro-Asians on these proposals, the second group campaigned for further qualifications. On February 4, Timberlake spent more than an hour with the President. In the next few days he testified, along with Williams, before the Senate Foreign Relations and House Foreign Affairs Committees. He told the members of Congress that the Administration was considering the release of Lumumba and formation of a coalition government and expressed his opinion in such a way that Williams considered his statements "disloyal." Emerging from a committee room, Senator Fulbright remarked that a coalition government with Lumumba "would be very dangerous." Senators Church and Aiken backed him up.[59] Meanwhile, Belgium and France expressed strong opposition to the new American plan.[60]

At a National Security Council meeting on February 9, Stevenson reported "encouraging first results" in his negotiations. However, "two significant amendments" were added to the Congo package "by senior Administration advisers, some with direct experience in the Congo." One eliminated Lumumba from a coalition government "because he would immediately climb into the driver's seat and initiate irresponsible policy." The object now "was to include representatives of Lumumbist forces—without Lumumba himself—in the broadened government." The liberation of political

[58] For descriptions of the plan, see *New York Times,* Feb. 4, 1961, p. 1; Feb. 5, 1961, p. 3; *Christian Science Monitor,* Feb. 4, 1961, p. 1; *London Times,* Feb. 4, 1961, p. 8; *Washington Post,* Feb. 3, 1961, p. A-1.

On the vagaries surrounding the release of political prisoners, see *Christian Science Monitor,* Feb. 7, 1961, p. 6; *Washington Post,* Feb. 8, 1961, p. A-3; Jane Stolle, "Gamble in the Congo," *Nation,* Feb. 18, 1961, p. 131. On the U.S. attitude toward removal of the Belgian advisers, see *ibid.,* and *Christian Science Monitor,* Feb. 8, 1961, p. 1.

[59] *New York Times,* Feb. 5, 1961, p. 3; *Libre Belgique,* Feb. 8, 1961, p. 7; Feb. 9, 1961, p. 4.

[60] *New York Times,* Feb. 7, 1961, p. 14.

prisoners was consigned to a late stage of the plan. The other amendment dropped disarmament and substituted retraining and reunification. If the Congo remained divided, this could imply assistance to the Central Government's army.[61]

Before negotiations could be resumed at the U.N., word arrived that Lumumba had been killed in Katanga. Tshombe's Minister of the Interior, Munongo, announced that Lumumba had escaped and been killed by villagers. He said that he would not pretend that the death of Lumumba made him sorry and continued: "People will accuse us of assassination. To this I have only one response: Prove it!" The world was shocked; marches, protests, and violent demonstrations occurred in more than thirty cities.[62] The Soviet Union reacted with predictable fury. It accused Hammarskjold of direct responsibility for the death of Lumumba and withdrew recognition of him as a U.N. official. It demanded sanctions against Belgium, the immediate arrest of Mobutu and Tshombe, termination of the U.N. operation within a month and the dismissal of Hammarskjold. Moscow also pledged "all possible help" to the "lawful" government of the Congo, headed by Antoine Gizenga. At the same time, the United Arab Republic and Guinea recognized the Stanleyville regime.[63] Suddenly a specter haunted Washington: the Communists and radical Africans would support a "war of liberation" against the Central Government. On February 15 President Kennedy said he was "seriously concerned at what appears to be a threat of unilateral intervention" in the Congo, and warned "there should be no misunderstanding of the position of the United States if any government is really planning to take so dangerous and irresponsible a step." He also denounced the "purported recognition of Congolese factions as so-called governments." [64] Williams flew to Khartoum to obtain a formal guarantee that the Sudan government would continue to bar transit for supplies to Stanleyville. The

[61] *Christian Science Monitor,* Feb. 10, 1961, p. 13; *New York Times,* Feb. 12, 1961, p. 12; *Washington Post,* Feb. 14, 1961, p. A-11.

[62] Hoskyns, pp. 315–318.

[63] *Ibid.,* pp. 323–324.

[64] *Department of State Bulletin,* Mar. 6, 1961, pp. 322–323. See also *New York Times,* Feb. 17, 1961, p. 3.

carrot of foreign aid was dangled before that weak regime.[65] At the Pentagon, contingency plans for limited war were drawn up. They contemplated the dispatch of 80,000 troops by air or sea. Five U.S. naval vessels appeared in the Gulf of Guinea off the Congo, ostensibly for "good will." However, they included two ships with 500 marines aboard and had a "possible emergency role." [66] Another important consequence of Lumumba's death was a stiffening of Afro-Asian demands. An "atmosphere of urgency" had been created and "moved the more moderate states much closer to the Casablanca position." [67]

On the 17th the consensus of most Afro-Asians was submitted to the Security Council by Ceylon, Liberia, and the United Arab Republic. Their draft resolution emphasized the withdrawal of foreign military, paramilitary, and political advisers, and strongly urged the reconvening of parliament. In addition, U.N. troops were given the right to use force as a last resort to prevent civil war. Although one provision called for the reorganization and depoliticization of the army, it was clear that the sponsors were putting their emphasis for neutralization on the other measures. Unlike most U.N. resolutions, the draft neither commended the past actions of the Secretary-General nor associated him with the implementation of its decisions.[68]

In Washington the Afro-Asian initiative provoked bitter disagreement. The Timberlake group argued against support of the resolution; it was necessary at all costs to strengthen Kasavubu, Mobutu, and Tshombe to resist compromise with Stanleyville. On the other hand, the Bowles faction, "though they felt the United States should press for certain amendments, was convinced that final support should be given to the Afro-Asians" whose proposals were "positive" and not associated with Moscow. Again, the Ad-

[65] Verhaegen, *Congo 1961,* p. 190.

[66] *New York Times,* Feb. 20, 1961, p. 2; *Christian Science Monitor,* Feb. 23, 1961, p. 1. According to one high official: "There was talk of sending troops. . . . In 1961 the Congo was as big as Vietnam."

[67] Hoskyns, p. 328.

[68] *Ibid.,* pp. 328–331.

ministration decided to compromise internal differences. Stevenson was instructed to submit amendments recognizing the legal authority of Kasavubu and expressing confidence in Hammarskjold. He was not authorized to vote for the Afro-Asian resolution if the amendments failed.[69]

Thus on February 20 the American delegation at the U.N. was campaigning for amendments which would entail a Russian veto and split the Afro-Asians. "Whether the resolution was accepted or not seemed in these circumstances to depend on just how determined the Americans were to force through their changes." [70] In its first month the Kennedy Administration was leaning toward a course which led from a weakening of the U.N. presence to a heavier U.S. involvement in the Congo, perhaps limited war. But on that Monday morning the U.N. announced the murder of six Lumumbists in South Kasai. "In a curious way this cold-blooded massacre seemed almost more shocking than the death of Lumumba and his companions, and in an atmosphere of horror and disgust the Security Council meeting was adjourned until 3 P.M." [71] During the recess Stevenson appealed to Kennedy to modify the American attitude, explaining the emotional state of the Afro-Asians and the prospect that the Soviets would now make much headway with the charge that the Americans had deliberately sabotaged the draft resolution. Some reports indicate Hammarskjold also made a direct appeal to the President.[72] In any event, Stevenson received permission to vote for the draft after expressing certain reservations. These had to do with the omission of any reference to implementation by Hammarskjold, possible abuse of the "force in the last resort," provision against civil war (America's allies feared it was aimed at Katanga), and the necessity to exclude not only foreign personnel but also arms and equipment (i.e., to weaken Stanleyville if Katanga was to be weakened). On Febru-

[69] The account is based on a reliable report in *Afrique Action* (later called *Jeune Afrique*), Feb. 27, 1961, pp. 11–12. It also draws on Hoskyns, p. 332, for certain details. The quotation is from the latter source.

[70] Hoskyns, p. 332. [71] *Ibid.* pp. 332–333. [72] *Ibid.*

ary 21 the Afro-Asian resolution was adopted by 9 votes to none with 2 abstentions (France and the Soviet Union).[73]

This episode showed that by institutionalizing neutral opinion, the United Nations could exercise some constraint on the actions of the big powers. But Stevenson's reservations suggested U.S.-Afro-Asian agreement was far from complete. The Americans would probably seek to moderate the application of the February resolution.

The Road to Lovanium

For the next two or three months American policy seemed ambivalent and indecisive. There was "discreet pressure" on Belgium to withdraw advisers from Katanga, but care was taken not to go too far and so "weaken the North Atlantic Alliance." [74] By April 15 the Afro-Asians were again estranged from the Secretariat's cautious diplomacy on Katanga. The General Assembly adopted a resolution deploring Belgian noncompliance with earlier resolutions, calling the adviser problem "the central factor in the present grave situation in the Congo," and demanding prompt action. Although the draft was approved by 61 votes to 5 with 33 abstentions, the U.S. abstained.[75] Stevenson explained he was "hopefully confident" that Belgium was cooperating with the U.N. and noted that the presence of foreign military and political personnel was only "one of the central factors" in the crisis.[76] In regard to the first point, it was, however, clear that "the Belgian government was in fact prepared to do very little without the consent of the Katangese." [77]

The American attitude on a political settlement verged from qualified approval of loose federation [78] to reiteration of the "American plan" with its emphasis on a gradual return to parlia-

[73] *Ibid.*, p. 333. [74] *Christian Science Monitor*, Mar. 17, 1961, p. 4.

[75] Hoskyns, pp. 350–352, 491.

[76] *Department of State Bulletin*, May 22, 1961, p. 782.

[77] Hoskyns, p. 391.

[78] Official comment on "Tananarive Agreement" in *New York Times*, Mar. 14, 1961, p. 1.

mentary government.[79] The American Embassy held aloof from the first efforts of U.N. mediators to reconvene parliament.

In this veritable fog of policy, certain Americans in the Congo felt free to advance their "hard-line" views. According to two reliable sources the CIA chief, Devlin, was vigorously backing Tshombe at this time; his positions "were said to differ from those of Consul Canup [the American Consul in Elizabethville]." [80] In Leopoldville, Timberlake told Western and American journalists that the U.N. should support an alliance between Kasavubu, Tshombe, and Mobutu and help the latter's troops defeat Stanleyville; some U.N. diplomats felt he was encouraging the Congolese to resist U.N. decisions.[81] It seems probable that the Ambassador imparted a certain toughness to American policy, and this must have influenced those Congolese officials who had been "made" by him and sustained by his government.

It was not until June that a clear sense of direction—favorable to the Bowles group—could be detected in U.S. actions. This was the result of several factors:

(1) Elections had produced a new Belgian government which took office on April 25. The Vice-Premier and Minister for Foreign and African Affairs was the veteran Socialist and former Secretary-General of NATO, Paul-Henri Spaak. He had criticized the previous government's policy in the Congo and inclined toward some measure of rapprochement with the U.N., provided the cabinet and Belgian public opinion did not become too excited.[82]

(2) Afro-Asian pressure for full application of the February Resolution was mounting. India, which had just contributed 5,000 troops to the U.N. Force was particularly active.[83]

79 Statement by Ambassador Stevenson to the General Assembly, Apr. 14, 1961, in *Department of State Bulletin,* May 22, 1961, pp. 782–783.

80 Gérard-Libois, *Sécession,* p. 205. From here through Chapter V below, the author has relied on an English translation for the rendering of direct quotations: Jules Gérard-Libois, *Katanga Secession,* trans. Rebecca Young (Madison: University of Wisconsin Press, 1966).

81 *Afrique Action,* Apr. 3, 1961, pp. 22–23.

82 Hoskyns, pp. 369, 394–395; Gérard-Libois, *Sécession,* pp. 244–245.

83 Hoskyns, pp. 364, 396.

(3) The political situation in the Congo strengthened the case of those who wanted to risk a meeting of parliament. Tshombe had shown no disposition to concert his forces with those of the Central Government—except on his own terms of virtual autonomy. Meanwhile the Stanleyville regime had secured some gesture of recognition from 20 Afro-Asian and Communist countries. Stalemate "seemed to favor Gizenga more." The reconvening of parliament might well bring the anti-Gizenga forces together and "smoke out and defeat" Lumumba's uncharismatic successor.[84] Such reasoning was persuasive with officials who were less zealous about improved African relations or more apprehensive about the "unmanageability" of parliament. For example, Secretary Rusk was said to have revised his position.[85]

(4) The African Bureau was strengthened by two important personnel changes. In May, Wayne Fredericks became Deputy Assistant Secretary giving the ever-traveling Soapy Williams a strong voice in Washington. On June 15, Timberlake was recalled. In spite of the presumption that all Ambassadors would be replaced in the new Administration, Timberlake had been held over due to the tense situation in the Congo. However, he was obviously out of tune with many themes of the New Frontier. According to one official, he "had gotten so deeply involved in high internal political activities since Independence that he represented something of a product of those experiences. A relative hard-liner on the Communist issue . . . he had strong opinions regarding the personalities involved." Others remembered his "disloyal" performance before Congressional committees. The exact timing of his demise resulted from the need to save India's face: the Western and Central Government vendetta against Dayal had finally succeeded, and it was thought that, if the American and British Ambassadors in Leopoldville also left, the political connotations would be muted.[86] But Timberlake "would have gone reasonably shortly anyway."

[84] Timberlake, pp. 132–133.
[85] According to two officials of the African Bureau.
[86] *New York Times,* May 26, 1961, p. 1; Oct. 22, 1961, IV, 9.

The United States had no objection when the U.N. moved against some of Tshombe's Belgian political advisers during May, June, and July. After all, Spaak himself was quietly cooperating with Hammarskjold.[87]

Of greater importance was the American role in arranging a parliamentary session. In early June, U.N. diplomats got Leopoldville and Stanleyville to agree to send their legislators to an insulated meeting at Lovanium University. Yet the Katangese were holding out. In addition, some important people in the Central Government feared the outcome of a parliamentary vote, especially if Tshombe's conservatives were absent. Among those concerned were Nendaka and the *Sûreté,* Mobutu and parts of the army, and possibly Bomboko. In these circumstances the conference was postponed, and there was considerable question as to whether it would actually take place.[88] But now the American government showed it was determined to have a meeting, to press Tshombe to send his delegates, and to influence the composition of a new cabinet.

The U.S. Embassy strongly supported the U.N.'s campaign to get parliament going. This must have impressed certain Congolese politicians who possessed first-hand experience in the realities of international politics. Embassy officials go so far as to maintain that "parliament came out of our contacts with Linner" (who had succeeded Dayal as Chief U.N. representative in Leopoldville), and "it was really a U.S. operation but using outstanding U.N. personalities."

The Embassy took a firm stand on Katangan participation. The Central Government had detained Tshombe when he tried to leave a political conference at Coquilhatville. In mid-June there was "some dispute between those who wished to have Tshombe released as a gesture of good faith and those who felt that he should be kept in Leopoldville at least until after parliament had met." [89] The U.N. and the American Embassy favored the latter course.

87 Gérard-Libois, *Sécession,* pp. 218–219.
88 *Christian Science Monitor,* July 5, 1961, p. 4; Hoskyns, p. 370.
89 Hoskyns, pp. 366–368.

But the Americans "gave the green light to releasing him when a real or imaginary threat of a *coup d'état* by *ultras* [extremists] was raised in Elizabethville." [90] Back in Elizabethville, Tshombe repudiated an agreement to send his parliamentarians to Lovanium. The State Department responded with "*démarche* after *démarche* urging the Katanga leaders to reconsider their decision and warning them of the dangers of allowing the new government to be formed without them." [91] Early in July the American Embassy sent a letter to Elizabethville,

> noting that the Americans, because of international tension, needed support from the Afro-Asians and that they would prefer eventualy to sacrifice the interests of Katanga rather than lose standing in the Stanleyville camp, recognized by thirteen countries, mainly Afro-Asian.
>
> The same note underlined the identity of views of the U.N. and the United States on the Katanga problem and pointed up the fact that if American influences had worked in extremis in favor of Tshombe's release, it was because the United States feared Katanga would sacrifice its president and shut itself off in total resistance.[92]

The U.N., which was working closely with the Embassy, made repeated attempts to persuade Tshombe to join a "triple summit" of Congolese leaders in Leopoldville as a prelude to Lovanium. The Americans also seem to have asked Britain and France to bring pressure to bear.[93] The British Foreign Secretary asked Roy Welensky, Prime Minister of Rhodesia, to intercede in Elizabethville. According to Welensky,

> Lord Home (in a message to me on July 10th) said that the absolute essential was, by getting these two together [Kasavubu and Tshombe], to isolate Gizenga and prevent him from getting a majority if and when the Congolese National Assembly met; and he thought this could be done without sacrificing a great deal of Katanga's claim to autonomy.[94]

[90] Gérard-Libois, *Sécession,* p. 208.
[91] Hoskyns, p. 372.
[92] Gérard-Libois, *Sécession,* p. 213.
[93] Hoskyns, p. 372.
[94] Welensky, p. 219.

Finally, the U.S. reportedly tried to persuade Union Minière—the huge European mining company which contributed approximately half of Katanga's revenue—to take a decisive stand.[95]

The American candidate to lead a new government was Cyrille Adoula. Williams told Welensky that "Adoula had been the Americans' choice for this job from the start." [96] This has been confirmed privately by U.S. officials. At least two weeks before parliament met to elect a government, U.N. mediators were advancing Adoula's candidacy. One of them, Mahmoud Khiary, showed Conor Cruise O'Brien (now U.N. Representative in Elizabethville) an envelope on which was written "the core of the government he hoped to see elected: Prime Minister, Adoula; Vice-Premiers, Gizenga, Sendwe, Bolikango." This was ten days before the election. O'Brien comments: "It all came true, except for Bolikango. Bolikango's trouble was that he was convinced that he was going to be President, replacing Kasavubu." [97] Adoula also benefited from the activities of CIA agents. As Senator Dodd noted on August 3, 1962, "I am not revealing any secrets when I say that during the period preceding the Lovanium Conference, and even during the Conference itself, there was considerable jockeying for influence by the U.N., by ourselves, by the Afro-Asians and by Soviet agents." [98] The following account—*by the New York Times*—has been generally verified by a member of the American Embassy:

> Money and shiny American automobiles, furnished through the logistic wizardry of Langley, are said to have been the deciding factors in the vote that brought Mr. Adoula to power. Russian, Czech, Egyptian and Ghanaian agents were simply outbid where they could not be outmaneuvered.[99]

[95] Hoskyns, p. 372; Gérard-Libois, *Sécession,* p. 272.

[96] Welensky, pp. 221–222.

[97] *New York Times,* July 18, 1861, p. 7; O'Brien, *To Katanga and Back,* p. 189.

[98] *Congressional Record,* Aug. 3, 1962, p. 15546.

[99] *New York Times,* Apr. 26, 1966, p. 30. Similar indications appeared in *Newsweek,* Aug. 14, 1961, quoted in *Courrier Africain,* Sept. 19, 1961, p. 7.

In the last week of July, American diplomacy neared its dénouement. On the 24th and 25th the first votes were taken at Lovanium. Thirteen out of fourteen legislative offices were captured by the Lumumbist alliance. The margins of victory indicated the Katangans might hold the balance of power. Apparently the Lumumbists now demanded a predominant role in the new government.[100] On the 28th, Michel Struelens and three visiting Katanga legislators were called to the State Department. They were asked

> to urge Moise Tshombe to send parliamentarians to Lovanium immediately in order to help the moderates create a moderate government. At that time it was pretty much touch and go between Gizenga and who would emerge as Prime Minister.

Agreement was reached on a telex to Tshombe from Struelens and the Katangans. This recommended the immediate dispatch of the parliamentarians, promised an American statement "praising your initiative," and implied the U.S. would not take a stand prejudicial to Katanga in the further political discussions that were bound to ensue.[101] After receiving the cable, Tshombe flew to Brazzaville in the former French Congo "to try to make contact with the Leopoldville authorities." (In view of his recent detention he was unwilling to cross the Congo River into Leopoldville.) On the 31st, Mobutu crossed over in "a final attempt to persuade Tshombe to send the Katanga deputies," but the local authorities and Katanga *ultras* prevented a meeting.[102] At the same time Struelens flew to the Congo—at the request of the State Department—for a personal encounter with Tshombe. Accompanied by an American

[100] Hoskyns, p. 376.

[101] U.S. Congress, Senate, Committee on the Judiciary, *Visa Procedures of Department of State: Hearings* before the Subcommittee to Investigate the Administration of the Internal Security Act and Other Internal Security Laws, Committee Print, 87th Congress, 2nd Session, 1962, pp. 31–39, 207–211, 288–294 (hereinafter cited as *Visa Procedures*). The quotation is from testimony by Jerome Lavallee of the State Department Congo desk, and is at p. 291.

[102] Hoskyns, p. 377.

diplomat, he arrived in Elizabethville on August 2.[103] The following day Tshombe finally agreed to send the parliamentarians. It was too late; a new government had just been chosen. Hampered by factionalism, wearied by weeks of isolation, bribed by Khiary and his Swiss *homme de main,* fearful of another Mobutu coup, the Lumumbist deputies had modified their attitude and accepted an Adoula government, in which half the ministries would be held by the Lumumbist alliance.[104]

[103] *Visa Procedures,* pp. 228–233, 239–246, 289; Verhaegen, *Congo 1961,* pp. 409–413, 590–598.

[104] This version of the Lovanium conclave is largely based on interviews with two Lumumbist participants. Information about U.N. bribery comes from a reliable European observer who was close to Khiary. Gizenga had vainly tried to fuse the MNC-L with his branch of PSA during the previous few months. The threat of a Mobutu coup was very much a possibility had Gizenga or Gbenye won; see *New York Times,* July 21, 1961, p. 3, and July 28, 1961, p. 6.

CHAPTER V

The Battle against Katanga

After August 10 CONAKAT deputies and senators attended the meetings of the central parliament. But there was no real change in Katanga's independent status. The Tshombe government still issued its own currency, prohibited the flying of the Congo flag, and convened the consular corps ("who invariably came") for discussions on "foreign affairs." [1] Tshombe controlled South Katanga, but exercised only sporadic and bloody authority in the North, home of the opposition BALUBAKAT. The present political balance—both internally and vis-à-vis the rest of the Congo—was assured by 512 foreign military personnel and mercenaries. Among the 604 officers and noncommissioned officers of the Katanga gendarmerie, there were 460 foreigners. Of these, 201 were Belgians who "took orders from the Belgian Ministry of Foreign Affairs and were assigned by the ministry to Katanga; the others were mercenaries of various nationalities," including an increasingly important group of French officers who left Algeria after the failure of the April putsch. The growing presence of forces not controlled by the Belgian government, many of them *ultras,* strengthened the die-hards in the Katanga government. It also narrowed the options of the European firms supporting Tshombe. If they made any move toward accommodation with the emerging international realities (e.g., the payment of taxes to the Central Government) they risked "retaliation by the secessionist author-

[1] O'Brien, *To Katanga and Back,* p. 207.

ities, which could be costly to mining installations for a long time." [2]

Operation "Rumpunch" and "Round One"

The continuation of Katanga's secession was especially disappointing to the African Bureau and its friends. It put Afro-Asian opinion at loggerheads with the West. It divided the new government and made Lumumbist militance more appealing. It jeopardized a U.N. "success" in the Congo. During August these concerns were intensified by two developments. At the U.N., the Afro-Asians were dismayed by the overall lack of progress in removing foreign personnel; rumors circulated that, along with the Soviets, they were planning to censure the Secretary-General publicly.[3]

In Stanleyville, Gizenga made clear to Adoula that "his condition for entering the government was that Adoula should take action against Katanga." [4]

Now Mennen Williams warned, "Separatism on the part of one province could only encourage separatism on the part of others, or civil war, or both." [5] The consequences would be instability in Africa, and Soviet influence in the Congo (supporting a new secession or helping a Central Government reintegrate Katanga).[6] Members of the African Bureau cautioned Tshombe's supporters that,

> if the Katanga did not come to an accommodation with the central government soon, it was to be expected that the government would seek to impose its will by force of arms and that the U.N. forces would

2 Gérard-Libois, *Sécession,* pp. 322, 235; Hoskyns, pp. 394, 388–389, 408.

3 Hoskyns, p. 401. "The Indians were especially critical, and on Aug. 2 the *Times* of India asked ominously whether it could really be said that the specific purposes for which the Indian contingent had been sent had been fulfilled." *Ibid.*

4 *Ibid.,* p. 400.

5 Stated publicly on Sept. 21, *Department of State Bulletin,* Oct. 23, 1961, pp. 668–670.

6 *Ibid.* See also Speech by Senator Hubert Humphrey in *Congressional Record,* Sept. 21, 1961, pp. 20607–20613; *Wall Street Journal,* Aug. 29, 1961, p. 16; and Sept. 22, 1961, p. 1.

be justified in intervening on the side of the central government on the grounds that it was the only legal government.[7]

Afro-Asian pressures, the stiffening of the American attitude, and the U.N.'s institutional interest in its recent success at Lovanium combined to bring about a more vigorous U.N. policy. Since Spaak's cooperativeness was causing him serious difficulty in Belgium and Katanga,[8] a direct move against Tshombe was indicated. On August 22, Adoula asked the United Nations for help in evacuating foreign officers from Katanga. On August 23, Hammarskjold cabled Khiary asking that the Central Government issue an order expelling foreign military men in Katanga and requesting United Nations assistance in executing the order (under the February Resolution). The government "should then inform us of this order in a new letter." When this was done, "O'Brien and his collaborateurs could take immediate measures. . . ."[9]

The Secretariat "hoped that a swift presentation of force would be enough to persuade these officers to cooperate and that there would be not actual fighting, but there seems little doubt than an initial use of force to persuade them to obey was envisaged." The expected protests from European countries would be neutralized by the brevity of the action and American support.[10] With regard to the latter, the coincidence of United States and United Nations policy toward Gizenga was underlined in Hammarskjold's cable:

> It goes without saying that if the government would take such measures, it would re-enforce its position not only with regard to Katanga, but also with regard to the so-called Stanleyville group.[11]

On August 27—the day before Operation "Rumpunch" was to unfold in Elizabethville—the U.N. impounded a plane flying regu-

[7] Welensky received this information from Williams on Aug. 26. Welensky, pp. 221–222. Struelens heard the same themes during a visit to the African Bureau around this time. *Visa Procedures,* pp. 48, 59, 235, 212.

[8] Hoskyns, p. 399.

[9] Verhaegen, *Congo 1961,* p. 463; the cable is reproduced in Lefever, *Uncertain Mandate,* p. 399.

[10] Hoskyns, pp. 402–403.

[11] Lefever, *Uncertain Mandate,* p. 229.

larly between Cairo and Stanleyville "that was recognized as one of the most important props of the Stanleyville group." This action allowed the Central Government to announce that no direct flights between Stanleyville and foreign countries would henceforth be permitted, "and it certainly weakened Gizenga." [12] The timing of this move suggests Hammarskjold may have been trying to make his American support just a bit more certain.

Early the next morning U.N. troops in Elizabethville seized control of communications facilities, raided army headquarters, and began to arrest foreign military officers. Similar action took place in North Katanga. The operation surprised the Katangese and encountered no resistance. At 1:00 P.M., Tshombe announced that all foreign officers were dismissed. At the same time the Belgian consul undertook to supervise their "orderly repatriation" to avoid bloodshed and humiliation. With 70 to 100 officers already rounded up, and these promises of cooperation, O'Brien called off the arrests.

The U.N. now had to deal with more powerful enemies: Belgium and Britain. On the 29th, the Belgian consul informed O'Brien that on instructions from Brussels he could take responsibility only for the Belgians who were under orders from their government. On the 30th, British representatives in Elizabethville and New York expressed opposition to the U.N. action. As a result of these moves, the success of "Rumpunch" was significantly qualified and Tshombe was encouraged to resist the U.N. By September 8, at least 104 mercenaries were still at large. With the removal of the moderates, i.e., those who would obey an order from their consul or were not afraid to return to their own countries, the field was left to the *ultras*. Thus,

> The hard core remained and, moreover, the U.N. had only the power to "evacuate" the military *Adeuxiens,* not to stop them from re-entering clandestinely and from reinfiltrating the gendarmery. And, now

[12] Arthur Lee Burns and Nina Heathcote, *Peacekeeping by U.N. Forces* (New York, 1963), p. 97. Like "Rumpunch," this action was justified by "the request of the Central Government for U.N. assistance." *Ibid.*

that the initial moment of surprise was past and the consuls had obtained a delay, what was to prevent the mercenaries from abandoning Katangan uniforms for civilian clothes and, provided with all the required official papers, blending into the mass of European technicians legitimately working in Katanga.[13]

The United States gave Hammarskjold tacit support during "Rumpunch." For example, Consul Canup dissociated himself from a joint *démarche* by his (Western) colleagues which served to indicate disapproval of the U.N. action.[14] But what would the U.S. attitude be toward the kind of operation that was likely to occur in the future: one with less surprise, bloody fighting, and more time for allied and domestic pressures to develop?

In the beginning of September, certain U.N. officials in the Congo were convinced that another show of force—proving the U.N. would not yield to European pressures—would cause Tshombe to give up his secession. These diplomats discounted the efficacy of the remaining mercenaries and wished to focus directly on the Katanga regime. On September 8 a closed-doors session of parliament was convened; a resolution was adopted asking the U.N. to arrest Katanga ministers, seize the radio, disarm the gendarmerie, and fly a special commissioner down to take over the administration. Three days later O'Brien received a detailed plan from Khiary which dropped the disarmament of the gendarmerie but added raids on the *Sûreté* and Ministry of Information. The operation was set for 4 A.M., September 13, even though Hammarskjold was to arrive in Leopoldville that same afternoon and would be severely embarrassed by any fighting. It was believed that even "determined resistance" could be ended in "at most, two hours." *All available evidence suggests that neither Hammarskjold nor Linner nor the American Embassy were aware of the full content of this operation.* They thought in terms of a "topped-off version of Rumpunch." However, only Hammarskjold was ignorant of

[13] Gérard-Libois, *Sécession,* p. 239. The above account is drawn from *ibid.,* pp. 238–239; O'Brien, *To Katanga and Back,* pp. 206–232; and Hoskyns, pp. 402–413.

[14] O'Brien, *To Katanga and Back,* pp. 225–228.

the timing.[15] In fact, it is practically certain that the timing (during Hammarskjold's flight) reflected a will to prevent the Secretary-General from stopping the operation.[16]

Operation "Morthor" erupted into "Round One" due to faulty execution and underestimation of the mercenaries. (It is also possible that Tshombe received encouragement from the British Consul at a decisive moment.) Fierce fighting broke out in Elizabethville, an Irish battalion was besieged at Jadotville, and a single Fouga jet (dubbed the "Lone Ranger") strafed U.N. troops. In Leopoldville Hammarskjold was shocked by these events, but quickly overruled the idea of rushing reinforcements into Katanga and adopting a more offensive strategy. Abhorring violence, he was not anxious to preside over a possible U.N. massacre in Katanga. Moreover, he did not think that the U.N. mandate justified an explicit attempt to end Katanga secession by force; hence he felt no compulsion to secure the success of his zealous subordinates. Politically he was under intense pressure from the British who threatened to withdraw all support from the U.N. Force. In the next few days these considerations shaped U.N. policy, qualified, however, by care not to offend the Afro-Asians or sacrifice U.N. prestige. Thus Hammarskjold consented to a limited reinforcement in order to right the tactical balance, but pursued a basically defensive strategy and sought a truce. On September 16 he agreed to a cease-fire and personal negotiation with Tshombe at Ndola, Rhodesia. The final accord had to be obtained by Hammarskjold's aides: en route to Ndola his plane crashed under mysterious circumstances, killing all aboard.[17]

15 *Ibid.*, pp. 235–253; Hoskyns, pp. 413–418; interviews with American officials involved. As in September 1960, Hammarskjold's instructions left his energetic subordinates considerable leeway. See Urquhart, pp. 559–564.

16 O'Brien, *To Katanga and Back*, p. 251. This account is confirmed by a foreign observer in Leopoldville who spoke directly to Khiary. It will be noted that even the alternative plan for this operation was for it to take place while Hammarskjold was en route to New York.

17 Gérard-Libois, *Sécession*, pp. 240–242. The best account of Hammarskjold's policy during "Round One" is in Arthur L. Gavshon, *The Mysterious Death of Dag Hammarskjold* (New York, 1962), esp. Chapters vi–x.

U.S. policy during "Round One" was consistent with, and possibly contributory to, Hammarskjold's. The State Department was startled by the fighting but came out at once in support of the U.N. action. However, Hammarskjold was quietly informed that President Kennedy and Secretary Rusk were "extremely upset" that there had been no consultation with the U.S. government, and that they urged him now to bring Adoula and Tshombe together.[18] On the 16th Hammarskjold's efforts toward a cease-fire and negotiations were applauded.[19] The same day Hammarskjold showed Ambassador Gullion the draft of his message to Tshombe and was assured of "broad U.S. support for the peace project." [20] Washington was also concerned about the vulnerability of the U.N. Force in Katanga. The State Department hoped that "the effective presence of the U.N. in all sections of the Congo" would be conducive to "the peaceful processes of reconciliation." [21] On September 21—a few hours after the cease-fire went into effect—two U.S. transport planes arrived in the Congo to help rectify the military balance in Katanga. Two more followed shortly.[22]

What were the ingredients of the American consensus? The Africanists were frustrated and disgusted by "Round One":

> Wayne Fredericks, recalling his days with General LeMay, Commander of the Strategic Air Command, put the feeling into simple words, "I always believed in air power," Fredericks said, "but I never thought I'd see the day when one plane would stop the United States and the whole United Nations." [23]

While there was much sentiment for strengthening the U.N. Force, there was no great pressure for an all-out attack on Katanga. Afro-

[18] Gavshon, p. 126. See also *New York Times,* Sept. 14, 1961, p. 1. Urquhart, p. 575, reports the Kennedy-Rusk initiative.

[19] *Department of State Bulletin,* Oct. 21, 1961, p. 550.

[20] Gavshon, p. 172.

[21] *Department of State Bulletin,* Oct. 21, 1961, p. 550.

[22] Lefever, *Uncertain Mandate,* p. 83. Urquhart, p. 577, observes that these planes were at first withheld, presumably due to U.S. reservations about "Round One."

[23] Hilsman, p. 251.

Asian opinion had not jelled; Ambassador Gullion had just arrived in the Congo and was not yet in a position to forward firm policy recommendations; Hammarskjold's view carried weight with the Bureau of International Organizations; Gizenga had joined Adoula in Leopoldville after "Rumpunch," so there seemed no immediate need for firm action; and some hoped that Tshombe might now move toward reconciliation with the Central Government. Other members of the State Department had to consider the extremely bitter denunciations of "Round One" by Belgium and Britain. The White House staff was concerned about a new focus of opposition in the Senate. Struelens' mailings to Congress had lit a fire under Senator Thomas Dodd, a powerful New England Democrat, hard-line anti-Communist, and member of the Foreign Relations Committee. In a series of speeches on the Senate Floor—September 8, 11, 13, and 16—Dodd maintained that the Adoula government was "so heavily weighted in favor of the Communists that, unless we do something to reverse the course of U.N. policy, the outcome is virtually a mathematical certainty." He urged support for Tshombe as "the most solid bulwark against Communism in the Congo, and indeed, in central Africa." And he submitted a resolution to establish a select committee to investigate the present situation in the Congo. Dodd's remarks received support from Senators Keating, Thurmond, and Yarborough. Senator Humphrey—the majority whip—was anxious to defend the Administration but admitted substantial ignorance about the situation.[24]

At the end of "Round One" the African Bureau took steps to curb its domestic opponents who by now included Senate Minority Leader Dirksen. Pro-Administration liberals received policy guidance at a meeting of the African Subcommittee of the Senate Foreign Relations Committee. Senators Church and Humphrey promptly offered informed rebuttals of Dodd on the Senate floor.[25]

[24] Dodd's speeches are reported in *Visa Procedures,* pp. 345–374; Humphrey's remarks are found in *Congressional Record,* Sept. 16, 1961, pp. 19883–19888.

[25] *Congressional Record,* Sept. 19, 1961, pp. 20195–20197; and Sept. 21, 1961, pp. 20607–20613.

Humphrey's speech writer was assisted by an emissary from the State Department's Bureau of Intelligence and Research. In a Boston address, Secretary Williams gave the "sophisticated anti-Communist's" case against Senator Dodd.[26] Most surprising, however, was the attempt by the "liberal" African Bureau to deport Struelens on the purely artificial pretext that his present activities were inconsistent with his visa status. In subsequent testimony before a Senate Subcommittee, George McGhee expressed the basic motivation quite candidly:

Now, Mr. Struelens appeared to be, as a good representative, carrying out this policy, and suddenly we in the State Department found that rather than a man who had been cooperative, that he appeared to be working against our policy in a variety of ways.

And the Department's natural instinct, because we think the people want us to carry out our policies vigorously with all the means available to us, was to protect ourselves against his efforts, what he thought, to undermine our policies. And among the other things that were considered was, well, what about his visa status. The people who are responsible for this in the Department looked into the matter and they found that in fact this visa that he had been granted was not the correct visa for him to have, and this really was probably the error of the consul who originally granted him his visa because Mr. Struelens had indicated the type of activity he was going to be engaged in and this visa was clearly only for people who are engaged in informational activities, and Mr. Struelens activities went broader than that. . . .

Now . . . there is the apparent anachronism that we had not previously discovered this, and I admit that that stands there in the face of it. On the other hand, what we finally did, we felt was entirely legal and proper as a means of protecting ourselves, and there is no occasion

[26] *Christian Science Monitor,* Oct. 26, 1961, p. 10. "Too much public discussion, too many news reports," he commented, "register on the negative factors at work in Africa. The danger of Soviet penetration is a category under which every possible item is faithfully entered, usually without too much background or perspective. . . . Is it fair to expect African States to forego diplomatic relations, trade and other contacts with the Communists when even their former colonial mentors engage in such atrocities?" *Ibid.*

for us to deny that we were using it as a means of protecting ourselves.[27]

It should be pointed out that the State Department had renewed Struelens' visa in August 1961, and was, at that time, fully aware of his activities. In the end, Struelens' visa was cancelled, but pressure from Senator Dodd and other members of Congress appears to have prevented his deportation.[28]

"Round Two"

At the beginning of November the Administration shied away from any new fighting in Katanga. Ambassador-at-Large W. Averell Harriman met Tshombe in Geneva "to underline the importance of reconciliation." [29] Harriman was quite impressed by Tshombe and later opposed military action against him. At the U.N., American spokesmen stressed their determination to avoid further military commitments. They resisted African demands for a new Council session and a strengthened mandate.[30] President Kennedy decided to take advantage of Senator Dodd's departure for the Congo to further the diplomacy of reconciliation. He asked Dodd to use his influence with Tshombe in favor of a summit meeting with Adoula.[31]

But, as in earlier months, circumstances in the U.N. and the

[27] *Visa Procedures,* p. 142. Bowles writes, "[Struelens] had for several months been effectively confusing the situation and had created considerable public and Congressional support for Tshombe's position. Now Struelens' visa was about to expire, and by simply refusing to renew it we could end his operation." *Promises to Keep: My Years in Public Life 1941–1969* (New York, 1971), p. 498.

[28] *Visa Procedures,* pp. 17–18, 6–8, 16–20, 379–380, 390–391.

[29] See speech by G. Mennen Williams on Dec. 27, 1961, in *Department of State Bulletin,* Jan. 22, 1962, p. 140.

[30] *New York Times,* Nov. 9, 1961, p. 7; Nov. 13, 1961, p. 1; *Christian Science Monitor,* Nov. 7, 1961, p. 1; Nov. 13, 1961, p. 4; Nov. 14, 1961, p. 4.

[31] *Department of State Bulletin,* Jan. 22, 1962, p. 140. Kennedy's interest in Dodd's trip reflected some narrower political concerns too. As one presidential adviser commented, "It was cosmetic . . . an effort to bring him over on our side."

Congo produced a "firming up" of American policy. The Security Council met on November 13 and heard "forceful speeches" by the Ethiopian delegate and Bomboko "stating that Katanga's secession was not a domestic issue, that it had been fomented and maintained by outside intervention, and that the United Nations mandate must be clarified in order that ONUC could deal more effectively with mercenaries and foreign personnel." It was clear that even "moderates" such as Ethiopia and Nigeria wanted a new test of force.[32] In addition, Soviet prospects in the Congo appeared to have brightened considerably. Shortly after "Round One," Gizenga returned to Stanleyville and re-established his political leadership in the eastern provinces. While he declared that he would not quit the Central Government "his intention was to renew the threat of secession in Stanleyville in order to encourage further action in Katanga." With him in Stanleyville were some old foreign supporters—diplomats from the United Arab Republic, Eastern Europe, and even, it is said, a few North Vietnamese. There were signs, though, that his position was not quite as firm as it had been before Lovanium. The Lumumbist Army Commander, General Lundula, defected to Leopoldville. Lumumbist leaders in Leopoldville, including Christopher Gbenye, Minister of the Interior, opposed Gizenga's move, "mainly on the grounds that by giving up the vice-presidency he had made it easier for the BND [Bloc National Démocratique opposition parties] to strengthen their position within the government." [33] Gizenga's departure led to two small offensives by Central Government and Stanleyville forces within Katangan frontiers. Neither army had much success; lack of discipline was obvious, and anti-European violence occurred, notably the massacre of thirteen Italian aviators at Kindu. The double offensive indicated political pressure on Adoula to end secession and the utter dependence of the Congolese on external

[32] Hoskyns, pp. 441–442; *New York Times,* Nov. 14, 1961, p. 38. Both Ethiopia and Nigeria had large contingents serving with ONUC.

[33] Hoskyns, pp. 438–440.

military assistance.[34] For the Africanists these events provided a persuasive argument—urgent anti-Communism—to bring the Administration closer to the Afro-Asian stand on Katanga. In fact, many officials indicate that the Africanists were not above exploiting or exaggerating what seemed to them a bonafide Communist threat. Experience in the State Department and in earlier intra-Administration wrangling on the Congo had taught them the uses of anti-Communist rhetoric. In any event, Gullion flew to the U.S. on November 19 and advocated firmness with Tshombe. Unless Katanga's secession was ended, "a strong Central Government" well-disposed to the U.S. "might fail and further secessions could occur." The Communists were already trying to be seen as "apostles and architects of Congo unity by any means." They were "almost bound to attempt by all means to recover a strong position of leverage in the Congo." [35] As for Tshombe, Gullion reportedly told Kennedy that his anti-Communism was a device to impress the U.S., and that his regime was sustained by mercenaries and Europeans.[36] In a lengthy justification of U.S. Congo policy on December 19, George Ball noted two possible paths for Communist influence:

> If Prime Minister Adoula should prove unable to deal effectively with the Katanga secession of Mr. Tshombe, militant extremists such as the Communists's chosen instrument, Mr. Gizenga, would bid to take over the Central Government—in the name of Congolese unity. In the resulting civil war our main objectives in Central Africa would be drowned in blood. . . .
>
> If the Congo is to be a nation, it can hardly permit provincial leaders to break off pieces of the country, especially when such provincial leaders are heavily influenced from the outside. What I am

[34] Gérard-Libois, *Sécession,* pp. 242–243; *Christian Science Monitor,* Nov. 7, 1961, p. 1; Nov. 24, 1961, p. 12.

[35] *Meet the Press,* Dec. 3, 1961, pp. 1–9; *New York Times,* Nov. 20, 1961, p. 16.

[36] *Jeune Afrique,* Dec. 13, 1961, p. 8; *Christian Science Monitor,* Dec. 7, 1961, p. 1.

saying applies not only to Katanga, but equally to the northern provinces and to any efforts of Antoine Gizenga, the agent of Communist designs, to set up shop as leader of a leftward leaning separatism in Stanleyville.[37]

The U.S. now took a stronger line. The effect was felt at the U.N., in Western capitals, and in the Congo. Support was given to a new Afro-Asian resolution authorizing "force, if necessary" to remove mercenaries and political advisers from Katanga. Through amendments and reservations the Americans again tried to incorporate measures against Gizengist separatism, and to prevent hasty or inappropriate use of the provision for force. When these failed, Stevenson received permission from the State Department to vote for the resolution anyway. But the issue was not as close as it had been in February. And after the vote, U Thant, the new Secretary-General, gave formal recognition to the American demands. Less legalistic than Hammarskjold, he indicated that Stevenson's points were implicit in either present or past resolutions.[38]

At this juncture the Foreign Ministers of Belgium and Britain tried to head off the use of force:

> The idea was to define a possible basis for reconciliation (reintegration of Katanga into a Congolese state of an accentuated federal type) and to entrust to a mediator, who could have been Leopold Senghor, the task of proposing it to Leopoldville and Elizabethville. A basis could easily have been elaborated by Brussels and London, whose points of view converged, but it had no chance of being carried out unless it won American backing at the U.N. and above all support in Africa, where logically the mediator could be recruited.[39]

It seems improbable that this initiative would have succeeded, given the increasing rigidity of both Adoula and Tshombe.[40] In any case, "the United States was reluctant, fearing 'to give too much importance to Tshombe in the resolution of the problem.' "[41]

[37] *Department of State Bulletin,* Jan. 1, 1962, pp. 47–48.

[38] Hoskyns, pp. 443–445; *New York Times,* Nov. 25, 1961, p. 1.

[39] Gérard-Libois, *Sécession,* p. 245. The Spaak-Home initiative took place in London, Nov. 30.

[40] Hoskyns, p. 447.

[41] Gérard-Libois, *Sécession,* p. 245.

After passage of the November 24 resolution the Secretariat hoped the threat of force would bring Tshombe to his senses. Instead, the mercenaries (reinforced by new recruits and aided by local Europeans) were brimming with confidence, and determined to provoke another round of fighting as quickly as possible. They encouraged Katanga politicians and soldiers to believe that the U.N. was planning an attack; a series of raids and assaults on U.N. personnel took place. Finally, roadblocks were set up jeopardizing U.N. communications and security. By December 5, all attempts to get the roadblocks removed had failed, and there were indications that an attack on the U.N. camps was imminent. U Thant decided that the U.N. should take full military action in self-defense and to restore freedom of movement. His conception of self-defense included (quite logically) assurances for the future; he also wished "to be satisfied that we shall be able to go ahead with the implementation of the Security Council and General Assembly resolutions, and especially the latest Security Council resolution of November 1961, without let or hindrance from any source." These objectives implied a strike at the center of Katangan power: key areas in the center of Elizabethville could not be left under the exclusive control of the gendarmerie. Obviously Thant's strategy of self-defense had important political consequences.[42]

According to George Ball, "The prompt action of the United Nations [was] made possible partly by our diplomatic support, our military airlift, and our financial contribution." [43] This is an understatement. The U.N. Force was politically dependent on American-Afro-Asian agreement. The United States paid nearly half of its expenses through mandatory and voluntary contributions. (Some countries which opposed the U.N.'s performance withheld their regular assessments, e.g., the Soviet bloc, Belgium, France, and Portugal.) [44] Thant could not hope to achieve a speedy and suffi-

[42] *Ibid.,* pp. 247–248; Gordon, pp. 142–144; Hoskyns, pp. 446–458; Burns and Heathcote, p. 134; Lefever, *Uncertain Mandate,* pp. 60–61.

[43] *Department of State Bulletin,* Jan. 1, 1962, p. 46.

[44] Lefever, *Uncertain Mandate,* pp. 199–206, 235–237.

cient concentration of forces in Katanga without a virtual fleet of long-range transports. Among his supporters, only the U.S. possessed the capacity and the planes to spare.[45] At a meeting of the National Security Council, U.N. action was effectively sanctioned.[46] This was a "tough, hard, controversial decision." The State Department was "split down the middle," with the U.N. and African Bureaus aligned against the European Bureau. Under Secretary McGhee opposed the use of force, but Under Secretary Ball went along. (Although he feared the possible impact on European relations and thought the Communist threat exaggerated, he agreed the Russians were trying to "fish in troubled waters" and felt "we were already committed" to the U.N.) The Pentagon seems to have sided with the "Europeans," fearing a precedent for intervention in Portuguese colonies which would jeopardize its bases in the Azores.[47] When a decision was reached, U.S. diplomats worked closely with Thant. "It seems that on 4th December an American official delivered an ultimatum to Tshombe (then in Paris on his way to Brazil) stating that if the roadblocks were not immediately removed, the organization would have to take action." [48] Thant's directive for military action was immediately supported by the U.S. which put 21 additional four-engine transports at his disposal.[49] Between December 6 and 21 these planes transported "a Swedish battalion, an Irish battalion, a Nigerian battalion, and Swedish armored cars from Leopoldville to Elizabethville. Approximately 100 flights were made, delivering 1,607 U.N. personnel, 901 tons of cargo, and 12 armored cars to Elizabethville and Kamina." [50] According to the State Department "It was this

[45] *Christian Science Monitor,* Dec. 6, 1961, p. 1.

[46] The following account is based on interviews and *Jeune Afrique,* Dec. 20, 1961, pp. 8–9. These sources are mutually confirming.

[47] *Ibid.* On the general attitude of the Pentagon toward Africa, see Hilsman, pp. 249–250. Bowles notes that the Navy considered South Africa to be "of great strategic importance." *Promises to Keep,* p. 492.

[48] Hoskyns, p. 451. "By all accounts," she comments, "the Americans were deeply involved [in negotiations at the U.N.]" *Ibid.*

[49] *Christian Science Monitor,* Dec. 6, 1961, p. 1; Dec. 7, 1961, p. 1.

[50] Lefever, *Crisis in the Congo,* p. 96.

internal airlift that permitted the rapid buildup in Katanga."[51] On December 8, London agreed "with strong encouragement from Washington" to supply twenty-four 1,000 pound bombs for the U.N.'s jet force (provided the bombs were used only in "preventive action against pirate aircraft on the ground").[52]

It was quickly apparent that "the military situation was not at all comparable to that of September." The U.N. was stronger in both personnel and equipment; the Katanga gendarmerie was "not so well led and less effective." The fighting "turned to the advantage of the U.N."[53] But the mercenaries were active, a significant group of local Europeans took up sniping, and the first mortar barrages and jet attacks on military targets in Elizabethville resulted in the unfamiliar sight of a "peace-keeping force" killing civilians and damaging a certain number of hospitals, schools, and churches. Since foreign journalists were nearly all ensconced in the heart of Elizabethville—which was controlled by the Katangans—the world began to receive a distorted, unfavorable perspective on U.N. tactics.[54] As the U.N. prepared for its big push into town, a group in the Secretariat was concerned that "protracted guerilla warfare" would compromise the organization's image and its future role in peace-keeping.[55] This group, which seems to have included Thant, wanted to use the *threat* of a takeover at Elizabethville to persuade Tshombe to enter meaningful negotiations with Adoula.[56] Given the opposition within the Secretariat and among the Afro-Asians to such a move, the American attitude would be crucial. This was recognized by Tshombe-supporter Roy Welensky on December 11 when he asked the U.S. to guarantee Tshombe's safety during a Tshombe-Adoula negotiation.[57]

[51] U.S., Department of State, *U.S. Participation in the U.N. 1961,* Department of State Publication No. 74-13 (Washington, 1962), p. 83.

[52] Lefever, *Crisis in the Congo,* p. 98.

[53] Gérard-Libois, *Sécession,* p. 248. The U.N. had jets this time and used them.

[54] Hoskyns, pp. 452–458.

[55] *Christian Science Monitor,* Dec. 12, 1961, p. 1.

[56] Hoskyns, p. 454.

[57] *Christian Science Monitor,* Dec. 12, 1961, p. 1.

At the start of "Round Two," Washington received the expected chorus of boos from Belgium, France, and Portugal; but Britain remained silent and even agreed to give the U.N. bombs. On the 11th, back-bench Tory MP's threatened to censure the government, and Prime Minister Macmillan cancelled the bombs.[58] On the 13th the British called for a cease-fire, and Secretary Rusk came under powerful pressure at the NATO Foreign Ministers Conference in Paris. ("The United States appeared to be isolated from all 14 of its NATO allies tonight in its support for the United Nations military action in the Congo," said the *Baltimore Sun.*) [59] Macmillan reportedly sent a personal message to President Kennedy warning that the absence of Western solidarity on the Congo could only benefit the Soviet Union.[60] An American official remarked that unless the situation in Katanga was quickly resolved, there would be wide differences in the West over Berlin and trade negotiations with the Common Market.[61]

Furthermore, the White House staff was getting nervous about a sudden spurt of domestic opposition. For some time Max Yergan—a conservative black educator who was a friend of Tshombe—had been trying to drum up support for Katanga within right-wing milieus. Among those he contacted were William Buckley, editor of the *National Review,* and Marvin Liebman, publicist for the Committee of One Million and Young Americans for Freedom. On December 8, Liebman received a fund-raising appeal from a group of conservative students at Yale. In anticipation of some New Left themes, they were organizing an International Brigade "to assist the troops of free Katanga" against U.S. and U.N. "aggression." This gave Liebman the idea for an "American Committee For Aid to Katanga Freedom Fighters." From a small office on Madison Avenue around 400 telegrams went out to potential contributors under the signatures of Yergan, Liebman, and several

[58] Hoskyns, p. 453.

[59] *Jeune Afrique,* Dec. 20, 1961, pp. 8–9; *Baltimore Sun,* Dec. 14, 1961, p. 1.

[60] *Jeune Afrique,* Dec. 20, 1961, p. 9.

[61] *New York Times,* Dec. 14, 1961, pp. 1, 16.

editors of the *National Review*. Cables of support from Tshombe were attached. The State Department began to receive a small flood of "right-wing mail" on Katanga. On the morning of December 14 a full-page ad appeared in the *New York Times* entitled "Katanga is the Hungary of 1961." Katanga was portrayed as an isle of stability, economic health, and popular government (black and white) in a sea of chaos. Tshombe was praised as "far and away the outstanding pro-Western and anti-Communist leader of the former Belgian Congo." Sympathizers were requested to contact their leaders in Washington and to support the Committee financially. The signers of the ad included many well-known conservative writers, professors, retired generals, and admirals—and Senator Dirksen (Dirksen quickly withdrew his sponsorship; a member of his staff indicated to Liebman that he had received an urgent call from the White House). The small group behind the American Committee "didn't know if we'd work on it after the ad at all." [62] The White House was worried that considerable mischief might be done in the present climate of anti-U.N. news reports. How many more Senator Dodds could it afford? [63]

These developments caused the Administration to re-examine its position. Over the objections of the Africanists, it was decided that the U.N. could not achieve all its objectives in sufficient time to forestall unacceptable opposition at home and abroad. There was, after all, no imminent threat of a Communist takeover, and there was at least the possibility that Tshombe might now agree to a negotiated settlement.[64] The U.S. immediately set about ending the U.N. offensive in Elizabethville.

First, Tshombe was persuaded to send a telegram to Kennedy expressing his desire to negotiate with Adoula and asking the

[62] The author interviewed a key figure in this lobby and obtained copies of all press releases and mailings to supporters.

[63] On his way home from the Congo on Dec. 7, Dodd called a news conference in Paris to denounce the latest U.N. action. *New York Times*, Dec. 8, 1961, p. 2.

[64] Hilsman's account, pp. 253–256, is essentially confirmed by other officials.

President "to designate a suitable negotiator and to stop at once useless bloodshed." [65] The next day—December 15—Ambassador Gullion was instructed to bring Tshombe and Adoula together for talks. A public statement implied that once Tshombe left Elizabethville fighting could be suspended.[66] Thant was closely associated with this diplomacy, and on December 18 he ordered the expected cease-fire. The Congolese leaders met at Kitona on December 20–21 with U.S. and U.N. representatives hovering in the background. When the talks threatened to break down, Ambassador Gullion appealed for perseverance. Nevertheless, at midnight the meeting broke up, and Adoula ordered his plane readied for the return to Leopoldville. At this point both Gullion and the U.N. representatives "used their powers of persuasion on the two men—who were in different rooms—to seek a satisfactory formula." Finally, at 2:30 A.M., an eight-point declaration was signed in which Tshombe recognized the authority of the *Loi Fondamentale*. It meant—in effect—the end of secession. (But in a covering letter, Tshombe said he would seek authorization by "the competent authorities of Katanga" to implement the declaration.) [67] The successful formula is said to have been provided by Khiary. "Round Two" was officially over.

A Peaceful Interlude

In accordance with the principles of "political realism," Tshombe refused to yield while his power base remained intact. His government passed the Kitona agreement on to its Assembly where it was accepted "as a possible basis for discussion" before being riddled with criticism. Henceforth Tshombe's purpose was to give

[65] *Ibid.*, p. 255; U.S. officials privately admit that Tshombe was asked to send the telegram by the American government. On Dec. 14, Spaak telexed the Belgian Consul in Elizabethville that "the Americans attach the greatest importance to the meeting between Tshombe and Adoula." Gérard-Libois, *Le Rôle*, pp. 64–65 reprints the telex.

[66] *Department of State Bulletin*, Jan. 1, 1962, pp. 10–11.

[67] The author interviewed three participants in the Kitona talks. The best account is found in Gordon, p. 146. For Tshombe's hedging of the agreement, see Gérard-Libois, *Sécession*, p. 250.

up nothing: "The mission of a central government . . . is to orchestrate fair and active cooperation between the governments of the diverse political units which constitute the Republic." He continued to insist on a settlement which "aimed, on essentials, 'to consolidate the internal regime instituted in Katanga' in July 1960, while admitting limited cooperation where prior agreement had been obtained." [68]

Ironically Tshombe's new breathing spell gave his American supporters time to organize and reach out to others. Alongside the firm stance of the Western allies, this established certain parameters for American and U.N. policy. The use of force was ruled out for nearly a year.

The American Committee for Aid to Katanga Freedom Fighters was a part-time activity of Marvin Liebman, in consultation with Max Yergan and the *National Review*. Yet it succeeded in developing a significant amount of support. Its basic constituency was conservative anti-U.N. and anti-Communist opinion. But it also attracted certain Southern whites who seem to have regarded Moise Tshombe as the African incarnation of Uncle Tom. The *Times* ad, and a mailing to known conservatives, produced upwards of $25,000 in two weeks from some 3,000 individuals. Furthermore, the ad was reprinted in at least nineteen newspapers throughout the country and paid for through locally raised funds. In a short time Senators Goldwater and Eastland signed on as sponsors, and the Committee's basic complaint was echoed by Richard Nixon, Senators Thurmond, Byrd (Harry F.), Morton, Lausche, Hickenlooper (the last two, along with Dodd, were on the Senate Foreign Relations Committee), several Congressmen, Herbert Hoover, and *Battle Line,* the organ of the Republican National Committee.[69] In the following months, there was a proliferation of regional and local committees, staffed by members of

[68] Gérard-Libois, *Sécession,* pp. 264, 266–267, 252.

[69] Nixon wrote an article: *New York Herald Tribune,* Dec. 19, 1961, pp. 1, 7. For other endorsements, see *New York Times,* Dec. 21, 1961, p. 7; Dec. 31, 1961, p. 10; Jan. 12, 1962, p. 2.

the John Birch Society, Young Americans for Freedom, and the Committee for One Million.[70] Sociologist Ernest Van den Haag was sent on a nine-day "survey mission" to the Congo (an attempt to get an African scholar was unsuccessful), and prepared a report on U.N. misbehavior in Katanga. Fifty thousand copies were distributed with special attention to "opinion molders." Ads in the *New York Times* (January 12, 1962) and the *Washington Post* (August 3, 1962) called for a Congressional investigation of Congo policy and suspension of legislative action on a bond issue to pay for U.N. operations in the Congo. The Committee issued numerous press releases. Of special note was one in October revealing a secret plan for U.N. military action in Katanga. This was said to have been leaked by a conservative black African delegate.

Some support for Katanga came from missionary organizations. Most active were the Methodist missionaries (Tshombe was a Methodist). Their contacts with the African Bureau were rather futile, but they seem to have had greater success in the Senate.[71]

A segment of business opinion caused the Administration some concern. A small but powerful group of Americans had economic interests in Katanga and in the white-controlled states of Southern Africa, and often minority participation in Belgian, British, and South African companies. It was felt that these interests were threatened by American support of U.N. actions in Katanga. Pro-Tshombe views were expressed by representatives of at least the following firms: American Metal Climax, Newmont Mining, Lazard Frères of New York, Morgan Guaranty Trust Co., Belgian-American Banking Corporation (Ryan-Guggenheim interests), Engelhard Industries (Charles Engelhard), General Motors, Euro-

[70] Jean Ziegler, "Le Katanga Lobby aux Etats Unis," *Courrier Africain,* Mar. 21, 1963, pp. 6–7. According to a leading member of the Committee, "The John Birch Society took over almost all the local right-wing groups that year."

[71] Senator Ralph Yarborough (Democrat, Texas) refers to their influence on his views in *Congressional Record,* Sept. 16, 1961, p. 19984. See also Senator Dodd's remarks in *ibid.,* Aug. 3, 1962, p. 15563.

pean-African Development Corporation (John van der Meersch), and probably Mobil Oil.

This group had a "low-key" approach to political influence.[72] Its main technique was the exploitation of personal and political relationships with decision-makers. F. Taylor Ostrander, assistant to the chairman of American Metal Climax, had lengthy discussions with Wayne Fredericks in his capacity as a fellow "African scholar." Two leading directors of that company, the Hochschild brothers, were in touch with their friend Adlai Stevenson. One official was taken to lunch by a Yale classmate whose investment firm disagreed with U.S. policy. Robert Murphy (chairman of Corning Glass and, in 1962, a director of Morgan Guaranty Trust), communicated a certain amount of business distress to old friends in Washington. Engelhard's opinion was known by the White House staff, and this prominent Democratic contributor is said to have contacted several Senators.

Institutional theaters of encounter between private and public leaders in international affairs were also exploited. In this respect, American Metal Climax was especially well situated. Its chairman, Harold K. Hochschild, was chairman of the Board of Trustees of the African-American Institute (AAI) from 1958 to 1965, an organization whose Board meetings were customarily held in the AMAX board room. The African-American Institute is, in the words of Professor Vernon McKay, "the most important" of U.S. organizations occupied exclusively with Africa.[73] Its activities are primarily educational, including scholarships for African students, and a short-term visitors program under which numerous African leaders have traveled to the United States. Its programs are closely coordinated with government agencies, and during the early sixties it received substantial support from the Agency for International

72 Most of this section is based on interviews with both businessmen and public officials.

73 Vernon McKay, *L'Afrique et les Américains* (Montrouge, France, 1967), p. 32.

Development (A.I.D.,) the Department of State, and the CIA.[74] Hochschild was also a leading figure in the Council on Foreign Relations, an important rendezvous and training ground for elites interested in foreign affairs.[75] In 1958–1960 Hochschild was chairman of the Council's discussion group on Africa South of the Sahara. In 1960–1961, his assistant, Taylor Ostrander, participated in a study group on U.S. policy in Africa. Hochschild and Ostrander also presided at several Council discussions on the Congo and Southern Africa. Government officials dealing with Africa were frequently present at these council meetings. Indeed, many officials were themselves long-time members (e.g. Fredericks, Bowles, Cleveland, Ball, Stevenson, McGhee). Although the proceedings of the Council on Foreign Relations and the African-American Institute are not available to the public, it can be said that AMAX officials regarded these two institutions as arenas for communication of their position to important policy-makers. It is, therefore, not excluded that other businessmen who were active in these organizations also had the opportunity to express pro-Tshombe views to government officials. Among those who seem to have been particularly concerned with Congo questions were Albert Nickerson (president of Socony-Mobil Oil) and Charles Spofford (associated with Morgan Guaranty Trust).[76] The Ameri-

[74] The CIA contribution was publicly admitted. On AAI programs and relations with the U.S. government, the author has profited from a 15-page detailed description of the Institute published in 1969 (no title), and AAI Board of Trustees, *Quarterly Reports on AAI Programs and Operations 1969* (New York, 1969). These materials were graciously provided by Ms. Jane Jacqz of the Institute, who also furnished lists of trustees present at board meetings from 1954 to 1964.

[75] On the political role of the Council, the best works are: Joseph Kraft, "School for Statesmen," *Harper's*, CCXVII (July, 1958), 64–68; and G. William Domhoff, "Who Made American Foreign Policy, 1945–1963," in Horowitz, pp. 28–36.

In the discussion below, the author has utilized the *Annual Reports* of the Council, 1958–1964, which list activities and members.

[76] Spofford was a director of Guaranty Trust which merged with the J. P. Morgan Company in 1959. According to a well-informed business source, Spofford stepped down from the board at that time only because of

can Eur-African Development Corporation (John van der Meersch) was in touch with Senator Dodd, as were other unidentified businessmen.

Undoubtedly, these economic interests had a restraining effect on American policy. At one point McGhee asked Murphy to explain to the business community "what we are trying to accomplish," and to endorse the official line.[77] He suggested that the Administration did not want to let a feeling among certain businessmen grow to an anti-Kennedy attitude on the part of the whole business community. This possibility seemed less and less remote after the Steel Crisis of April 1962.

Finally, there were some foreign influences on American opinion. Struelens continued to send information to Congressmen and was particularly close to Senator Dodd's office.[78] Material also went to the increasing number of friendly journalists and conservatives. In July, Katanga Information Services purchased time for 52 advertisements on WWRL, a New York radio station serving the black community.[79]

Société Générale de Belgique had a separate public relations organization based in New York. The Belgo-American Development Corporation was originally formed to publicize Société Générale's activities among U.S. businessmen interested in the Common Market, and to locate possible investment opportunities in the U.S. The office was run by Herbert Farber, a young American who had formerly worked for the Belgian Information Service. In the early sixties, Farber began to spend most of his time on

---

a limitation on the number of persons on the new board. Spofford's law firm, Davis, Polk, Sunderland, has been described as a Morgan legal representative. Perlo, pp. 320–321.

77 Murphy, p. 338.

78 A former member of Senator Dodd's Congressional staff writes, "I can state unequivocally that Mr. Struelens provided most of the information used in Senator Dodd's Senate speeches on the Congo issue, that Struelens was frequently in Senator Dodd's office, that he arranged Senator Dodd's trip to the Congo in late 1961 and that he served as a message center between Senator Dodd and Tshombe." Letter to the author, Aug. 15, 1968.

79 *New York Times,* July 10, 1962, p. 3.

Congo problems. Annual reports, a quarterly newsletter, press releases, background sheets, and production statistics put forth the company's point of view and defended it from attacks in the press. Literature was forwarded to all major newspapers (the top 100), general news magazines, business periodicals, and individual businessmen, right-wing publications like the *National Review,* U.N. correspondents, columnists writing on U.S. foreign policy, U.N. delegates and officials, etc. . . . The press campaign was considered a success, particularly with regard to the "average businessman." As one participant later commented, "I felt we got our point of view expressed in the stories that were written. We also got answers and blunted the effect of attacks." Belgo-American Development also had contacts with officials in the executive branch of government (especially the African Bureau). These talks seem to have revolved around "economic problems" in the Congo.

In Washington, Charles Meyer, another American representative of Société Générale called from time to time on Arthur Krock, the sympathetic columnist for the *New York Times.*

Business pressures in favor of the Central Government were relatively unimportant. No doubt this was partly due to the fact that government policy was already traveling this road. But a central part of the explanation lay in the comparative weakness of the business faction that had a stake in the unity of the Congo. Tempelsman's position was well known to higher officials. In addition, it seems that the Rockefellers gave some quiet support to the embattled African Bureau. According to one member of the African Bureau, "The Rockefellers were, I think, more logically concerned with the *whole* Congo." One director of the Chase Manhattan Bank (John McCloy) agreed to support the U.N. operation in a Congressional appearance. Another Chase officer writes, "I, as one officer of the Bank having to do with African affairs, felt all along and continue to do so, that the U.S. and U.N. policy toward the Congo was the right one and that that policy has been successful." Possible channels of communication with relevant policy-makers were the African-American Institute (Dana

S. Creel of the Rockefeller Brothers Fund was one of several active trustees) and the Council on Foreign Relations (David Rockefeller had participated in the Council's discussion group on Africa South of the Sahara and presided at one meeting on the Congo in the summer of 1960).

One index of the growing strength of the Katanga Lobby was Congressional debate on the U.N. bond issue. By the end of 1961, the U.N. Congo operation was $76.9 million in debt due to unpaid assessments. As a stopgap measure, the General Assembly authorized a $200-million bond issue. This would wipe out the deficit and finance the operation into 1963. On January 30, 1962, President Kennedy asked Congress to approve the purchase of $100 million in 25-year bonds at 2 percent annual interest. A bill was reported out by the Senate Foreign Relations Committee in March. The President's request was modified: $25 million would be purchased outright, but the rest would be bought on a matching basis; annual payments of principal and interest would be deducted from the regular U.S. contributions to the U.N. Even with these amendments, the bill was barely approved (10-6). In the full Senate the Administration accepted language critical of U.N. financial management in order to prevent a heavy negative vote leading to a defeat in the more conservative House. The bill passed the Senate by 70–22. In the House the Administration made an extraordinary effort. Henry Cabot Lodge and John McCloy (director of the Chase Manhattan Bank and member of the foreign policy establishment) endorsed the bond issue in Committee hearings. Statements of support came in from former Presidents Eisenhower and Truman. An Advisory Opinion of the International Court of Justice, rejecting legal arguments on behalf of ONUC's delinquent payees, helped too. The House Foreign Affairs Committee approved a bill which provided, however, that the *entire* $100 million should be purchased on a matching basis. This was adopted by the House on September 14 by 257-134. A motion to recommit the bill and amend it to bar purchases until the General Assembly formally adopted the International Court decision was defeated, 171-219. Debates in both houses showed that the central issues were: Katanga, the delinquency of others, and U.N. financial responsibility. They indicated that a significant number of Republican and Southern Democratic Congressmen were reluctant to sponsor a mere continuation of the U.N. presence in the Congo, let alone a new round of fighting in Katanga.[80]

In the first half of 1962, American policy stressed peaceful reconciliation through diplomatic persuasion. At the request of the State Department, Admiral Alan G. Kirk—President of a U.S. affiliate of Union Minière—conferred with company officials in Brussels in an effort to win endorsement of the Kitona agreement.[81] Washington also tried to enlist the cooperation of American businessmen to "twist Union Minière's arm." For this purpose Ambassador Stevenson contacted several New York firms including Lazard Frères and American Metal Climax. There was some hope that business and "old boy" relationships could be manipulated. In the absence of any progress on this front, the U.S. and U.N. encouraged further discussions between Tshombe and Adoula. This was, for the most part, a repeat performance of Kitona. The Congolese held to established positions: Adoula insisted on a federal structure with only slight modifications of the *Loi Fondamentale;* Tshombe demanded a loose confederation. The differences were "even deeper in regard to the so-called transitional period," before a new constitution was laid down. U.S. and U.N. diplomats used all their influence to prevent the permanent departure of either delegation. If agreements were reached, "they were often the fruit of U.N. mediation or of 'advice' given the two parties by interested Western countries." Ambassador Gullion was said to be responsible for certain concessions on the part of

[80] *Congressional Quarterly Almanac, 1962* (Washington: Congressional Quarterly Service, 1963), pp. 2, 47, 141, 180, 257, 262, 289, 444, 537–539, 580, 629, 1261, 1369, 1561.

[81] *New York Times,* Jan. 2, 1962, p. 1; *Jeune Afrique,* Jan. 31, 1962, p. 10.

Adoula. This time, however, there would not be even the illusion of success. The talks ended on June 26, at 5:30 A.M., in "a declaration of bankruptcy with the parties refusing even to sign a joint communique." [82]

Once again, events in the U.N. and the Congo forced the Secretary-General and the Americans into a more militant position. Upon the breakdown of negotiations in Leopoldville, India and Ethiopia threatened to withdraw support from ONUC unless new action was taken against Katanga. As a result, Thant visited several European capitals where he tried to persuade the British and Belgian governments to use their influence with the private corporations supporting Tshombe. The Secretary-General offered a military guarantee for the protection of the mining installations should they become the object of Katangan vengeance. By the middle of July this piece of diplomacy seemed no more successful than its antecedents. The governments were either unwilling or unable to control the corporations; the corporations were either unwilling to dump Tshombe or afraid of the damage that could be done to them by a few well-placed demolition charges, U.N. guarantee or no.[83]

Cleveland and Williams now went to Europe to see if there was support for economic sanctions against Katanga.[84] These measures might have had the advantage of directing further pressure on Tshombe without the use of (politically unacceptable) force. At the same time, the Adoula regime began to look rockier than ever. On July 16 a reconstituted cabinet received 66 votes against 44 with 6 abstentions in the lower Chamber. The opposition rallied both the left and the right, and it appeared that Adoula lacked an absolute majority (69 votes) in the Chamber.[85] Ambassador Gullion hurried to Washington to warn that unless Adoula

[82] Gérard-Libois, *Sécession,* pp. 258–270; Gullion's influence is noted in *New York Times,* Mar. 25, 1962, p. 1; and *Jeune Afrique,* July 9, 1962, p. 20.

[83] *Jeune Afrique,* July 16, 1962, p. 19.

[84] *Department of State Bulletin,* Aug. 6, 1962, pp. 214–215.

[85] Gérard-Libois, *Sécession,* p. 285.

reintegrated Katanga his position would be untenable, the Lumumbists or Mobutu would take over, and the prospects for civil war and Soviet influence would be enhanced.[86] Furthermore, a setback for U.N. policy would strengthen the position of white and black extremists in Africa, and make more difficult America's association with the moderates.[87] From the end of July to the middle of August, U.S. officials took the initiative in formulating a U.N. plan for economic sanctions. After lengthy negotiations with British, Belgian, and French representatives, a plan was drawn up in the State Department.[88] With only slight revisions this became the U.N. "Plan of National Reconciliation" or "Thant Plan" on August 10, 1962. It provided certain guidelines for a new "federal constitution" to be drawn up with the assistance of U.N. legal experts. It envisioned a transition period in which Katanga would keep 50 percent of the revenues from taxes, duties on exports and imports, and royalties from mining concessions; also 50 percent of the foreign exchange originated in the province. Other points were: integration and unification of military forces and gendarmerie troops within 90 days, a general amnesty, cabinet posts for members of CONAKAT, and a phased plan for currency unification. This package was slightly more generous to Tshombe than Adoula's proposals in the Spring. But it was now backed by a 4-phase "course of action." If Tshombe did not act within specified time periods, he would face an ascending scale of pressure including American military equipment for the Congo army, cutting off all communications between Katanga and the outside world, and an international boycott of Katanga copper and cobalt. Since the Belgians expressed reservations regarding the pace of pressure,

[86] *New York Times,* July 20, 1962, pp. 1, 5; July 29, 1962, sec. 4, p. 3; *Jeune Afrique,* July 30, 1962, pp. 18–19.

[87] *New York Times,* July 29, 1962, sec. 4, p. 3; Aug. 5, 1962, sec. 4, p. 4.

[88] *Ibid.,* July 19, 1962, p. 1; July 26, 1962, p. 4; Aug. 2, 1962, pp. 1, 5; Aug. 10, 1962, p. 1; Aug. 15, 1962, p. 1; Aug. 16, 1962, p. 2. Hilsman, pp. 258–260, presents an unusually candid account of the (American) genesis of the Thant Plan.

and the British took a dim view of any economic sanctions, detailed steps of the course of action were not publicized. As both countries were substantial consumers of Katangan products, the success of the Thant Plan was in doubt from the beginning.[89]

For this reason many of the Africanists had little confidence in the Thant Plan. Even a "Europeanist" like George McGhee thought sanctions would never be invoked.[90] In retrospect, American sponsorship of the Thant Plan was essentially an effort to arrive at a consensus among allies, public opinion, and intra-Administration factions. It had very little to do with the Congo. It did not proceed from a rational analysis of alternative policies in Katanga and their requirements. The Africanists secretly hoped that the failure of the Thant Plan would create a stronger case for military action. The Europeanists secretly hoped that an impasse would bolster the case for disengagement. Unaware of these private sentiments, the President seemed confident that a solution was now at hand.[91]

By October the implementation of the Thant Plan was hardly begun. Tshombe was stalling as usual. The Americans now moved to head off the application of sanctions. At Senator Dodd's suggestion, George McGhee flew to the Congo to parley with Tshombe. The outcome was not expected to be "a fulfillment of the Thant Plan," but made provision for "certain gestures" such as the deposit of two million dollars in Leopoldville, the reopening of the Lubilash Bridge (allowing the Central Government to collect added export taxes), and the resumption of Elizabethville-Leo-

89 Gérard-Libois, *Sécession,* pp. 273–276. The Plan is reproduced at pp. 337–342. France, another important consumer, would definitely not participate in the boycott. Indeed, France was boycotting the entire U.N. operation in the Congo.

90 Hilsman, p. 263 notes, "There were [in Dec. 1962] a number of people in the White House and the State Department among those of both the 'New Africa' and the 'Old Europe' persuasion who had long thought that economic sanctions would not work."

91 According to a diplomat who spoke with Kennedy at Newport that summer.

poldville telecommunications.[92] At the end of November, negotiations between the U.S. and Belgium produced a variant of the Thant Plan dubbed the "McGhee Plan." This was believed to allow Katanga somewhat better than the 50-50 division of Union Minière revenue formerly proposed and greater autonomy in the projected constitution.[93] For both Adoula and Thant these modifications were politically unreal: they were under overwhelming pressure to reject them.[94] In the end, the McGhee initiatives only postponed a necessary re-examination of American policy. Thant had to delay sanctions.[95]

By the end of November the consensus in the Administration was breaking apart. Gullion returned to Washington with the feeling that "the solution was to unleash the U.N. troops and let them destroy Tshombe's army." [96] McGhee advocated an indefinite postponement of sanctions since the cooperation of America's allies was still quite uncertain. Ralph Dungan and Carl Kaysen, who were following the Congo for the White House, "had become openly critical of deeper American involvement in the Congo." As protectors of the presidential interest they were concerned about the domestic risks of further intervention. (The situation was "unknown, unknowable, savage, hard to sell . . . defending freedom where heads are cut off, hard to find decent guys.") As "pragmatic" Kennedy liberals, they asked why Africa couldn't take responsibility for its internal problems, rather than call for outside help. They wondered aloud whether the "bleeding hearts" in the African Bureau were not exaggerating the imminence of a Communist takeover for "African policy reasons." [97] The President now recognized the problems involved in sanctions. The need for an

[92] Gérard-Libois, *Sécession,* p. 281.

[93] *New York Times,* Nov. 29, 1962, p. 1; Nov. 30, 1962, p. 12.

[94] For their rejections, see *ibid.,* Oct. 19, 1962, p. 30; Dec. 2, 1962, p. 1; Gérard-Libois, *Sécession,* p. 281.

[95] *New York Times,* Oct. 20, 1962, p. 1; Nov. 6, 1962, p. 7; Nov. 18, 1962, sec. 4, p. 11; Nov. 24, 1962, p 12; Nov. 27, 1962, p. 12.

[96] Schlesinger, p. 532.

[97] Part of their view is presented in *ibid.,* pp. 532–533.

urgent reappraisal of policy was highlighted by (1) the increasing difficulties of the Adoula regime; (2) the scheduled withdrawal of Indian troops, "now the mainstay of the U.N. operations," in February; and (3) the prospect of wider domestic opposition when Congress convened in late January.[98]

"Round Three"

In the first three weeks of December the American position gradually stiffened. On the 3rd the United States resumed an airlift of men and supplies to strengthen U.N. forces in Katanga.[99] On the 6th the Immigration Service ordered Struelens to leave the country voluntarily within fifteen days or face deportation.[100] In the following days U Thant invited various governments to apply economic pressure against Katanga—reflecting the new momentum of American policy.[101] At the same time President Kennedy asked the State Department for a new appraisal of the real options in the Congo. Skeptical about sanctions, he told Ball that "the only alternative, given the mood on Capitol Hill, India's troubles, and so on, seemed to be either using force to end the secession of Katanga or pulling out of the Congo entirely." [102] On the 17th the National Security Council decided to *give the U.N. whatever equipment was necessary to reintegrate Katanga by force.*[103] It put off a decision on a proposal that "we persuade U Thant to accept in addition a squadron of U.S. fighter aircraft, to be flown by our Air Force, thus ending Katanga's resistance in a hurry." This plan was sponsored by leading lights in the African and U.N. Bureaus and a section of the military. In the National Security Council it

[98] Hilsman, pp. 260–263; Sorenson, p. 638.

[99] Burns and Heathcote, p. 199.

[100] *New York Times,* Dec. 7, 1962, pp. 1, 22. This action was politically motivated and planned in advance. Hilsman, pp. 261–262.

[101] On the day Thant moved to apply sanctions, Secretary Rusk said that Adoula was under pressure and that movement toward unity was needed "very soon." *Department of State Bulletin,* Dec. 30, 1962, p. 999. See also Hilsman, p. 261.

[102] Hilsman, p. 263.

[103] *Ibid.,* p. 267; *Christian Science Monitor,* Dec. 20, 1962, p. 1.

was backed by many of the "doves" in the Cuban missile crisis. However, "most of the 'hawks' were highly skeptical," and the President felt it would be "hard to explain to the Congress, the allies and the American people . . . unless we could make a better case for the threat of a Communist takeover." Moreover, both Adoula and Thant were hesitant to request it. Therefore, Kennedy demanded proof that the air squadron was necessary and deferred decision.[104]

With the decision to use force in Katanga, a decision taken against the advice of the European Bureau and Defense Department,[105] the U.S. buried the policy of the preceding year and adopted a coherent alternative. The scene would be set by the dispatch of a U.S. military mission to the Congo "to signal our intentions effectively to Tshombe." There would be "close coordination with our allies" and a "special effort to brief the press and key Congressmen on the evidence that had been accumulating of renewed Soviet activities in the Congo and the long-run danger of a Communist takeover in Leopoldville from which they could subvert not only Katanga but all the neighboring African states as well." [106] For months the U.N. command had been developing a three-phase plan for ending Katangan secession by force, "though in legal terms it was called a plan for extending 'freedom of movement' throughout the province." Operation "Grandslam" was now scheduled for the third week in January.[107]

What considerations lay behind the new thrust in American policy? Of utmost importance was the fear that unless Katanga was reintegrated swiftly, Adoula would fall and Lumumbist and Communist influence would rise dangerously. Toward the end of November a diverse and even contradictory opposition cartel reached an accord on parliamentary strategy. The cartel included Lumumbists, Tshombists, and even members of ABAKO, Presi-

[104] Sorenson, p. 638. The sponsors of the plan were disclosed in interviews with the author.

[105] Bowles, *Promises to Keep,* p. 498. [106] Hilsman, p. 267.

[107] Lefever, *Uncertain Mandate,* p. 62; *Jeune Afrique,* Jan. 7, 1963, p. 12; Burns and Heathcote, p. 206.

dent Kasavubu's party. Their aim was to overthrow the government and establish a new coalition. The first part of their strategy succeeded on November 23 when the Chamber voted to end the state of emergency in Leopoldville and demand the immediate release of political prisoners. On the 27th, pro-government deputies narrowly defeated a motion of censure against the government. The vote was 50-47-2 in favor of Adoula, but it demonstrated the vulnerability of the American-sponsored regime.[108] Only last minute concessions by the Prime Minister and profuse bribery by the CIA prevented an unfavorable vote.[109] On December 7 the Chamber censured the Minister of Justice, 76-4.[110] Meanwhile, the Soviet Ambassador was noticed cornering Congolese politicians at cocktail parties and criticizing U.S. Katanga policy in Leopoldville beer halls. His agents were said to have "crystallized" the opposition in parliament. According to one high official, who was intimately involved in policy-making at this time, the American Embassy reported that Soviet diplomats were offering military assistance to possible successors of Adoula, even "moderates." From these events and reports, American officials drew the following conclusions: The future of the Adoula government was extremely uncertain. Its collapse would bring about a new Lumumbist regime or a new Mobutu junta. Any new government would encounter irresistible political pressure to move against Tshombe. The Communists would "attain a position of considerable influence through a military aid program, including Soviet technicians to train the Congo army, a program which their representatives in Leopoldville were offering anyone who would listen." One could easily see that from a base in the Congo, the Communists could play hell with affairs in much of Central and Southern Africa. Therefore,

108 Jules Gérard-Libois and Benoît Verhaegen, *Congo 1962* (Brussels, 1963), pp. 89–93, 102–105; *New York Times,* Nov. 29, 1962, p. 1.

109 *New York Times,* Nov. 29, 1962, p. 1. The bribery is confirmed by U.S. officials; *ibid.,* Apr. 26, 1966, p. 30, presents an account which is only slightly inaccurate. Soviet and Tshombist representatives reportedly bribed the other side.

110 *Ibid.,* Dec. 8, 1962, p. 1.

U.S. policy should be to strengthen Adoula by reuniting the Congo for him. If this was not done, the U.S. "would be dragged back into full engagement on much less favorable terms than [the U.S.] now had, unpleasant though these often seemed." [111]

Again there are strong indications that the Africanists were playing up the Communist threat as much as possible. In particular, Embassy reports of Soviet military aid offers have been questioned. One very high official who analyzed these dispatches later spoke to newsmen in Leopoldville. He came away with a strong impression that the Embassy "exaggerated the Soviet aid thing deliberately." In interviews with the author, Embassy and African Bureau officers said they did not recall any such offer specifically. This seems odd since the alleged offer was one of the major considerations of Washington policy-makers.[112] In any case, it is likely that the available facts and the Administration's expectations of Soviet behavior would have led to the same conclusions even without the apparent zeal of some Africanists.

The basic, and probably sufficient, cause of the shift in American policy was the Communist threat. For example, George Ball was a waverer whom the Africanists needed in their camp. He was, however, a Europeanist, and wondered whether the Soviets really cared about Africa or found it particularly subvertible.[113] On the other hand, he had a strong feeling that once the American government had "committed" itself to a certain objective, it was not good to "back down." [114] According to Roger Hilsman, chief of the State Department's Bureau of Intelligence and Research at this time, the Communist threat resolved Ball's dilemma: "the

[111] Hilsman, pp. 264–266. See also speech by G. Mennen Williams, Nov. 9, 1962, in *Department of State Bulletin,* Nov. 26, 1962, pp. 804–805; *New York Times,* Dec. 18, 1962, p. 6; Dec. 19, 1962, p. 1; *Christian Science Monitor,* Dec. 13, 1962, p. 4; Bowles, *Promises to Keep*. pp. 497–498.

[112] Hilsman, pp. 264–266.

[113] Ball, pp. 233–234.

[114] A good example of this attitude is Ball's discussion of Vietnam policy in *ibid.,* pp. 293–342, esp. pp. 332–342. This tendency in Ball's thinking is confirmed by other officials.

notion of getting out was tempting, he said, but when you thought it all through the risk was just too great." [115]

Another set of factors contributed to—or eased—the decision to use force. By early December there were signs that some of the venom had gone out of the liberals' European opponents. Belgium and Britain were still unwilling to apply economic sanctions, much less military ones, against Katanga.[116] Yet they were likely to be less upset than before if a third round occurred. On November 27, Spaak had gone so far as to join in a statement with Kennedy that, "if there is not substantial progress within a very short period of time, the United States government and the government of Belgium fully realize that it will be necessary to execute further phases under the United Nations Plan which include severe economic measures." [117] On December 4, Spaak warned Tshombe that if there were no solution by the 21st, Thant would have to return to his Consultative Committee and the Security Council and there "one would have to expect tough resolutions . . . against Katanga." [118] On the 11th Spaak called Tshombe a "rebel" and said he was prepared to support the U.N. Force and the Central Government if they resorted to armed force to end Katanga's secession.[119] Much of this was bluff (Spaak could not get that far ahead of Belgian opinion and interests), but it served to allay the worst fears of the Europeanists.[120] At the end of November the British informed Roy Welensky that while they would never employ economic sanctions, they were powerless to oppose or prevent them.[121]

[115] Hilsman, p. 266.

[116] Welensky, p. 264; *New York Times,* Nov. 18, 1962, sec. 4, p. 11; Gérard-Libois, *Sécession,* p. 270.

[117] *New York Times,* Nov. 28, 1962, p. 1.

[118] Gérard-Libois, *Sécession,* p. 282.

[119] *Ibid.,* p. 288, n. 1; Lefever, *Uncertain Mandate,* p. 61.

[120] Hilsman, p. 266: "Those of the 'Old Europe' persuasion were, of course, most reluctant of all to abandon the current policy. . . . Spaak's statement carried the day so far as the State Department was concerned."

[121] Welensky, p. 264.

Many have claimed credit for the attenuation of allied opposition. Some Africanists maintain that long hours of rational persuasion finally paid off.[122] Some Europeanists say the cautious diplomacy of 1962 soothed many sore spots. While these explanations may contain some degree of truth, they are obviously self-serving and fail to account for changes in the *objective situation* which America's allies confronted at the end of 1962. Tshombe's position had deteriorated in the past year. The Central Government had his forces on the run in North Katanga. The morale of the Katanga gendarmerie had sunk to a new low. Tshombe had brought himself some new mercenaries after the second round, but their discipline and effectiveness were uncertain. Rhodesian aid, which was both fact and promise, "lost its importance in the medium and long run" as London came to accept the breakup of the Rhodesian Federation and thus a black government in Northern Rhodesia. (This also made the Katanga buffer less important to Britain than it had been in 1960 and 1961.) Union Minière "was conscious that the secession was weakening, even if its directors hardly dared act openly in accordance with the belief." [123] On the other hand, the U.S. and U.N. were exerting steady pressure toward unification of the Congo. (Allies of the United States know they must bend a little when their senior partner wants something badly.) It is perhaps significant that Spaak's warnings to Tshombe became more frequent and uncompromising as American policy became manifestly more stringent.[124] Given these circumstances, it would be surprising if some European leaders did not occasionally ruminate about the virtues of a short bout of fighting which could end secession with minimal damage to the mining installations.

"The state of tension prevailing in Katanga after December 15

[122] Hilsman, p. 261.

[123] Gérard-Libois, *Sécession,* pp. 286–289; *Christian Science Monitor,* Dec. 14, 1962, p. 1; Lefever, *Uncertain Mandate,* pp. 62–63.

[124] Spaak's statements of Dec. 4 and 11, for instance, both came one day after (1) the U.S. resumed its airlift in Katanga December 3, and (2) the U.S. supported the application of economic sanctions Dec. 10.

was almost bound to give rise to incidents which could degenerate into a trial of strength between the U.N. in the Congo and the Katanga gendarmerie. After the 24th there were numerous exchanges of gunfire, and the Katangans brought up roadblocks. On the 28th the U.N. activated—prematurely—phase one of its three-phase plan for the subjugation of Katanga. Within two days "the Elizabethville zone, that is, the city and the zone within a radius of 20 kilometers, was entirely under the control of the U.N." [125] The U.N. Force was stronger than in 1961, whereas the opposition was extremely demoralized.[126] At this moment the Belgians and British demanded an immediate cease-fire and the resumption of negotiations with Tshombe. In Washington the surprisingly easy victory of the U.N. produced new divisions. One group seems to have argued that the action had disclosed Tshombe's weakness and had shown that the remaining phases could be implemented without significant damage in lives or property. A second group was frightened by Tshombe's threat to carry out a "scorched earth" policy, i.e., to blow up dams and mining facilities. It advocated another stab at negotiations in the new, more favorable military situation. At the United Nations, Thant was, as usual, anxious to avoid uncharacteristic behavior by a "peace-keeping" force. On December 31, with the approval of Washington, Thant announced that the ONUC operation had been completed and that he would allow a period of two weeks in which to implement the Thant Plan "before other measures might have to be weighed." [127]

Suddenly, with the help of the State Department, events took an unexpected and decisive course. There had been a failure of communications between the U.N. in New York and the U.N. in Elizabethville, and an Indian company crossed the Lufira River on January 1 and proceeded toward Jadotville with little resistance (Jadotville was the principal target of Phase Two). The State De-

[125] Gérard-Libois, *Sécession,* pp. 290, 292.

[126] See above, n. 123, and *New York Times,* Dec. 31, 1962, pp. 1, 62.

[127] Gérard-Libois, *Sécession,* p. 292; *Washington Post,* Jan. 1, 1962, p. A-1; *Christian Science Monitor,* Jan. 2, 1962, p. 1. For indications of the division in Washington, see Schlesinger, p. 533; and Hilsman, p. 268.

partment knew of the approach to the Lufira, and its crossing, even before the U.N. command. (Ambassador Gullion's air attache was following the Indians' progress minute by minute.) Instead of calling for an immediate halt and the resumption of negotiations, the Americans decided to let the U.N. try and exploit its chance opportunity. According to American officials, the U.N. Secretariat was "skittish," and "if we'd joined them the generals would have had to stop." On the other hand, if the U.S. said "go to Jadotville, a lot of people would have complained about our policy." Since the Indians were "doing OK," the U.S. officials decided to "do nothing for two or three days while they were going to the river and after." Thus "we were influential in restraining the U.N. from calling off the local U.N. initiative."[128] U.N. diplomats put it even more strongly. "Determined action" was possible "due to" Washington's political support.[129] On January 2, Thant sent a message to Tshombe saying, "It is now too late for negotiations. . . . Past experience with cease-fire agreements with the Katangan gendarmerie indicates their futility, since they are not respected."[130] The U.S. followed this statement with an announcement that trucks, armored personnel carriers, and transport aircraft would arrive in the Congo by mid-January.[131] On January 3 the U.N. took Jadotville without opposition. Greatly encouraged, the State Department urged Tshombe to "end promptly the Katanga secession by recognizing the U.N.'s full freedom of movement throughout Katanga . . . and by exerting his influence with Katangese military personnel and the civilian population to prevent sabotage and damage to important installations."[132] The Belgians, British, and Union Minière now urged

[128] On U.N. Representative in Leopoldville Robert Gardiner's decisive initiative and its political roots, see Gendebien, pp. 234–239. However, in the author's view, Gendebien too quickly accepts the idea that U.N. headquarters in New York knew nothing of the operation until Jan. 3.

[129] *Christian Science Monitor,* Jan. 4, 1963, p. 1.

[130] *New York Times,* Jan. 3, 1963, p. 1; Hilsman, p. 270 (Hilsman misdates the quotation however).

[131] *Washington Post,* Jan. 3, 1963, p. A-19.

[132] *Department of State Bulletin,* Jan. 21, 1963, p. 91.

Tshombe to surrender peacefully. On January 14 the Katangan ministers proclaimed the end of secession and granted the U.N. liberty of movement throughout Katanga. On the 15th Union Minière signed in Leopoldville an agreement on foreign exchange. On the 21st, U.N. forces entered Kolwezi. They found Tshombe there to welcome them. The secession was truly over. "Thanks to special financial contributions, which amounted to bribes, to foreign mercenaries by Belgian companies, and the efforts of the European consuls and certain Belgian advisers close to Tshombe there was no serious deliberate damage to Katanga's industrial infrastructure." [133] The Africanists were exultant. On January 17 Harlan Cleveland declared,

> The Congo is about to be free and whole again. It is moving toward law and order. The secessionist bubbles have burst. There are no uninvited foreign troops, no Communist enclaves, no "army of liberation," no reason for a single American soldier to die there, no excuse for a Soviet soldier to live there. . . . No other organization could have done so much. If the United Nations had not existed, the responsible members of the world community might have had to invent it.[134]

A Note on Decision-making in the Kennedy Administration

Ultimately Kennedy's policy was shaped by men who looked forward to America's increasing involvement in Africa and who had a relatively sophisticated response to the "Communist threat." Profiting from events—and occasional exploitations of events—they were men who could survive the twists and turns motivated by Europeanist and hard-line opponents.

Yet Kennedy's Congo policy was more than the interaction of ideologies and events. Unlike Eisenhower, Kennedy had to *choose*

[133] Lefever, *Uncertain Mandate,* p. 145. See also Gérard-Libois, *Sécession,* p. 294.

[134] Address, Jan. 17, 1963, *U.S. Department of State Press Release,* No. 34, p. 2.

between different recommendations. The way the President made decisions had important consequences for American policy. The evidence presented in the last two chapters indicates the President's inability to impose a coherent conception of policy on his Administration, his disposition to compromise internal differences even when these differences were uncompromisable on the level of external reality. The extremism of Kennedy's caution was responsible for some of the tottering, the ambiguity, and the blind alleys of American diplomacy; it was one reason why events—even the most fortuitous events—had such a determinative influence on policy. I am not suggesting that compromise and moderation should be excluded from the making of American foreign policy. I am merely saying that thoughtful compromise entails a modification of ends and a consequent tailoring of means and that it is the result of dispassionate analysis, not fear. Too often Kennedy's compromises left the ends confused or untouched and the means confused or inadequate. Too often they were the product of pure caution.

Thus in February 1961, Kennedy was confronted with a split between hard-line Europeanists and soft-line Africanists. One policy implied support for the "pro-West" forces and an increasingly unilateral involvement in the Congo. The other entailed some sort of political compromise and continuing multilateralism. Characteristically Kennedy borrowed from both sides and ended up with an approach that disdained unilateralism but was not sufficient to project a basis for further multilateralism. At this point the Administration was saved from its own irresolution by a chance massacre in the Congo which Stevenson used to alter our position at the U.N. But in the next few months the basic confusion reasserted itself. Uncertainty in both means and ends produced impotence. Power descended to low-level officials whose objectives were much clearer than their responsibility.

The Thant Plan is another example of a compromise which did not bring means and ends into rational relation. Again, events in the Congo—and the way the Africanists interpreted them—finally jarred the U.S. into a more realistic stance. Kennedy's attempts to develop an independent "presidential" viewpoint were gimmicky and futile. The Congo-watchers on the White House staff tended to interpret the presidential interest as domestic protection. When they offered their own analyses—as they did in December 1962—their opinions had little weight vis-à-vis the entire "expert" structure of policy-making. In December 1962, Kennedy also called on the Bureau of Intelligence and Research of the State Department to analyze the alternatives for American policy. But this was only *after* he had concluded that the alternatives were military force or disengagement, i.e., after events had exposed the absurdity of the Thant Plan. Furthermore, while Hilsman makes much of his Bureau's memorandum—which recommended military force—other policy-makers are convinced that Kennedy's course was not especially influenced by this "independent analysis." And it is true that the new momentum of American policy pre-dated the Hilsman memorandum.

Kennedy's caution comes out clearly in his panicky response to the first efforts of a minuscule right-wing lobby, a group that was extremely uncertain of its own future. The shortsightedness of this caution was shown when the failure to finish the job in Katanga gave the Katanga Lobby a chance to organize and increase its strength. Lacking a firm conception of policy, Kennedy even produced some of the divisions within his own Administration. All accounts indicate that he did not consider the policy implications of replacing Bowles and promoting Ball and McGhee (two Europeanists) in November, 1961. This was viewed as an administrative change but it built into policy-making a certain schizophrenia.

The Kennedy style in decision-making was not restricted to the Congo. In the planning of the Cuban invasion, Kennedy also balanced incompatible policies. As Arthur Schlesinger observes,

> The Pesident had insisted that the political and militay risks be brought into balance: given the nature of the operation, this was impossible, and someone should have said so.[135]

[135] Schlesinger, p. 276.

And, again, faced with conflicting recommendations on Vietnam, Kennedy tried to adopt both a "military" and a "political" approach to the problem. He acquiesced in the military thrust of the Taylor-Rostow report but withdrew from the commitment of large numbers of regular troops. He told Diem that he must make political and social reforms but was reluctant to force the issue. The ambiguity of this policy produced a situation in which the implementation was determined by such considerations as the relative aggressiveness of Dean Rusk and Robert McNamara. The inadequacy of policy by potpourri produced a situation in which the number of military "advisers" in Vietnam gradually escalated, and the Administration was again faced with a choice between military and political commitments, but this time at a higher level of involvement. Schlesinger labels this process "the politics of inadvertence," a phrase which has the effect of obscuring the necessary object of criticism. The Congo was only an instance of Kennedy's most glaring failure: his incapacity as a statesman.

CHAPTER VI

Liberalism: The View from Leopoldville

Only a year after Harlan Cleveland's trumpet burst of optimism, liberal policy was a shambles. In 1964 the Congo was wracked by rebellion. By August approximately half the country was controlled by antigovernment forces.[1] The revolt was marked by localism, traditionalism, and factionalism, characteristic features of the unintegrated or "syncretic" societies of Africa. Yet the revolt was "clearly distinguished from dissidence elsewhere on the continent during the past decade by its scope, by the massive violence engendered, by its long-term consequences for the affected areas, and by its international implications." [2] It was, in fact, "a revolution rather than a rebellion," a widespread movement for major social change. It had "nothing in common with minority-group subversion or any other superficial challenge to an existing government or political system." In effect, "the established government was completely overthrown, and the vast majority of the people supported the revolution in the affected areas." [3]

An understanding of the roots of the rebellion should cast light on the adequacy of liberal perspectives in the Congo. Many explanations have been offered for this unusual and almost unique development in African politics. One of the most important of

1 CRISP, *Congo 1964: Political Documents of a Developing Nation* (Princeton, 1966), p. 542.

2 Crawford Young, "Significance of the 1964 Rebellion," in Kitchen, p. 111.

3 CRISP, *Congo 1964*, p. ix (Introduction by Herbert Weiss).

these calls attention to the history of "rural radicalism" in the Congo.[4] Belgian colonialism had been thoroughly dense and disruptive. It required extensive expropriations of village lands for plantations, parks, and mines. These incursions, and a campaign against sleeping sickness, led to forced regroupments of villages, sometimes to famine, and to the beginnings of a rural labor force prey to the fluctuations of the world cash nexus. In addition, nearly a million families were covered by the system of obligatory cultivation (mainly cotton in the East). The villagers were also subject to such corvées as road maintenance and portage. The Administration intervened, often out of ignorance, against traditional authorities. So too, the missionary effort, which included a rudimentary primary education, hurtled against traditional beliefs and customs. Such a system, which was not a 19th-century aberration of King Leopold II, but a pulverizing reality up to and beyond Independence, generated frustration, anomie—and rebellion.

The resistance at first was set in motion by certain traditional structures, particularly the secret societies, which employed fetishes and other protective magic of the clan against the white invaders. Sometimes, as in an economic crisis, there were open revolts within the villages where the people showed their displeasure by "not buying imported goods, refusal of corvées, abandonment of obligatory cultivation in the expectation of a fantastic and imprecise event which would overthrow the European power, abandonment of villages situated along the trails." [5]

Rites of immunization and customary terrorism also reflected the

[4] The term was invented by Herbert Weiss, *Political Protest.* An essential source for the study of this phenomenon is Merlier, *Le Congo.* Of particular importance is his discussion of secret societies and Messianic movements, *ibid.,* pp. 231–250. Young, *Politics in the Congo,* pp. 216–231, has a valuable discussion of the effect of colonialism on the Congolese peasant. Verhaegen's work on the rebellions is essential for understanding "rural radicalism." See *Rébellions au Congo,* I (Brussels, 1966); and *Rébellions,* II. For a stimulating interpretation of mass-elite relations at Independence and beyond, see Benoît Verhaegen, "Lutte des classes au Congo," *Révolution,* X (July–Aug. 1964), 31–38.

[5] Merlier, p. 231.

attempt to maintain the integrity of traditional units in the face of foreign intrusions. As the colonial impact deepened, this form of protest was often susperseded by that of the syncretic religious movements. With their synthesis of modern and traditional forms and ideas, they were able to mobilize the oppressed rural masses in larger (ethnic and even regional) and less backward-looking struggles. According to Young:

> This represents a period when no secular remedy to the frustrations engendered by the colonial situation seemed available. The disequilibria introduced in traditional communities by colonial contact found temporary remedy through the millennial dream, or through adaption of Christian symbols to supplant ritual functions which had been suppressed by the colonial administration; or to cope with an outbreak of witchcraft symptomatic of social dislocation.[6]

These movements, such as Kimbanguism in the Lower Congo, and Kitawala in the East, announced the imminent reversal of white power, and brought about boycotts of the colonial system—of its administrative organs, its taxes and obligatory cultivation, its missions, censuses, hospitals, and productive apparatus. Prophets for these movements heralded a new age in which modern aspirations (European riches and well-being, instruction in white science) and traditional ones (return of wrongly deposed chiefs, resuscitation of ancestors) were inextricably entwined. The rise of secular nationalism, traversing the economic recession of the late fifties, resulted in a further development of radical rural protest. Now, an urban elite that burned above all for promotion and equality *within* the administrative and economic structures of colonialism, marshaled, behind the slogan "immediate independence," a rural mass which demanded the *negation* of most of these structures as the first condition of emancipation. In 1959 and 1960, those parties which sought to contact the masses directly rather than through their traditional leaders found themselves immersed in a newer version of rural radicalism, one that some-

[6] Young, *Politics in the Congo,* p. 284.

times threatened to surpass their own efforts. The mood of the masses, their spontaneous boycotts, the exceeding of instructions for limited civil disobedience, and the demands that the parties assume wider representative functions (for example, in economic life), forced party leaders and propagandists to adopt a harder anticolonial line and to promise radical improvements in everyday life of a kind for which they as yet had neither program nor the means to realize one.[7] In the wake of the triumph of militant mass parties in May 1960, rural protest assumed more modern but still syncretic forms: the secular sphere (politics) is predominant, but it is invested with mythic capacities and qualities; in certain places Kitawala presents itself as "the religion of independence"; semischooled youths are at violent odds with a customary authority they have learned to question and a colonial structure that limits their entry into a modern world whose superiority they have been taught to accept; the stimulus of political competition exteriorizes old clan, ethnic, and religious conflicts whose future becomes bound up with that of the nationalist party; new religious sects endow the day of Independence with a millennial significance:

> In certain rural areas and notably in Kwilu and the Lower Congo, the awaiting of the day of independence took on magico-religious forms: the ancestors would return to take the place of the Whites and would recover their power; the country would be governed by them in conformity with traditional customs.
>
> The departure of the Whites and the return to a system of customs whose content was very imprecise and mythic, did not exclude the maintenance and development of the practical advantages of colonisation; the riches reserved before Independence to the colonizer and burdened with negativism and alienation, would be transferred the next day to the Congolese population and would produce a general well-being.[8]

In conclusion, the rural masses, and particularly those in the Lumumbist fiefs, had demonstrated a propensity for violent

[7] See especially Weiss, pp. 186–250; and Verhaegen, *Rébellions,* II, 94–104, 111–117.

[8] Verhaegen, *Rébellions,* I, 24.

revolt, and a radicalism which is not adequately described by Western political terminologies. However, it should also be noted that many of the Lumumbist leaders and secondary cadres had become more conscious of the need to do something to make Independence meaningful to the villagers,[9] and that any co-ordinated, hence serious, uprising would depend on the availability (i.e., the political fall) of these catalyzing elements.

Other causes of the rebellion were more recent. The crisis at Independence interrupted the growth of a unifying nationalism and dealt a heavy blow to political parties. Then the death of Lumumba removed the Congo's only charismatic, nationally oriented leader. And the sudden exodus of thousands of Belgian administrators after the mutiny caused the cadres of all the major parties to be "almost entirely absorbed into the (bureaucratic) establishment." Inevitably there was "a rapid shriveling of the roots of parties. Once within the government or administration, even party militants tended to see little reason for vigorous party activity." Following the political breakdown and secessions of 1960 there were severe economic dislocations which further widened the gap between leaders and masses.[10]

All observers agree that, in addition to the above factors, the character and performance of the Adoula government was an important cause of the 1964 rebellion.[11] This regime came to power under American and U.N. sponsorship. It benefited from the political and economic support of the United States. American advice influenced its activity. In the end, with the U.N. Force gone and the Eastern Congo in flames, the Central Government was dependent on American and Belgian military aid for its very survival. While the militarization of American policy occurred under the administration of a middle-of-the-road Southern Democrat, its development resulted from the inadequacy of earlier, more subtle

9 Referred to above, n. 7.

10 Crawford Young, "Congolese Political Parties Revisited," in Kitchen, pp. 74–78.

11 See below, pp. 200 ff.

policies. As the political incapacity of the Kasavubu-Mobutu alliance reflected the limitations of a "responsible conservative" approach to the Congo, so the failure of the Adoula government suggests the inapplicability of a "liberal" prescription.

The Adoula Government

After the collapse of the army and administration, and the death of Lumumba, the Congo "could only be governed by striking a bargain between the local leaders." [12] Adoula himself lacked a popular following. He had, however, a knack of soothing and unifying those with whom he worked. His success would "depend upon the skill with which he could balance the various interest groups against each other and make himself indispensable." [13] One might add that in a fragmented and increasingly polarized society, with little experience of pluralistic compromise, there were bound to be winners, losers, and no small numbers of victims. In concrete terms, Adoula's success would depend upon (1) his summoning up enough political force to moderate the violence of local and national conflicts, and (2) his capacity to integrate, perhaps even to favor, the most popular and militant elements (the Lumumbists and their followers).

As it turned out, under Adoula the militant Lumumbists were excluded from power at all levels of government and administration. In January 1962, Gizenga was arrested because he had refused to rejoin the Central Government in Leopoldville. Taking advantage of divisions within the Lumumbist bloc, Adoula got the Chamber of Deputies to remove Gizenga's parliamentary immunity. In the following months other Lumumbists lost their ministries. For instance, Minister of Interior Gbenye was deposed in July, along with a number of "right and left extremists." The increasing narrowness of Adoula's cabinet endangered its majority in parliament. This produced a steady movement toward repression. An attempt by parliament to censure Foreign Minister Bomboko brought out soldiers and police who surrounded parliament and

[12] Hoskyns, p. 381. [13] *Ibid.*, pp. 381–382.

prevented a vote. In the Fall of 1962, the refractory legislators were sentenced by the Adoula government to a "holiday." Convened again in November, they witnessed the arrest of several of their Lumumbist colleagues—including Gbenye—on trumped-up charges. At this time, seven Lumumbist deputies were in prison and three were in exile abroad. Even so, it took CIA money (admittedly in competition with Soviet and Tshombist money) to maintain the government's majority. In subsequent months, parliamentary resolutions demanding the release of Gizenga, who was detained on the Isle of Bule-Mbemba, were ignored.[14]

Within the government, the purge of the Lumumbist factions was completed, except for a few turncoats. Thus, of 23 ministers who left the cabinet in 1962, 15 were Lumumbists. Of seven ministers and two secretaries of state from Gizenga's regime who had been incorporated into the government at Lovanium, only one remained in April 1963.[15] By the end of 1963, the Lumumbist parties in Leopoldville were repressed, parliament was closed on account of obstinacy, and the chief Lumumbists had fled to Brazzaville where they formed the Committee of National Liberation (CNL), a "government of public safety."

To a large extent this pattern was reproduced at the provincial level. The Lumumbist parties were displaced from local power bases, often by the intervention of the central authorities. As Verhaegen has shown in his studies of the rebellions, the Central Government contributed to a cumulative chain of violence which had begun with the fall of Lumumba and the conflict with Gizenga. Unambiguously taking the side of the "moderates," the customary chiefs and the Europeans, backing their purges and repression with the force of the state, Adoula's government cleared the terrain for an even more violent revenge. It will be noted that the political divisions in the provinces were even more stark and

14 Gérard-Libois and Verhaegen, *Congo 1962,* pp. 16, 22, 26.

15 *Ibid.,* pp. 56–57, 111; Jorge Beys, Paul-Henry Gendebien, and Benoît Verhaegen, *Congo 1963* (Brussels, 1964), pp. 12–13; Verhaegen, *Congo 1961,* pp. 182–183, 417–418.

consequential than those in Leopoldville, because the followers of the contending groups were present and because political disputes tended to develop an "ethnic contagion." [16]

Thus it is not surprising that the 1964 rebellion was a phenomenon of the Lumumbist provinces. The top leaders—such as Gbenye, Mulele, and Soumialot—were Lumumbists who had formerly been members of national or provincial governments. The middle-level activists were often the same young people who had served as party auxiliaries in 1960 and suffered greatly in succeeding years. The greatest support for the revolution came from ethnic groups that had sustained severe political casualties:

> Even though grievance was rather generalized [throughout the Congo], the perception of it was fragmented and often fused to regional or ethnic conflicts. In Kwilu for example, the exploited community tended to view itself as Bapende-Bambundu, with Mupende Antoine Gizenga as the martyr. In southern Maniema, the Batetela-Bakusu believed they had been systematically victimized by "Leopoldville," beginning with the assassination of their favorite son, Lumumba; they reacted with a high degree of communal support for the revolt.[17]

Cut off from the most strongly nationalist segment of the political elite, from that section of the *petit-bourgeoisie* whose self-seeking was at least tempered by *some* feeling for the needs of the masses and which had laid down the embryo of mass organizations in the interior (including demanding secondary cadres and "youth"), the Adoula regime fell prey to forces of fragmentation and social division.[18] Unwilling to press its foreign sponsors to

[16] The process took a particularly clear and vicious form in Maniema: Verhaegen, *Rébellions,* II. See also Gérard-Libois and Verhaegen, *Congo 1962,* pp. 55, 272–280; Verhaegen, *Rébellions,* I, 50–74, 265–273, 277–292, 415–420; Catherine Hoskyns, "The Congo as the U.N. Leaves," *World Today,* XX (June, 1964), 231–234; Beys, Gendebien, and Verhaegen, *Congo 1963,* pp. 308–309, 314–315, 330–344.

[17] Young, "Significance of the 1964 Rebellion," in Kitchen, pp. 112–113; and Fox, de Craemer, and Ribeaucourt, "The Second Independence."

[18] The following discussion is based on a number of excellent economic analyses which never lose sight of the fact that (as one wrote), "the ensemble of economic phenomena remains dominated by political events."

take a stronger position on Katanga, it had to wait 18 months before recovering crucial revenues and foreign exchange. Setting up 21 "provincettes," it incurred substantial budgetary expenses for new administrative and political institutions. In his political weakness, Adoula was a virtual captive of influential pressure groups in African politics.

There was, for example, little restraint on the army, which "lived off the land" and behaved brutally in the rural areas. The budget was in thrall to avaricious soldiers, politicians, and higher civil servants—85 percent of expenditures went for salaries to state employees. The deadly combination of a large budget deficit, the spending patterns of the new privileged class, and the loss of confidence in the franc engendered by the first devaluation, produced inflation. In turn this gave rise to illegal exportations that drained foreign exchange, and encouraged a host of parasitic businessmen and foreign adventurers who profited from the speculative atmosphere and the derangement of traditional circuits of distribution. Entrepreneurs in the interstices of a foreign-controlled but sick economy, these profiteers knew how to obtain the collusion of politicians and high civil servants in such mutually rewarding schemes as the "illegal exportation of Congolese merchandise payed for in foreign exchange—which gave profits of more than 500 percent and concerned almost half of Congolese exports in 1961" and "the concession of import licenses either for fictitious merchandise or for products sold in the black market

---

Fernand Herman, "La Situation économique et financière du Congo en 1962," *Etudes Congolaises,* IV (Mar. 1963), 1–27; "La Situation économique et financière du Congo en 1963," *Etudes Congolaises,* VI (Apr. 1964), 1–36; Hugues Le Clercq, "Analyse générale de l'inflation congolaise," *Cahiers Economiques et Sociaux,* I (Oct. 1962), 3–40; Bernard Ryelandt, "Evolution des prix à Léopoldville," in *ibid.,* pp. 57–65; Michel Merlier, "L'Economie congolaise de 1960 à 1965," *Le Mois en Afrique,* No. 4 (Apr. 1966), pp. 22–36; Verhaegen, "Lutte des classes au Congo"; Jules Gérard-Libois, "The New Class and Rebellion in the Congo," in Ralph Milliband and John Saville (eds.), *Socialist Register 1966* (New York, 1966), pp. 267–279; CRISP, *Congo 1964,* pp. 81–82.

with a long and costly system of distribution."[19] The corruption that cemented this new administrative-political-commercial class acquired such weight that it became itself "one of the essential factors of the [economic] crisis."[20] The inflation had seriously diminished the standard of living of ordinary people, especially in the rural areas, and resentment against a new, postcolonial class of "exploiters" escalated.[21] In November 1963, alarmed foreign exporting interests and Western governments succeeded in obtaining a "compromise" devaluation; however, this was paid for by the same classes that had suffered for the previous three years, and the inflation did not subside as quickly as expected. Already some of the rural radicals were in motion.

American Influence

The U.S. wanted a "moderate" government run by the "sincere nationalists." But the Lovanium settlement gave prominent posts to "extremist elements" who were "all too ready to invite hostile outside intervention which could plunge central Africa into chaos, with the Communists as the only winners." As the Adoula regime grasped the reins of power and began to make progress in Katanga, and as the Lumumbist bloc showed signs of fragmentation, American officials expressed a desire to see the extremists "dealt with effectively by the genuine nationalists in the Congo government." Coalition appeared to be a *temporary, tactical necessity* which could be conveniently discarded, as the Adoula regime accumulated strength and nationalist prestige. For liberal Africanists, the real object of American policy was to "oppose revolutions from the right or the left," to achieve "a strengthened Congo *fully able to defeat subversion from within* or attempts at outside domination," to get a "government *impervious* to outside infiltration" [emphasis added]. There was a dynamic here that tended to undermine Lo-

[19] Verhaegen, "Lutte des classes au Congo," p. 38.

[20] Merlier, "L'Economie congolaise," pp. 35–36.

[21] Crawford Young, "Significance of the 1964 Rebellion," in Kitchen, pp. 111–125.

vanium. For these liberals, Adoula was a fine choice to lead the Congo. He was, after all, "an able and dynamic leader of a trade union organization that is affiliated with the free trade union movement, the ICFTU." With economic aid from America and the West, it was thought that the moderates would take up their "overwhelming task of progressive modernization." [22]

It is convenient to distinguish two kinds of American influence on the Adoula government: generalized support and specific interventions. Of course, the existence of the former is the precondition for the latter.

From July 1961 to July 1964 the United States pumped $178.6 million of economic aid into the Congo, first through voluntary contributions to the United Nations, and then bilaterally.[23] Given the pathetic state of the Congo treasury this meant that "the Adoula regime was being largely supported by American financial aid." The Congo "thus became the first country in Africa to be dependent to this extent on American assistance." [24] Under "Buy American" clauses in its aid programs, the United States became the largest importer in the Congo. The sudden and widespread introduction of American products and commercial practices disturbed certain Belgian interests greatly, even though American investment remained small.[25] Adoula was also sustained by American military support. This provided crucial backing for the U.N. Force which subdued Katanga and kept a lid on ethnic and political violence, before being phased out in the first half of 1964. In the provinces, the U.N. Force was used effectively against the opponents of Adoula.[26] In the fall of 1962, the United States "informally and

[22] Quotations are from speeches by G. Mennen Williams, George Ball, Adlai Stevenson, and Dean Rusk in *Department of State Bulletin,* Jan. 8, 1962, pp. 43–50; Jan. 22, 1962, pp. 136–139; Feb. 5, 1962, pp. 216–218; Mar. 19, 1962, p. 450; Apr. 8, 1963, pp. 524–525.

[23] Figures obtained from the Congo desk of the Agency for International Development (A.I.D.), Department of State, Washington, D.C.

[24] Hoskyns, *Congo Since Independence,* p. 474.

[25] Beys, Gendebien, and Verhaegen, *Congo 1963,* pp. 101–102.

[26] Verhaegen has demonstrated this for the province of Kivu in *Rébellions,* II, 132, 176, 184, 188.

quietly" inaugurated a bilateral-aid program for the Congolese army. In late 1963, a three-man military mission was established in Leopoldville. The program was essentially logistic and was run in conjunction with training efforts by other Western nations.[27] By July 1964, the U.S. had spent $5.1 million, a modest but significant sum.[28] Furthermore, American aid to the Congo was of such importance that it constituted an implicit endorsement of the Adoula government and its policies.

It was also the basis for explicit interventions in the governmental process. This is not to say that the American Ambassador had the Congo government in his hip pocket. The relationship was more subtle and not so all-inclusive.[29] When, for example, Ambassador Gullion urged Adoula to tighten up his administration of finances, the Prime Minister was unable to conform (because his supporters were greedy). The Ambassador's recommendation that American rather than Italian oil companies build a refinery at Moanda was spurned.[30] And, when Gullion asked Adoula to release labor leaders who had been arrested on the eve of a visit by American labor officials, and was turned down, it was apparent that Adoula put his own fears of revolution ahead of American interests.[31]

Still, American influence was quite important. A key official admits, "At the big crucial turnings we'd have something to do," i.e., some responsibility for the direction of internal Congo politics. A

[27] Lefever, *Crisis in the Congo,* pp. 127–130.

[28] Figures obtained from the Congo desk of the International Security Affairs Division of the Department of Defense, Arlington, Virginia.

[29] The following paragraph is based on statements to the author by members of the American Embassy during the Adoula regime.

[30] Beys, Gendebien, and Verhaegen, *Congo 1963,* p. 104.

[31] Upon their arrival, the labor leaders protested to Mobutu, Bomboko, Adoula, and Gullion. According to one of them, "Whether our protests and pressure were effective or not is subject to speculation since [the Congolese labor leaders] were in jail for about a month. However it has been acknowledged that our constant raising of the issue did embarrass the government and at least the treatment of the trade unionists during their incarceration was quite good." Letter to the author, July 1, 1970.

former member of the American Embassy states that "we were in on" the Central Government decision to arrest Gizenga. In January 1962, Struelens told a Congressional subcommittee that "Mr. Gullion personally was working very hard in Leopoldville to make the policy of the State Department appear very clear for this country's opinion, and [he] influenced Mr. Adoula, and we know it by Congolese sources, to make Mr. Kalonji of South Kasai Province and Mr. Gizenga both deprived of the parliamentary immunity." [32] *New York Times* correspondent David Halberstam reported from Leopoldville that Adoula opposed Gizenga due to "personal contempt" and "the need for strength in the eyes of the West." [33] The U.N. Force helped the Central Government arrest Gizenga by disarming his private guard of 300 soldiers, even though an American amendment authorizing such action had been rejected by the Security Council several weeks before. Thus, many observers assume that the U.N.'s action in Stanleyville reflected the organization's dependence on American political support.[34] This assumption is shared by the relevant officials in the U.N. Bureau of the State Department.

The Americans were "elated" [35] by the arrest and imprisonment of Gizenga. Shortly, Halberstam warned that Adoula might soon "cut some ministers that he feels tried to undermine his government. He must watch the danger of forming a fairly conservative government that, while pleasing to the United States, would lose touch with the nationalist sentiment in the Congo." [36] It seems likely that American influence was one factor, for example, in the demise of Gbenye and some other Lumumbists. Gbenye was well aware of the relationship between the American Ambassador and his posi-

[32] *Visa Procedures,* p. 122. [33] *New York Times,* Jan. 10, 1962, p. 6.

[34] Burns and Heathcote, pp. 155–160; Hoskyns, *Congo Since Independence,* pp. 458–460.

[35] The account here is based on statements to the author by members of the U.S. Embassy. Verhaegen, *Congo 1961,* p. 441, observes, "Of all the Western countries, it was the U.S. which was most closely and manifestly associated with the policy of the Adoula government."

[36] *New York Times,* Jan. 21, 1962, sec. 4, p. 3.

tion in the government. At one point Gbenye believed that Mobutu was about to kill him and pleaded with Gullion to intercede with the government and save him. Gullion did talk to Adoula and Mobutu and was assured that Gbenye's fears were unfounded. However, when Gbenye fell, the Americans tried to "keep him hitched" by getting him a scholarship in the United States. But it was plain they had little use for him in a position of power.

American interest showed itself in various guises. The CIA kept Adoula's legislature in line by periodic "rentals" of deputies and senators.[37] It learned of a plot to assassinate Mobutu and passed the information along to him (Mobutu was grateful, so the CIA's influence grew). Economists in the American Mission furnished continuous advice on the Congo's currency. In the summer of 1963 an important devaluation was held up while the Embassy sought to persuade the Belgians and the International Monetary Fund to accept a particular method of devaluation. To show it meant business, the Embassy got permission to suspend, temporarily, some aid programs. Nevertheless, the Americans lost, and the Congo got an economic reform in November that it could have had in July. And, when the revolt began in late 1963, the American Ambassador flew to Kwilu Province, not to inform himself but to "dramatize" to the Congo government the seriousness of the situation. Thus the American government not only supported Adoula; it was, in many different ways, part of his government. *It was very directly involved in his successes and failures.* A sad and rather ugly aspect of American wheeling and dealing was the kind of rationalization used by Embassy officials to justify their manipulations. When this author asked whether the Communist threat was not rather remote, he was told that the Congolese had "a short span of attention," hence were easily influenced by outsiders; that "bribery is the basis of Bantu politics," and that Gizenga was, anyway, "primitive," and "like an illiterate moron." (Needless to say these insights do not appear in the usual literature on the Congo,

[37] *Ibid.*, Apr. 26, 1966, p. 30.

and Gizenga, whatever his political and moral deficiencies, was a teacher before he was a politician.)

The kind of regime which liberals favored in the Congo subverted liberal notions of foreign aid. Uncorrected inflation caused the diversion of large quantities of surplus food to Brazzaville where they fetched a high price in hard currency. The distribution system was unimaginably corrupt, and some of the aid was simply "lost." Urgently needed American trucks "often" went to "political brokers" or "the highest bidder." Limited by its political context, aid had ambiguous results. It kept the Congo afloat economically, and it benefited most the politically favored elites in Congo society.[38] In the 1964 rebellion,

> there was an external "enemy" as well, against which the "mass" must be rallied. The new class of "exploiters" were able to protect their authority, it seemed to many, because they had the material support of the "imperialists," above all Americans. . . .[39]

American policy-makers never confronted the *political* problems of foreign aid. They seemed incapable of such self-criticism. Thus "obstacles to progress" in "nation-building" were reduced to *technical* problems. Harlan Cleveland headed an aid mission to the Congo in January 1963. His report concluded that external assistance would be most effective if the Congo developed "the admintistrative capacity to rehabilitate the national army," brought "the fiscal system under control," and constructed "a political system featuring a strong executive." [40] In his 1966 essay, *The Obligations of Power,* Cleveland remarks that a "fashion" which remains to be discovered in foreign aid is "political organization." He suggests the U.N. should have included in its mandate the establishment of one

[38] The discussion of American aid is based on interviews with two former A.I.D. officials, and *ibid.,* May 28, 1963, p. 1 (interview with Robert L. West, A.I.D. Director in the Congo); and Jan. 20, 1964, p. 45 (economic analysis of the Congo).

[39] Young, "Significance of the 1964 Rebellion," in Kitchen, p. 112.

[40] *Department of State Bulletin,* Apr. 1, 1963, pp. 481 ff.

or more national political parties to counteract "tribalism."[41] Actually, the CIA did just that by providing financial backing for Adoula's new RADECO (Rassemblement des Démocrates du Congo) party. But RADECO never received any popular support.[42] Cleveland's amended approach seems too manipulative, too technological—at base too provincial—for the real world of politics.

41 Harlan Cleveland, *The Obligations of Power* (New York, 1966), p. 112.

42 CRISP, *Congo 1964*, p. xxvi; Marvin D. Markowitz and Herbert F. Weiss, "Rebellion in the Congo," *Current History*, XLVIII (Apr. 1965), 213; John Hatch, "Hostages, Mercenaries and the CIA," *Nation*, Dec. 14, 1964, p. 11. CIA support for RADECO has been confirmed by a Belgian diplomat who was in Leopoldville during that period.

CHAPTER VII

From Kennedy to Johnson

Sophisticated anti-Communism and liberal Messianism led toward American military intervention in the Congo. On the international plane such attitudes undermined the political and financial basis of the multilateral force. In Leopoldville their political results generated pressure for an American military presence. The militarization of American policy began during the Kennedy Administration when a military aid program was established, and reached a high point under President Johnson when, in 1964, American planes, equipment, and personnel were used to defeat the rebels. Throughout, the militarization took place under the auspices of Kennedy appointees—mainly liberals. If Johnson imparted a nuance of toughness, impatience, or indifference to this process it was, after all, only a nuance.

Toward a Belgo-American Protectorate

During the Katangan secession, Western influence in the Central Government was submerged. American support was usually routed through U.N. channels. The Congo operation appeared to represent a broad international consensus on behalf of Congo unity and independence. Although Belgium kept a foothold in the Central Government via advisers and a quiet military training program,[1] her behavior in Katanga attracted all the attention.

By mid-1962, however, American planners were anticipating the eventual withdrawal of the U.N. umbrella. The refusal of

[1] See Lefever, *Crisis in the Congo,* pp. 30, 125; *Christian Science Monitor,* Apr. 17, 1963, p. 1; July 1, 1963, p. 7.

France and the Soviet bloc to pay peace-keeping assessments—reflecting strong disapproval of U.S. and U.N. policies—had precipitated a financial crisis.[2] The White House understood that the U.N. bond issue was just a holding action, and it did not relish the prospect of returning to a cranky Congress for more scotch tape. So the Americans counted themselves lucky to have gone so far with the U.N. and prepared to bow to "international realities." (Indeed, after completing its major business by winning Round Three the U.N. Force began to phase out. Only a virtuoso lobbying performance by Ambassador Gullion persuaded the State Department and the U.N. to maintain a small contingent during the first half of 1964.)

With a U.N. retreat in view, American officials worried about an "internal security gap" in the Congo.[3] They realized that the presence of the UNF had been a deterrent to political violence and that the weak Adoula government needed a dependable military arm. But the ANC had lost its trained leadership at the time of the mutiny, and subsequent events had produced fragmentation, politicization, and poor discipline.

"Recognizing that the United Nations was making little progress in reorganizing the ANC or providing a reliable officer corps for it,"[4] Washington dispatched a military advisory team to the Congo in July 1962, led by Colonel Michael J. L. Greene. On February 26, 1963—a month after Round Three—Adoula introduced the "Greene Plan" to the world. He informed the U.N. that his government had decided to ask five NATO powers and Israel for help in modernizing the armed forces. The key roles would be played by Belgium (which would supply "technicians for ANC headquarters and units" and help "in the matter of bases, the gendarmerie and the various military schools"), and the United States (which would "do no more than provide the equipment necessary to ensure the

[2] Lefever, *Uncertain Mandate,* pp. 199–206, 236–237.

[3] See the report of the Cleveland mission on aid to the Congo, Mar. 1, 1963, in *Department of State Bulletin,* Apr. 1, 1963, pp. 481–484.

[4] Lefever, *Uncertain Mandate,* pp. 68–69.

success of . . . [all the] technical assistance measures"). Adoula also requested U.N. help, principally in the coordination of the various bilateral programs.[5] Thus the "Greene Plan" envisaged U.N. "cover" for Western military aid. A majority of Africans and Arabs on Thant's Congo Advisory Committee were not in the mood, however, so in late April the Secretary-General was forced to reject the plan.[6] Adoula proceeded to sign bilateral agreements with the U.S., Belgium, Israel, and Italy. Canada and Norway withdrew from the Greene Plan after it failed to obtained U.N. approval.[7]

Beginning in July 1963, the U.S. gave significant assistance to the ANC. By March 1964, this included an eight-man military mission, ordnance, and English-language-training teams (the latter for 51 soldiers slated to receive short-term specialist training in the United States), 60 two-and-one-half ton trucks, 40 jeeps, 50 trailers, 3 vans, and several shipments of spare parts, tires, and tools. A large shipment of communications equipment was "in the pipeline." [8] In addition, about a dozen Congolese officers had received training at Fort Knox. This training was part of a larger American program for emerging African states, one purpose of which is to develop "a cadre of strictly professional officers prepared to protect the legally constituted governments against subversion and domestic disorder." [9] Such were the beginnings of an American military commitment in the Congo.

It was not that the U.S. was particularly eager to fill the Congo's

[5] U.N., *Annual Report of the Secretary-General on the Work of the Organization,* June 16, 1962–June 15, 1963, A/5501, pp. 14–15; see also U.N. Security Council, *Official Records, Supplement for Jan., Feb., Mar., 1963,* S/5240 (Feb. 4, 1963), p. 104; and *Supplement for Apr., May, June, 1963,* S/5240 Add. 2 (May 21, 1963), pp. 4–7.

[6] *Ibid.* The Belgian and Israeli contributions were particularly resented; see also *Christian Science Monitor,* July 1, 1963, p. 7; *New York Times,* May 2, 1963, p. 10.

[7] *New York Times,* Mar. 25, 1964, p. 19; Lefever, *Uncertain Mandate,* p. 70.

[8] Lefever, *Uncertain Mandate,* p. 88; CRISP, *Congo 1964,* pp. 96–97; *New York Times,* Mar. 25, 1964, p. 19.

[9] Lefever, *Crisis in the Congo,* p. 131.

security vacuum. Even during the Kennedy Administration, Africa was an area of residual interest, consuming no more than 10 percent of American aid. But both the international power structure and America's past policies precluded other means of assuring "American interests." The weak, poorly organized African states could not by themselves modernize the ANC. Among the Western powers, Belgium had the most impetus to become involved, but U.S. officials doubted she had the capacity or will power to fill the void alone. Other alternatives included a U.N. training mission or a Western one with significant African participation. But here the Americans were limited by past policies. General Mobutu was a pro-Western creation of the Eisenhower Administration. As head of the army his power had risen in direct proportion to the political weakness of the regime favored by the Kennedy Administration. And Mobutu insisted on white, Western aid:

> In October 1961, at the request of Leopoldville, Major General Iyassu Mengesha of Ethiopia made preparations for a U.N. officer training school with a multinational staff. General Mobutu never sent any cadets because he preferred direct assistance from governments of his own choice. From the outset he retained a small group of Belgian advisers on his staff and in the Defense Ministry and he was anxious to get additional officers from Brussels. On the wall of his office in 1962 hung the pictures of all but one of the past commanders of the Belgian *Force Publique;* the exception was the last one, the blunt General Janssens. When Mobutu was asked why the pictures were there, he replied that even though there was political discontinuity in the Congo, there should be military continuity.[10]

Some time in 1962 the American Embassy wondered whether Mobutu might accept some (pro-Western) Senegalese trainers. He reportedly responded: "Je ne veux pas ces nègres."

The Nature of the 1964 Rebellion

The general causes of the Congolese rebellion were discussed in Chapter VI. As was indicated, similarity of grievance did not result

[10] Lefever, *Uncertain Mandate,* p. 68.

in a common organization or tightly-knit leadership cadre. There were also some ideological differences. Thus Congo experts have preferred to describe the rebellion within the framework of its main structural subdivisions.[11]

In July 1963, Pierre Mulele returned to his native Kwilu (a province in the western part of the country near Leopoldville). A former minister in Lumumba's cabinet, he had supported the Gizenga regime and then spent long months in the United Arab Republic and the People's Republic of China. New he established forest camps in which idle out-of-school youths, students, teachers, and workers received a thorough and rigorous preparation for revolutionary warfare. When the stage of action was reached, these training camps were superseded by *équipes de partisans* living in close symbiosis with individual villages. Available descriptions of this period suggest the "syncretic" nature of the revolutionary movement. Each *équipe* was led by a President (military leader) and a Political Commissar, accompanied by a *soigneur* (healer) who was usually a practitioner of traditional magic and medicine. Mulele, the Leader-Savior,

> presents himself to his partisans as possessing a superior power to all of his enemies; he appears invulnerable to bullets and does not hesitate to prove it by having himself shot by blank cartridges; he is omnipresent and can transform himself into an animal, a serpent for example. . . .[12]

His magic was the source of their own invulnerability as well. A *"Code des Partisans"* evoked the military recommendations of past practitioners of revolutionary war, particularly Mao Tse-tung. Many of these recommendations would be put into practice, but the partisans would also rely on the force of magical tabus whose

[11] The following discussion is based on CRISP, *Congo 1964;* Young, "Significance of the 1964 Rebellion," in Kitchen, pp. 111–125. Fox, de Craemer, and Ribeaucourt, "The Second Independence"; Weiss, pp. 291–299; David Reed, *111 Days in Stanleyville* (New York, 1965); Verhaegen, *Rébellions,* I and II; *New York Times* and *Christian Science Monitor,* 1964.

[12] Verhaegen, *Rébellions,* I, 126.

observation was supposed to assure personal immunity and, hence, ultimate victory. Arms were rudimentary and largely traditional.

Ideological training appears to have consisted of "a summary introduction to Communist doctrine." Three major themes were developed: the class struggle, the necessity of revolutionary struggle, and the need for partisans to be "fish" in the "sea" of villagers. In the new society, all would have work; he who did not work would not eat. Foreigners would not be able to come to steal the wealth of the country, and no one would be able to steal from another. Each would have a new house. The population was promised a "Second Independence." [13] But it was the military effort itself which best revealed the radical intentions of the rebellion's leaders. In addition to eliminating local authorities and non-cooperators, the Mulelists destroyed (rather than took over) the administrative structure, halted (even through destructive sabotage) major economic activity, and forced foreign missionaries to leave (instead of trying to collaborate with them).

If the Mulele rebellion was the most radical and most modern of all the Congo rebellions, it was nevertheless heavily influenced by the characteristics of Congolese rural society. The Bapende-Bambunda rallied en masse to the revolution, but other ethnic groups in the same general social position kept their distances. The first large offensive weakened the will to observe Mao's rules of conduct toward the civilian population. The advent of the Congo army, and hence the first real challenge to the rebels' magical beliefs, resulted in a sharp rise of indiscipline and a lessening of Mulele's control. It also shook the loyalty of many of the villagers who ceased to believe in the rebels' magical invulnerability and were alienated by excessive executions and acts of indiscipline. On the other hand, even as late as 1965 observers of the rebellion were impressed by the idealism of the Mulelists, by the close communal life of the soldiers, and by the revolutionary organization and enthusiasm in some villages. Of all the Congolese leaders who have

[13] *Ibid.*, pp. 129–133, 166–172; Fox, de Craemer, and Ribeaucourt, pp. 94–97.

tried to "organize this desperate resistance of the past at the level of modern conceptions,"[14] Mulele appears to have had the most success. Because of the limited information available, it is difficult to estimate Mulele's achievement. However, his action clearly illustrated some of the difficulties of revolutionary movements in rural Africa.

A further point concerns the development of ideology during the rebellion. At first it was the Congolese bourgeoisie which was attacked. The harmful influence of foreigners was "evoked only in general manner or as a means for the corruption of national politicians." But later, after the first rebel defeats and the intervention of American T-28 aircraft, "attacks against foreigners became more precise and more virulent."[15]

Revolutionary Mulelism had some minor resonance in a separately organized, small attack on Bolobo and Mushie from training camps across the river in Congo-Brazzaville. However, this lone attempt to create an ideological and perhaps geographical link-up with the rebellion in Kwilu was quickly suppressed.[16]

The Eastern Congo having been the principal terrain of rural nationalism in 1960, it was, logically, the main theater of rebellion in 1964. The revolt was mounted by emissaries of the dominant "Gbenye faction" of the CNL (the Lumumbist exile front in Brazzaville). From Bujumbura (Burundi), Gaston Soumialot worked with local opposition forces in Kivu to organize a rebel army with a national orientation. Although it was a youthful, rural force without modern arms, the Armée Populaire de Libération (APL) took over nearly half the country in three months—due to its prestige in magic and its first popularity. Political leadership returned to the MNC-Lumumba, whose cadres and *jeunesse* (youth wing) were rapidly absorbed into the civil and military institutions of the rebellion. The Eastern *simba* (Swahili for lion) troops received a

14 Merlier, "L'Economie Congolaise," p. 36.

15 Verhaegen, *Rébellions,* I, 131; Fox, de Craemer, and Ribeaucourt, pp. 95, 97, 108.

16 Verhaegen, *Rébellions,* I, 189–206.

much less systematic military-political training than the Mulelists. Correspondingly, the role of magical-religious tabus in sustaining cohesion was more significant.

But the greatest difference between the Kwilu rebellion and the rebellion in the East lay in the latter's nonradical ideology. If the disappointments and violence of the years since Independence had brought the MNC-L cadres to insist upon a division between "the rich, that is to say the high administrators and politicians who were automatically thieves and sell-outs" (to foreign interests) and "the people, poor and suffering,"[17] they had scarcely changed their comportment before the economic and administrative structures of colonial society.

> The *simbas* call themselves nationalists and not communists. They insist on the distinction. That corresponds besides to their convictions in matters of economic organization. If they wish to attack social inequality, they do not intend to suppress private property nor foreign capitalist enterprises; to the contrary, they proclaim that they will never attack foreign enterprise and capital and that they will appeal to all capital, from the East as well as the West, to invest in the Congo. They promise "the second independence," but that is just synonymous with prosperity and liberty. . . . Their attitude regarding religion was tolerant and with several even favorable.[18]

After purging and executing the old power holders in the villages, towns, and cities, the rebel "counterelite" invested the existing bureaucratic structures. Some popular measures were taken. Most taxes were abolished, school fees were eliminated, price controls were attempted. There were a few pragmatic nationalizations of small businesses (for example, to assure the army's nourishment). Some representative organs (*Conseils des Sages*) were established. But the administrative hierarchy was retained, as was the tension between the different categories of the pay scale. The bureaucratic world of paper, routine, and channels reasserted itself even at the expense of urgent, external needs. The party elite succumbed to the habit of command, alienating local cadres who

[17] Verhaegen, *Rébellions,* II, 372. [18] *Ibid.,* p. 375.

staffed the *Conseils des Sages*. Tribal favoritism and corruption marred even some dynamic and popular performances. The lower categories of state workers complained that they were not paid.

A notable effort was made to keep foreign enterprises running. Soumialot even permitted the Compagnie des Chemins de Fer du Congo Supérieur aux Grands Lacs Africains (CFL) railroad to bring Union Minière's copper through the rebel zone. As rebel officials in Kindu would "rely on foreign economic enterprises and help them because they appear the most apt to contribute to economic development," [19] so Gbenye would give Belgian Foreign Minister Spaak all assurances regarding the future safety of Belgian capital in the Congo.[20] In spite of numerous vexations, particularly in the interior, where controls and discipline were lacking, foreign missionaries benefited from a general tolerance. They were encouraged to keep the school system going and warned to stay out of politics. Soumialot went to church as did many of the *simba*.[21]

Less systematic and more opportunistic than Mulele, yet operating on a larger scale, the CNL elite took upon itself the conflicts of a ruthlessly fragmented society. Ethnic suspicions and antagonisms cut off potential allies and divided the rebels. An urban, bourgeois political elite was opposed by essentially rural, populist *Conseils des Sages* (Maniema). An alienated, wild urban *jeunesse*, and the temptations of city life, sapped the discipline of the first, rural *simbas*. Ultimately, it was the contradictions of rural revolution, personified by the APL, which discredited the rebellion—thus permitting it to be repressed so quickly. With their cohesion assured by magical beliefs and sanctions (as well as hemp-smoking) the *simbas* attained the purity of an isolated caste. They could free themselves to a cruel and spectacular repression without

19 *Ibid.*, p. 714.

20 In a memorandum prepared for their Aug. 23 meeting in Brussels. A copy appears in *Courrier Africain*, Feb. 18, 1967, pp. 33–37.

21 However, a political program drafted by Soumialot's advisers did envision "state control" of the Catholic school and clinic system to end "discrimination in education" and "injustices by Catholic nurses." Verhaegen, *Rébellions*, II, 728.

considering the generalized insecurity it created among a population which admitted the principle of executions. After their first defeats—partly the result of American military technology—the military system based on magic collapsed, and so did discipline. The civilian population lost faith in the ultimate triumph of the rebellion, and everyday life became an endless round of requisitions, thefts, and violence by disoriented soldiers. As suggested above, Mulele was able to neutralize some of this deterioration by ideological indoctrination and by application of the theory of revolutionary war with its close association of soldiers and peasants. He also had the advantage of an ethnically homogeneous, rural redoubt which could provide short-term security and keep alive the hope of victory. Yet even Mulele could not wholly escape the difficulties of rural-based revolution.

Withal, the CNL leaders' ability to maintain their own unity and control the general direction of the rebellion (so long as the APL was a coherent force) was impressive. Had a compromise been arrived at between Leopoldville, its foreign supporters, and the CNL, the author believes that the agreement probably could have been "sold" to the rebel cadres and militants.

It was only in 1963 and 1964 that Lumumbist ideology became overtly anti-American. And it was not until the "moment when Belgo-American military assistance broke the power of the popular army" that " the Americans became the principal adversaries. The *simbas* had the conviction that only American aid permitted the Leopoldville government to resist." In his exhaustive study of the rebellion in Maniema, Verhaegen shows that American air attacks caused the rebels to use the foreign population as hostages against further bombardments. And "according to the majority of foreign witnesses, the *simba*'s hatred of Belgians and Americans came only later [in the rebellion] because of the aid given to the ANC by Belgium and the United States." [22]

Another question concerns the role of external powers in the Congo rebellions. Mulele was the only important rebel who had

[22] *Ibid.*, pp. 313, 654.

spent time in China, and he seems to have taken some important lessons from this experience. Little is known about the depth of his commitment to Communist ideology. What is certain is that his movement was not dependent upon the power of international Communism, and that foreign revolutionary theory was severely modified by the endemic processes of the Congo. Mulele received moral, but not material, support from the Chinese. In return, there were a few vague references in Mulelist literature to that "country of happiness" which would some day help the Congolese and teach them manufacturing.[23] If success had meant Communism, it would certainly have been a "national" one, deeply rooted in African rural society.

As for the CNL left-bourgeois exiles, they undoubtedly "received some funds from the Chinese and Soviets."[24] Chinese officials in Brazzaville and Bujumbura provided training manuals and films and possibly occasional tactical advice. Yet it was not until late Summer or Fall, *when the rebels came under heavy pressure from Western mercenaries and planes,* that substantial quantities of Communist-made (mainly Soviet) arms appeared in the Congo. Significantly, these seemed to come from Algeria and the United Arab Republic, with transshipment arranged through Sudan, Tanzania, and Uganda.[25] At best, Soviet and Chinese influence was indirect and dependent upon the preferences of certain African states. The arms arrived too late and were not used effectively. The American Embassy was unaware of any Communist personnel in the rebellion. It seems fair to conclude, with Young, that the "Communist role" in the Eastern rebellion was "very small."[26]

[23] Fox, de Craemer, and Ribeaucourt, p. 96.

[24] Young, "Significance of the 1964 Rebellion," in Kitchen, p. 121.

[25] The consensus in the African Bureau was that most of the arms shipments were initiated by African countries with promises of replacement given by the Soviet Union. For evidence of independent planning by ten African nations, see CRISP, *Congo 1964,* pp. 492–494.

[26] Young, "Significance of the 1964 Rebellion," in Kitchen, p. 122.

American Perspectives on the Rebellion

Most of the officials involved placed the Congo rebellion in a Cold War context. This does not mean that they challenged the *factual* judgments of experts such as Professor Young. As before, the judgment that certain political forces carried with them a Communist threat was based on *expectations* of their future course and consequences. In 1964 these expectations flowed from the world view of sophisticated anti-Communism.

Since they accepted Communist aid, Gbenye and his ilk were considered "unreliable." Moreover, they were regarded as "not economically or indigenously strong enough to preserve a separate identity if they won and the Communists were associated with them." Hence no political arrangements should be worked out with the rebels. Finally, given the organizational looseness of the rebellion, its success would entail a fragmented Congo, perhaps even the release of centrifugal forces in neighboring countries. In such a situation the Communists "could establish a position." Soviet activity in Africa was old hat; now the Chinese were also currying influence—not only in the Congo but in Dar es Salaam, Nairobi, Bujumbura, and Brazzaville.

For the liberal crusaders who headed the African Bureau, anti-Communism was not enough (indeed, three years of experience in Africa had convinced them that the Communist threat was in some degree overrated). Here was a "free" government besieged by "radical," "irresponsible," "racist" opponents. Of course, the U.S. shouldn't make deals with such a bunch. Ultimately Gbenye could be expected to pitch up an internally radical regime in Stanleyville and to seek assistance from "more radical" countries like the United Arab Republic and Algeria. And this would be "disruptive" for the whole Congo.

The notion that America was already "committed" to the Congo government, and therefore "had" to oppose the rebellion, recurred frequently in conversations with policy makers. Previous support for the U.N., Adoula, and the Congo Army was interpreted as "an important economic investment" in the Central Government. It was also said that the U.S. was "associated" with that government's fate "in the eyes of the world." Such thinking was particularly strong in the bureaus which dealt with the Congo on a day-to-day basis. And it carried some weight with other officials (especially George Ball).

The policy-makers agreed that the rebellion should be crushed without a major American commitment. (Trouble in South Vietnam served to re-emphasize Africa's low rank in U.S. strategic planning.) However, there were somewhat different emphases regarding tactics.

Under Secretary of State Harriman approached the Congo within the perspective of "confronting the Communists." As a "hard-headed" student of power realities he was not impressed by the abstraction—"African opinion." In pursuing his overriding objective he evinced little interest in such matters as the Leopoldville regime's "African image" or the impact of Western intervention on African sensibilities. On the other hand, the African Bureau naturally cared about African views. It was afraid that inexperienced outsiders would overlook intangibles, like public opinion, in managing the African Cold War. Most important, men like Williams and Fredericks had objectives which surpassed anti-Communism. They envisioned an association between the U.S. and African nationalism which would have the effect of liberalizing the latter and improving the racial climate of the former. Such an ambitious goal obliged America to "play it cool" in the Congo, to be sensitive to African nationalist opinion. Both orientations contributed to the tactics of counterrevolution.

Harriman's background helps explain his outlook. His family had been concerned with Russian-American relations since the beginning of the century. His father, Edward H. Harriman, was a railroad and steamship magnate "who had worked to establish economic ties with Tsarist Russia in the 1906–1909 period" in order to secure control of the Manchurian railroad system. W. Averell Harriman "carried on his father's activities as a railroad and steamship power in the United States and, in addition, had entered the banking business." In 1925 he signed a contract with the Soviet government to exploit certain manganese deposits and to construct a railroad in Russia. However, actions by both sides led to "a negotiated abrogation of the contract that brought Harriman a sizable payment from the Soviets to compensate for his original investment." [27] During World War II he was Ambassador to Moscow and attended nearly all the wartime conferences. By 1945 he was arguing for a firm stand against Stalinist expansion in Europe and the Far East; he was deeply involved in the onset of the Cold War.[28] He ran the Marshall Plan in Europe and was Truman's national security adviser during the Korean War. On the eve of the Kennedy Administration he explained his preoccupation with the Communist threat to Arthur Schlesinger, Jr.: "Everyone worries about the thing he knows best. Jack knows the Senate better than anything else, so he worries about that. For just the same reason, I worry most about the Russians." [29]

Harriman's domestic views were not such as to incline him toward a civilizing mission in the Third World. He fell somewhere between enlightened conservatism and moderate liberalism. Heir to one of the great American fortunes, he did not become a Democrat until 1932; even afterwards he served as chairman of the Business Council and Secretary of Commerce. Yet he was liberal enough to run a conventional Democratic administration as Governor of New York. He is characterized by what his friend, Schlesinger, Jr., calls "a certain unsentimentality of personality." [30] (In a generally sympathetic vignette, Kraft remarks, "for the common run of humanity, Harriman seems to have no feelings at all." [31] While Harriman's sophisticated anti-Communism and appreciation of power realities often led him to reach the same

[27] William Appleman Williams, *American-Russian Relations 1781–1947* (New York, 1952), pp. 217, 51, 212–213.

[28] Gar Alperovitz, *Atomic Diplomacy: Hiroshima and Potsdam* (New York, 1967), *passim.*

[29] Schlesinger, p. 144.

[30] *Ibid.*, p. 281.

[31] Joseph Kraft, *Profiles in Power: A Washington Insight* (New York, 1966), p. 149. I have drawn upon Kraft's essay for some of the biographical details above.

conclusions as those who were also influenced by liberal Messianism, this was not invariably so. One has only to recall his initial skepticism about a "nationalist" solution in Laos,[32] his differences with Bowles on the latter's concept of a "neutralized" Southeast Asia,[33] and his aforementioned sympathy for Moise Tshombe.[34] Additional factors which may help to explain Harriman's sympathy for Tshombe are: his predominantly European diplomatic experience, his banking firm's (Brown Brothers Harriman's) concentration on Europe, and his family's holdings in Anaconda Copper (his brother, E. H. Harriman, the head of Brown Brothers Harriman, was a director) which might occasion a primal sympathy with Union Minière.

The emergence of a Harriman strain in Congo policy (counterbalancing what one cynic calls "the noble African" strain) was related to the advent of the Johnson presidency. In early 1964 Harriman was "cut out entirely from Vietnamese business" and assigned special responsibilities in Africa. In part this reflected Johnson's preference for a conventional military solution in Vietnam and his desire to compensate Harriman for his loss of influence in Asian policy. But it is also clear that Harriman's Congo views tended to coincide with Johnson's own instincts. As Vice-President he is reported to have "silently admired" Tshombe's secessionist efforts.[35] While his preoccupation with the presidential campaign left him little time for the Congo, Johnson gave many the impression that he wanted a quick anti-Communist solution and had little empathy for African opinion. Top people in the African Bureau felt that the White House was less sensitive to their problems. The President's outlook can be traced to his Southern roots, inexperience in foreign policy (except for the military aspects), deference to Congressional opinion (especially Southern seniors and protégé Dodd), and election year caution.[36]

32 Hilsman, p. 135.

33 Schlesinger, pp. 503, 898–899.

34 See above, p. 161.

35 Philip Geyelin, *Lyndon B. Johnson and the World* (New York, 1966), p. 38.

36 This analysis is based on *ibid., passim;* Kraft, *Profiles in Power,* pp. 9–18; interviews with informed individuals in Washington.

Intervention before the Fall of Stanleyville

As the rebellion grew, American officials attempted to distribute the burden of repressing it. When their efforts fell short, the Defense Department and CIA came in and picked up the slack.

Earlier events had fostered the habit of cooperation between local U.N. officials and the American Embassy. For instance, in late 1963 Gullion participated in a U.N. rescue operation in Kwilu to bring home to Adoula the seriousness of the situation.[37] Yet with a reduced contingent and just a few months to go, the UNF commander, Major General Ironsi of Nigeria, understandably sought to avoid direct clashes with the rebels. He was sustained by the "psychology of disengagement in the Secretariat" and waning African interest in the UNF after Katanga's defeat.[38] The result was a quieter and less significant U.N. contribution to U.S. objectives than before. In Kwilu, U.N. planes and helicopters carried equipment and supplies for government soldiers and airlifted the wounded; they also evacuated "threatened missionaries including American nationals, and U.N. civilian personnel." In the East, ONUC put transportation and communications facilities at the disposal of the Congo Army and collected military intelligence for the government. On May 22 a U.N. reconnaissance flight in Kivu was ended by ground fire; all on board survived including the local Congolese commander and Colonel William A. Dodds, U.S. Army, a counterinsurgency adviser. Under U.S. prodding, the U.N. formulated contingency plans for a "temporary military presence" in the strategic city of Bukavu, which was threatened by rebel forces. U.N. officials felt such a presence "might be decisive." On May 24 Adoula orally signified his intention to request U.N. assistance at Bukavu. A Nigerian company was ordered to stand by in Leopoldville. According to Thant the Nigerians would not "subdue or conquer" the dissidents but simply maintain law and

[37] See above, p. 208.

[38] Lefever, *Crisis in the Congo,* pp. 132–133; *Jeune Afrique,* June 15, 1964, p. 7.

order, ensure the safety of U.N. personnel and property, and evacuate the endangered. However, they could use force in "self defense." In the end the Nigerians were not sent. Adoula could not get Mobutu's consent for a written request until the government drive on Bukavu collapsed on May 31. At that point the Nigerians had only ten days to go in the Congo, and Ironsi was reluctant to become involved. Thant now offered to send the Nigerians to nearby Goma (as a bluff). Adoula replied that surplus military equipment would be more useful.[39]

> Substantial quantities of material and equipment, including armored vehicles, weapons, ammunition, quartermaster items, air transport, vehicles and surplus rations, were accordingly sold or otherwise transferred or made available to the ANC. Some of the transfers in question had in fact occurred or were being negotiated well before 6 June.[40]

During the Spring of 1964 American diplomats sought additional aid from Africa and Belgium. The African Bureau pressed Adoula to request African troops as a partial substitute for the retiring UNF. This plan envisaged bilateral accords with Nigeria and Tunisia (and Ethiopia?) to be approved by the Organization of African Unity (OAU). The U.S. would indirectly finance the program.[41] There was tremendous skepticism in the Defense Department and the Embassy concerning these countries' capacity to provide meaningful assistance. In any case, Mobutu thwarted the project. Fearing for his prestige and control of the army, he forced Adoula to postpone his appeal. The Americans had a little

[39] Gendebien, *L'Intervention,* p. 221, states that Mobutu again opposed the use of U.N. troops at this time.

[40] U.N. Security Council, *Official Records, Supplement for Apr., May, June, 1964,* S/5784 (June 29, 1964), pp. 262–272. The presence of Col. Dodds on the U.N. plane is noted in CRISP, *Congo 1964,* p. 72. Some details regarding the American role, Ironsi's attitude, and the bluff at Goma were provided by U.S. officials.

[41] CRISP, *Congo 1964,* p. 98; *New York Times,* June 7, 1964, sec. 4, p. 7; June 19, 1964, p. 10; *Jeune Afrique,* June 15, 1964, p. 7; *Christian Science Monitor,* Apr. 8, 1964, p. 2.

more success in Belgium. On May 9, Spaak and Rusk met in Brussels to discuss coordination of military aid. A month later a detachment of approximately 120 members of the Belgian Air Force arrived in the Congo. Its assignment was to pilot and maintain U.S.-donated transport planes and helicopters which would provide much-needed mobility for the Congo Army.[42] At this time some American officials began to advocate the encadrement of Belgian military instructors in the Congolese officer corps. However, Belgium was reluctant, worrying about the consequences for Belgian citizens in rebel-held areas.[43]

Recognizing that its client was in danger and receiving inadequate external support, Washington stepped up military assistance. Harriman is said to have been the "spark plug" here, although there was no dissent from other policy-makers. In March he traveled to Ghana, Nigeria, and the Congo seeking information on the repercussions of the UNF's scheduled departure at the end of June. After six days in the Congo he concluded that the country faced two external threats: that of the Communist-aided Brazzaville exiles and that of the Portuguese-aided Tshombist mercenaries, some of whom were awaiting a new call to arms in Angola. The U.S. decided to furnish land and air transport with instructors to the Congo.[44] According to the *Financial Times,* quoted by *Le Monde* April 30,

> The Americans are arming on a war footing six Congolese battalions grouped in Katanga. They have given the Congo Army six H-21 heavy helicopters, five C-47 transport planes, and will deliver before June 30 five other C-47s and six combat planes of a type not yet specified.[45]

[42] CRISP, *Congo 1964,* pp. 97–98.

[43] The Belgian attitude at this time is conveyed by a cable from the Belgian Ambassador in Leopoldville, quoted in *ibid.,* pp. 378–379.

[44] *Ibid.,* pp. 87–88; Lefever, *Crisis in the Congo,* p. 131; *Christian Science Monitor,* Apr. 8, 1964, p. 2.

[45] Quoted in CRISP, *Congo 1964,* p. 97. Even before Harriman's African tour, a covert U.S. operation was mounted in order to hold off the first rebels in Kwilu. An account is given by Belgian Colonel e. r. Frédéric Vandewalle, who later directed the Belgo-American-Congo government

The threat to Bakuvu provoked a speed-up and step-up of American aid. In the interest of covertness and immediacy the CIA was asked to produce an "instant Air Force." Front organizations in Miami and London quickly acquired Cuban exile pilots and European mechanics to handle six T-28 fighters armed with rockets and machine guns.[46] With the knowledge of the State Department, a few American civil pilots signed contracts to instruct the Cubans in the peculiarities of the T-28. It was understood in Washington that the Americans would not fly combat missions, but this understanding was surpassed by local feelings of emergency among CIA—and possibly Embassy—officials. When American journalists spotted their countrymen flying sorties in Kivu, the State Department first denied their reports, then embarrassedly referred to new information from its Embassy and announced the flights would be curtailed. The Department was "barely disguising its

---

military campaign against the rebellions, in *L'Ommegang: Odysée et reconquête de Stanleyville, 1964* (Brussels, 1970), pp. 63–64.

"At the beginning of 1964, things were going badly in Kwilu. Some one, probably the head of the Central Intelligence Agency (CIA) in Leopoldville, had the idea of using some armed T-6s [Italian training planes] to help contain the rebellion. Contracts were signed with Cuban refugee pilots in Florida. . . .

"A special organism was to be created for the exploitation, if one can use the word in this particular case, of Congolese combat aviation. It had its own house in the principality of Liechtenstein, with the sign WIGMO (Western International Ground Maintenance Operation).

"At $2,000 per month it engaged men determined to risk their skins in the Congo. Measured risks, that is. Soon they refused to accept the least mission without the certainty that a helicopter was ready to pick them up in the bush, if such an eventuality should occur. . . .

"On February 13, 1964, an attack on Kikwit was beaten back with the help of rockets from two T-6s. [Cuban pilots and maintenance crews] shared the mediocrity of [airport] installations with the crews in charge of 3 helicopters and the Otter airplane of the U.N.

"The officers of the United Nations Force pretended to ignore the nature of their neighbors. These mercenaries, introduced in contempt of the Security Council resolutions, provided them with protective sorties for their rescue operations at various times."

46 *New York Times,* Apr. 26, 1966, pp. 1, 30.

displeasure with other arms of the government."[47] It is unclear whether the Washington office of the CIA was informed fully about the activities of its agents in the Congo.

The Defense Department dispatched "several" counterinsurgency experts to advise Congolese commanders, notably in Kivu.[48] Their efforts, along with those of the C-47's and T-28's, played a major role in the temporary reversal of enemy momentum near Bukavu.[49] By June 30, Washington had sent almost 100 "military technicians" to the Congo, mostly to teach the Congolese how to use the growing influx of American equipment.[50] Toward the end of the month General Paul Adams of the U.S. Strike Command arrived, "presumably" to ascertain military needs.[51] Meanwhile, large chunks of territory slipped from government control; the rebels scored important victories in Kivu and North Katanga.[52]

On the last day of June, President Kasavubu accepted Adoula's resignation. In little more than a week he installed a new cabinet (since parliament had expired without new elections taking place, Kasavubu claimed full power of appointment). The head of the new government was none other than Moise Tshombe, fresh from a year of self-imposed exile and elaborate plotting in Spain.[53]

Tshombe's amazing climb to power was another mark of that political talent which had enabled him to hold out so long in Katanga. This time his skills coincided with the conceptions of self-interest held by the most powerful political forces in the Congo. Foremost among these was the dominant clique in Leopoldville, the "Binza group." This included Mobutu, Nendaka, Bomboko, Ndele, and Kandolo. With the army floundering in the

[47] *Ibid.*, June 7, 1964, p. 27; June 16, 1964, p. 13; June 17, 1964, p. 1; June 18, 1964, p. 1; June 20, 1964, p. 1. This point was also confirmed by interviews with the appropriate officials.

[48] *Ibid.*, June 7, 1964, p. 7.

[49] CRISP, *Congo 1964*, pp. 71–74.

[50] Lefever, *Crisis in the Congo*, p. 131.

[51] *New York Times*, June 24, 1964, p. 6.

[52] CRISP, *Congo 1964*, p. 78.

[53] The next few paragraphs are largely based on the excellent account of Tshombe's return to power in *ibid.*, pp. 123–185.

East and the U.N. withdrawing from Katanga, they were afraid that Tshombe would seize the occasion to renew the secession or throw in with the rebels. Tshombe's cards included an estimated 15,000 ex-Katanga gendarmes, armed and hiding in the bush, an undetermined number of ex-gendarmes and white mercenaries training and awaiting their leader's call in Angola, and certain sporadic advances in the direction of the CNL. Anxious to buttress its position, a preponderant faction of the Binza group recognized the strong feeling among moderates in Leopoldville for a "government of national reconciliation"; it also hoped that Tshombe might be able to detach some of the CNL leaders. For all these reasons the Binza group came to favor first the reintegration of Tshombe, and finally his accession to the top governmental post.[54]

La question Tshombe provoked the first major split in the Binza group. The following rundown of individual positions comes from a Western diplomat who was actively concerned with this issue. Ndele and Kandolo felt it was "too risky" to deal with Tshombe from a position of weakness. On the other hand, Mobutu was impressed by the Katangan's military assets. Besides, Mobutu had remained on excellent personal terms with Tshombe even during the secession period. Nendaka's ambition was frustrated by Adoula. For example, Nendaka wanted to be President of RADECO, the CIA-financed government party. But he was forced to withdraw his candidacy in favor of Adoula when the U.S. Embassy threatened to cut off the party's funds. So Nendaka now tried an alternative alliance with Tshombe. Bomboko's stance was ambivalent. In the end, however, he joined Mobutu and Nendaka.

Rivalry between Adoula and Kasavubu was, according to the

54 According to a principal in the negotiations, Adoula, Bomboko, and Mobutu would have contacted Tshombe as early as Aug. 1963, and offered him the Ministry of Economic Affairs. Tshombe declined, probably under the influence of rightist advisers. It must be noted that, at this moment, Tshombe's bargaining position was not as strong as it would be later. A comparatively effortless "absorption" of Tshombe into the government was envisioned. After the birth of the CNL and the beginning of the U.N. withdrawal, the reintegration of Tshombe seemed more necessary *and* more costly.

same authoritative source, equally important in Tshombe's success. Both were maneuvering for power in view of the new Constitution which provided for a transitional government, new elections and a strengthened presidency. Adoula came to favor Tshombe's return as a means of bolstering his own sagging regime, and as part of his plan to be *the* architect of "national reconciliation." (Other aspects of this plan were the liberation of Gizenga and the restoration of party activity.) Kasavubu's strategy was to maintain the existing Adoula government during the transition period, then preside personally over a "round table," regrouping all political forces. This conference would achieve "national reconciliation," and the President would emerge as "the father of the Congo."

Against this background, one can better follow Tshombe's labyrinthian path to power. On June 15th, Adoula and Mobutu summoned two Belgians to Leopoldville: Pierre Davister, a journalist close to Tshombe, and Roger Lallemand, a Belgian Socialist adviser to Adoula. Several days later, Davister was given a mandate to return to Europe and bring back Tshombe. As it turned out, Adoula had underestimated Tshombe's ambition to be "top dog," the support he could find in the Binza group, and Kasavubu's political acumen. On July 1, the President played *his* Tshombe card—partly on the recommendation of the Binza group and partly to upstage Adoula. As *formateur,* Tshombe's first impulse was to form a broad, moderate government including three Vice-Ministers: Adoula, Zola (ABAKO, a rival of Kasavubu), and Kiewewa (MNC-Lumumba, but not in the CNL). However, he was dissuaded from this course by rightist European advisers and Kasavubu. The latter was determined to keep his new Prime Minister in a dependent position, and to let events "wear him out" as they had Adoula.

Yet it would be wrong to leave the impression that Congolese political calculations were wholly independent of external influences. Key Western powers were increasingly sensitive to the advantages of reintegrating Tshombe in some important capacity. And successful Congolese leaders had developed the habit of consulting certain Western representatives. This could only have been reinforced by the Congo's increasing dependence on Western military support. General Mobutu traveled to several European capitals in April and May seeking equipment for the ANC. According to the Centre de Recherche et d'Information Socio-Politiques (CRISP), he returned "partisan d'une entente avec M. Tshombe" (at the time this did not necessarily imply a change of prime minister). *Sûreté* chief Nendaka also sojourned in Europe in early 1964. There, French intelligence appears to have encouraged him in his distaste for Adoula and toward increasing sympathy for Tshombe. On June 12, Spaak informed Adoula that Belgian "technicians" could not organize antirebel operations unless it was demonstrated that a political solution ("sans compromettre l'essentiel") was impossible. Noting that Tshombe and a number of CNL representatives had declared their willingness to open discussions, he suggested that "aid to maintain order" would be facilitated by the "impression" that national reconciliation was occurring. In this regard he urged an official amnesty for Tshombe to hasten his reintegration. The next week Spaak met separately with Tshombe and Bomboko. At this stage the American Embassy was not taking an active role. However, as early as April, certain members had begun to ask themselves whether it would not be best to "incorporate Tshombe in the government rather than see him help the revolutionary forces or try a new secession which the Army would be incapable of defeating."

In the last days of June, Tshombe returned to the Congo. On his way back he conferred with Spaak in Brussels; afterwards, the Belgian Foreign Minister remarked that the Adoula government was "running down" ("en parte de vitesse"). Belgium now formally abandoned the idea of reintegrating Tshombe into Adoula's regime pending new elections: "Un nouveau government au Congo, estime-t-on beneficiera toujours d'un préjuge favorable," repeated sources close to Belgian officials. The Belgian Embassy was described as favorable to national reconciliation and wishing Kasavubu to adopt a "positive attitude" toward the Katangan leader.

While Belgian representatives clustered around the returned prodigal, the Americans held aloof. They still preferred Adoula and expected Kasavubu to fulfill his own plan to keep Adoula on. At the same time the Embassy was "not screaming against" the notion of including Tshombe in a government which someone else would lead. This was perfectly consistent with past attempts to forge a moderate nationalist-conservative alliance against the Lumumbists with a moderate in the top spot.[55]

At this moment, cautions our diplomatic informant, one ought not to exaggerate U.S.-Belgian differences. The Belgians wanted a new government, but this could conceivably be a totally revamped Adoula government. They were not opposed to a Tshombe *équipe* however, and they soon learned from Davister that this was under serious consideration. The Americans manifested greater support for Adoula and were distinctly less keen for Tshombe. Having received Davister's report second hand, they may not have rendered it its full significance. In any case, the U.S. Embassy did not take a clear-cut stand against a possible Tshombe government.

July 1, Kasavubu asked Tshombe to explore the basis for a transitional government. It was five more days before Tshombe was asked to *form* a new government. In this time there appears to have been no U.S. effort to block his appointment, although American aid programs constituted significant bargaining power.[56] Ameri-

[55] The phrase just cited was used by a high official of the U.S. Embassy in an interview with the author. The urge to reintegrate Tshombe was undoubtedly stimulated by memories of Katangan secession. "The immediate worry here," reported the *New York Times* State Department correspondent on July 1, "is that a breakdown of central authority—leading to new secessionist movements in various Congolese provinces and the strengthening of extreme leftists—will occur now that the United Nations military shield has been removed." *New York Times,* July 2, 1964, p. 1. Most U.N. troops had been stationed in Katanga.

[56] *Ibid.,* July 25, 1964, p. 2. (This report notes that some "observers" in Leopoldville believed a "massive effort" could have succeeded in blocking the appointment, but that the U.S. made no such effort.)

Paul-Henri Spaak, *Combats inachevés,* II (Paris, 1969), 269, states that

can officials seem to have been impressed by Tshombe's support among influential politicians in Leopoldville. Hopeful that he would produce a stronger government to compete with the rebels, they acquiesced in his nomination. Unlike the Belgians, they did not react with any enthusiasm. In the African Bureau it was feared that Tshombe's ignominious past would make it harder for the Congo to obtain African military and political support.

In conclusion, the return to power of Moise Tshombe was not exactly contrary to American wishes and policies. The U.S. contributed to the notion that Tshombe should return and be reintegrated into the Central Government. Given the United States' reluctance to furnish ground troops against the rebellion, it was perhaps to be expected that the Binza group and the Belgians would turn toward Tshombe and that here would be some latitude for the play of personal rivalries. Still, the Americans did not attempt to use the great influence they did possess. It would seem they were not *that* unsatisfied with Tshombe as Prime Minister. If he was not their first choice, he was perhaps an acceptable second.

A change of Ambassadors may have affected the Americans' decision not to challenge Tshombe. At the end of 1963 Gullion was relieved for reasons which remain obscure. Gullion detested Tshombe and would have found it difficult to work with him. In his last weeks in Leopoldville he had successfully fought Tshombe's efforts to come to an agreement with the hard-pressed group in power.[57] Even in the new context of 1964 it seems questionable whether this energetic and influential Ambassador might not have resisted the clamor for Tshombe. His successor, G. McMurtrie Godley, was a capable career officer of a more conventional stripe. His previous overseas assignments were nearly all European, including a stint in Belgium during the 1950's. Although he was Gullion's deputy in 1961 and 1962 and subsequently served in the African Bureau, he felt that Guillion's attitude was too anti-

the U.S. and Belgium were not for Adoula's cashiering by the "ambitious" Kasavubu. This is the truth, but not the whole truth.

57 CRISP, *Congo 1964*, pp. 126–127.

Belgian. Godley was also more skeptical of the virtues of African nationalism, an attitude not wholly unrelated to a kind of ethnocentrism (or racism) which is prevalent in the diplomatic corps (see above, p. 208, for earlier examples).

Intervention after the Fall of Stanleyville

During Tshombe's first weeks in office, there was a further deterioration of the government's position vis-à-vis the revolution. Rebel forces gained control of virtually the entire Eastern Congo (except for Tshombe's home, South Katanga). The Congo Army generally withdrew without fighting. In Kwilu the Mulelists maintained their hold on half the province. At the end of July, Leopoldville itself was threatened when CNL commandoes (trained in Brazzaville) briefly held an area in the Western Congo only 150 miles from the capital.[58]

Tshombe's own actions had destroyed the already slim possibility of a political solution. In mid-June, various CNL leaders had responded favorably to the idea of Tshombe's return and even of political cooperation. At the time, the CNL issued four conditions for national reconciliation: freeing of political prisoners including Gizenga, resignation of Kasavubu and Adoula, halt in operations against the rebels, provisional government of public safety (presumably including some rebel leaders). Except for Kasavubu's ouster, these conditions were acceptable to many moderate groups in Leopoldville.

But at the crucial moment Tshombe chose the easier route to power (via the Binza group and its international supporters) over the more uncertain strategy of allying with the CNL and pressing Leopoldville to agree to national reconciliation. He rejected some advisers' suggestion that he fly to Brazzaville to treat with the CNL instead of accepting Adoula's invitation to return to Leopoldville immediately. In forming his government he antagonized the CNL by proceeding while Gizenga remained in prison, by trying to include a few CNL turncoats without dealing with CNL leaders in

[58] *Ibid.*, pp. 224–227.

Brazzaville and Bujumbura, and by spending a good part of his days with Nendaka and Mobutu. In the end, Tshombe produced a cabinet which was so narrow politically that even the Belgians were disappointed. The main portfolios were held by Tshombe and Munongo, the former Minister of Interior of Katanga who was widely believed to have been implicated in Lumumba's murder. Albert Kalonji, Tshombe's old ally and fellow secessionist from South Kassi, was Minister of Agriculture. Prominent moderates were absent. Only one CNL turncoat participated. Mobutu and Nendaka—who had the most to lose in any political settlement—stayed on as heads of the Army and the Police. In no time at all Tshombe's old entrouge of rightist Belgian advisors and South African mercenaries began to appear in Leopoldville.[59]

On August 4 the rebels captured Stanleyville, the former capital of Lumumbism. In addition, Bukavu was again threatened. The Eastern rebellion neared its high-water mark. It also entered a stage of extreme brutality in the main towns:

> The lack of cohesion and control permitted diverse groups to seize the occasion to liquidate their rivals on various pretexts. Many of the executions were public, performed in front of Lumumba monuments, with grotesque cruelty. . . .[60]

Now neither the high-riding rebel leaders nor the personally threatened hard-liners in the government saw any possibility of a negotiated compromise.[61] Enter the U.S. and Belgium with more military aid.

Shocked by the fall of Stanleyville, the U.S. and Belgium moved to concert new strategy. On August 7, Harriman met in Brussels with Spaak and the directors of key Belgian companies in the Congo. The U.S. position was: additional American equipment will not be effective unless an "orderly army" emerges in the Congo. It was hoped that Belgian officers would set the ANC's house in order by assuming a combat role. However, Spaak reiter-

[59] *Ibid.*, pp. 142–148, 164–198.
[60] Young, "Significance of the 1964 Rebellion," in Kitchen, p. 123.
[61] CRISP, *Congo 1964*, pp. 209–224.

ated his previous reluctance to endorse such a role. An African peace-keeping force within the cadre of the Organization of African Unity was still plausible, although less so since the return of Tshombe. Yet it could take months to organize and might not be sufficient unto the task. Confronted by these difficulties, Harriman and Spaak agreed to the following general plan: [62]

(1) Colonel Vandewalle, former Belgian representative in Elizabethville, would return to the Congo to organize the repression. Belgium would provide more staff and training officers, some of whom would be acting in close support of combat troops. Immediate steps would be taken to recruit white mercenaries. They would go into action within a few weeks.

(2) The United States would provide additional transport planes, trucks, communications, and finances to underwrite the Congo Army and its new helpers. For the sake of efficiency and the American image in Africa, the Belgians (especially Vandewalle) would have overall responsibility for the organization of the mercenaries and other aspects of the antirebel campaign.

(3) A concentrated effort would be made to "Africanize" the

[62] *New York Times,* Aug. 7, 1964, pp. 1, 2; Aug. 8, 1964, pp. 1, 4; Aug. 13, 1964, p. 6; Aug. 25, 1964, p. 3; Aug. 30, 1964, sec. 4, p. 8; Mike Hoare, *Congo Mercenary* (London, 1967), p. 27.

In an article in *Jeune Afrique* (Sept. 7, 1964, pp. 8–9), Simon Malley places the crucial decisions a few days before the fall of Stanleyville. He reports a discussion within the National Security Council which seems, in the light of author interviews, generally correct. According to Malley, CIA Chief McCone took a strong anti-Communist position and urged Western military intervention. Rusk minimized the importance and extent of the Chinese role, emphasizing factors such as tribalism, economic grievances, and general anarchy. But he was alarmed and convinced of the urgency of the situation. He noted that African and European assistance was unlikely. Finally, he suggested two inevitable consequences of American intervention: charges of neocolonialism and opposition by American blacks. McNamara endorsed U.S. military aid but feared that a limited effort would risk defeat and a loss of prestige. Johnson—some say because he thought a victory would add votes—opted for limited military intervention preceded and followed by diplomatic efforts to get African and European help. If these efforts failed, Tshombe would be helped to recruit white mercenaries who would receive U.S. material support.

counterrevolution. Tshombe would be encouraged to actively recruit African diplomatic and military support. At the least, this could provide diplomatic cover for Western military intervention. At best, it would result in some sort of peace-keeping force which would limit the number of mercenaries needed. Thinking again of her African relations, the United States took the lead in this area.

With impressive celerity the Americans brought forth their equipment. On the 13th, four Air Force C-130 long-range transports arrived with full crews (50) and a "guard" of 56 parachutists from Fort Bragg [63] (a few days later it was explained that the parachutists would also be available to ride helicopters on "rescue and support" missions).[64] On the 18th, three twin-engine B-26 fighter-bombers put down in Leopoldville; in a short time the CIA staffed them with anti-Castro Cuban pilots and European mechanics.[65] A total of four or five B-26's were eventually delivered.[66] Other significant American material arriving in August and September included ground vehicles (substantial quantities of jeeps, trucks, and light tanks), communications equipment, ammunition, and heavy machine guns.[67]

This assistance was essential for the reconquest of the Eastern Congo. At Bukavu in mid-August pro-government forces defeated a rebel attack with the help of the C-130's which brought in reinforcements and supplies at a crucial moment. (The T-28's and American counterinsurgency advisers also made important contributions.) [68] By October, Vanderwalle had organized the Fifth Brigade which was to be the main instrument of the repression.

63 CRISP, *Congo 1964,* pp. 359, 363–364.

64 *New York Times,* Aug. 14, 1964, pp. 1, 4.

65 CRISP, *Congo* 1964, p. 357; *New York Times,* Apr. 26, 1966, pp. 1, 30.

66 Officially, seven B-26's were "lent" to the Congo government, but only 4 or 5 were delivered. Figures obtained from the Department of Defense.

67 CRISP, *Congo 1964,* pp. 357–359, 363–364.

68 *Ibid.,* pp. 232–238; *New York Times,* Aug. 21, 1964, p. 1. Verhaegen, *Rébellions,* II, 539–540, emphasizes the importance of armored cars and European settlers, "two types of adversary against which their [i.e. the rebels'] magical protection was without effect."

This consisted of six columns of selected government troops, each spearheaded by white mercenaries—mostly South Africans and Rhodesians. Belgian officers remained in the background but held the key command posts and took care of the logistics. American vehicles and communications provided necessary mobility for the practically autonomous columns. And, their advance was very well protected by rocket and machine-gun firing B-26's and T-28's.[69] (The *New York Times* reported, "Most troops term the air cover as decisive in their success on the ground.") [70] The psychological impact of the airplanes was at least as important as their physical threat.[71] The mercenaries and planes quickly overwhelmed the militarily inexperienced and poorly equipped *simbas,* driving them out of the main centers, and effecting a terrifying carnage. In one town alone, Kindu, the mercenaries admitted killing at least 3,000 Congolese of all ages.[72] By November, parts of the Fifth Brigade were driving toward their ultimate target—Stanleyville, capital of the revolutionary government.

As in the past, U.S. military policies had to be coordinated with those of its Belgian and Congolese partners. A recurrent source of controversy was the employment of white South African and Rhodesian mercenaries as spearheads of advancing government troops. American policy-makers were disturbed that the most available gunfighters—aside from the CIA's Cubans—were so unsavory, and were placed up front of the blacks in the manner of a classic colonialist police operation. American military officers who were assigned to work with Vandewalle in organizing the Fifth Brigade persistently sought to modify its structure in order to conceal the mercenaries. They also pushed the Belgian commander to win his war as quickly as possible even if poorly trained Congolese troops had to be thrown into the fray. With victory the mercenaries could be eased out and the mopping up Africanized.[73] A most revealing

[69] CRISP, *Congo 1964,* pp. 358–363, 370–376; Reed, pp. 117–130, 173–183.

[70] *New York Times,* Nov. 22, 1964, p. 4.

[71] *Verhaegen, Rébellions,* II, 544–546.

[72] Reed, p. 180.

[73] Vandewalle, pp. 157, 159–160, 221, 277–278.

picture of the State Department's concerns emerges from its cable to the Leopoldville Embassy in October which was shown to—and pocketed by—Colonel Vandewalle:

> It is probable that the OAU's concern with the subject of Tshombe's use of mercenaries, in particular South Africans and South Rhodesians, will increase. The ad hoc committee could require a departure program and will probably not be satisfied with a symbolic reduction of effectives.
>
> You are asked to examine this question with Van der Walle and to proceed with a study of an elimination of South African personnel as soon as the military situation permits.
>
> VDW's comments will be solicited for he is the best qualified person to furnish the information. You can give him the assurance that the government of the United States continues to be guided by the military necessities of the situation and realizes that the VDW plan is based principally on the employment of mercenary spearheads.
>
> However, in pursuing our examination of the delicate subject of South African mercenaries, we would like to benefit from VDW's discussion of the following aspects of the problem:
>
> 1. What is the distribution of mercenaries by nationality? Is it possible to give an opinion on their effectiveness as groups of the same origin?
>
> 2. What are VDW's plans for the use of mercenaries now and during the period following the hoped-for military success against the rebels?
>
> 3. Is it wise to envisage the employment of mercenaries in another branch of Congolese security forces, which we believe envisaged in Commissioner Decelle's police plan in Katanga?
>
> 4. What credit does VDW accord to the stories of brutality and pillage by mercenaries engaged in combat?
>
> 5. Is there a practical means of preventing the mercenaries from giving impromptu press interviews?
>
> 6. What does VDW think of the elimination of the South Africans after the capture of Stanleyville, according to this plan:
>
> —their services will be terminated and they could be replaced, if necessary, by recruitment of volunteers of Belgian and other nationalities;

—the mercenaries maintained, other than the South Africans, could be transformed into "military technicians" or "advisers" and integrated individually in units of the ANC, in an attempt to make them acceptable to African opinion.

7. What is VDW's estimate of the possibilities of supplementary recruitment in order to make up for the departure of South African mercenaries?

8. What is VDW's attitude, as military leader and a Belgian, on the subject of his compatriots who, for example at Bukavu, take up arms to defend their life, their house, and their property? [74]

Vandewalle's account of the mercenary episode in the Congo naturally suggests the practical difficulties and ultimate hypocrisy of America's "indirect wars." Shying away from an overt link with the mercenaries, the Americans tried not to transport them in U.S.-piloted C-130's; Belgian-piloted U.S. C-47's were entrusted with the grimy task. On the other hand, war material (including American civilian aid trucks) and Congolese troops being led by the mercenaries traveled by C-130. Still, in the heat of a military campaign, this division of labor was often violated.[75] The U.S. military attaché, Col. Raudstein, tried to stay clear of the mercenaries. But several American military officers were prominent in Vandewalle's headquarters, and certain ones even *fought* alongside the South Africans.[76] The Belgian Commander was struck by the ironic juxtaposition of Raudstein's scrupulous distance and another American's rather pushy interest:

However Colonel Vandewalle had met the first secretary of the Embassy of this country, Benjamin Hilton Cushing, a representative of the CIA. This ambidextrous diplomat had picked up some rumors that the

[74] *Ibid.*, pp. 207–208. [75] *Ibid.*, pp. 221, 244, 285, 180–185, 189, 297.

[76] *Ibid.*, pp. 203, 221, 230, 290, 313, 315, 325, 350. U.S. Army Col. Donald Rattan was the American "observer" in Vanderwalle's headquarters. He worked largely on logistical problems as well as those of coordination. He was assisted by an unidentified U.S. Air Force major and an army sergeant interpreter, Sam Wiesel. On a higher bureaucratic level, Vandewalle's American consultants were Col. Frank Williams, a Col. Thomas, and the U.S. military attache, Col. Knut Raudstein. Rattan and Wiesel fought in one of the mercenary columns driving toward Stanleyville.

[military] plan was in difficulty for financial reasons. He let it be known that if such should be the case, he could subsidize all or part of the recruitment from outside the Congo. The offer was mentally recorded but it wasn't necessary. The obstacles were especially administrative in character.[77]

As it increased its military aid, Washington also pressed the political-diplomatic side of its policy. The African Bureau took the lead in a U.S.-Belgian attempt to effect a rapprochement between Tshombe and key African states. According to several State Department sources Harriman had little enthusiasm for this effort. On August 11 Soapy Williams flew to Leopoldville for several days of talks with Tshombe, Munongo, Nendaka, and Mobutu. After considerable persuasion, Tshombe appealed for troops to Malagasy, Nigeria, Ethiopia, Senegal, and Liberia. It was understood that the U.S. would underwrite the cost of an African expeditionary corps. Coincidentally it was announced that Tshombe's request for the B-26's was being granted. On the other hand, Tshombe rejected Williams' entreaties to broaden his government in the direction of Adoula, Bomboko, and their ilk in order to enhance his African image.[78] This request was frequently renewed in later weeks—by the American Ambassador, by Joseph Palmer, II (head of a new interdepartmental task force on the Congo, who talked with Tshombe and Spaak), and by the Belgians. But Tshombe remained adamant.[79]

A few days after Tshombe's appeal for African troops, the two most important potential donors—Nigeria and Ethiopia—declared they could only act within the cadre of the Organization of African Unity. It was doubtful that a majority of the OAU would sanction troops, especially since Tshombe was now employing South African and Rhodesian mercenaries.

Another difficulty was Mobutu's insistence that any African

[77] *Ibid.*, p. 203.

[78] CRISP, *Congo 1964*, p. 357; *New York Times*, Aug. 18, 1964, p. 1; Moise Tshombe, *My Fifteen Months in Government*, trans. Lewis Bernays (Plono, Texas, 1967), pp. 51–52.

[79] CRISP, *Congo 1964*, pp. 522, 380.

force be placed under his authority. With their hopes for African forces now "faint," [80] American officials concentrated on increasing Tshombe's "African legitimacy." Various countries were appealing to the Secretary-General of the OAU for an extraordinary session of the Council of Ministers to take up the Congo situation. The U.S. decided to sponsor Tshombe within the OAU and other inter-African contexts as a reformed man and a true African nationalist.

After representations by the American Embassy,[81] Kasavubu asked the OAU to convoke its ministerial council. The council met at Addis Ababa from September 5–10. Tshombe asked it to provide troops to be stationed in "already pacified regions" enabling government forces to focus on "troubled regions." In return he offered to dispense with the services of the mercenaries (but not those of the Belgians and Americans). A high-ranking member of the American Embassy claims that American advice contributed to Tshombe's "noises about getting rid of the mercenaries." Bitterly divided, the OAU passed a watered-down resolution which all sides claimed as a victory. Nigeria, Liberia, and Senegal offered an amendment giving Tshombe the military aid he requested, but it failed, 9–9.[82]

America's attempt to sustain good African relations while supporting Tshombe encountered increasing obstacles. Under the OAU resolution an *ad hoc* commission was given the task of "encouraging" the Congo government's efforts in favor of a cease-fire and national reconciliation.[83] The seven-nation commission assembled in Nairobi on September 18 under the aegis of its chairman, Kenya Prime Minister Jomo Kenyatta. After prodding by American diplomats, Tshombe reversed his own prior judgment and flew to Nairobi. But he overestimated his persuasive powers and left after only two days—much to the discomfort of U.S. Ambassador to Kenya, William Attwood. Tshombe's early departure

[80] *Ibid.*, p. 464; *New York Times*, Aug. 22, 1964, p. 3; Aug. 28, 1964, p. 3; Aug. 30, 1964, sec. 4, p. 8.

[81] CRISP, *Congo 1964*, pp. 464–465.

[82] *Ibid.*, pp. 467–473.

[83] *Ibid.*, p. 471.

offended Kenyatta (who hoped to mediate the civil war), and left the field to rebel representative Thomas Kanza and his African supporters who told Kenyatta that, if America pulled her planes out, there could be a cease-fire. On the 23rd, the OAU commission decided to send a delegation to Washington immediately to see the President after stopping military aid to the Congo. This put Washington in just the position it was trying to avoid. As Attwood has written,

> If we received the OAU mission, this would drive a wedge between us and the Congolese government; if we refused, it would justify all the suspicions that we cared more for Tshombe (and our mythical investments) than for African opinion as expressed by the OAU. Hostile propagandists would have a field day.[84]

The U.S. first announced that it would not receive the delegation since any meeting should include Tshombe. After a few embarrassing days a compromise was worked out which included a luncheon with Rusk and a communiqué saving everyone's face. But a residue of strain persisted. In early October the American Embassy advised Tshombe to attend the Conference of Non-Aligned States in Cairo. Tshombe writes that he went in order "to convince the Africans of the soundness of my views." [85] Such was not to be the case, however, for Egyptian President Nasser, backed by militant African leaders, barred Tshombe from the conference. For a few days Tshombe languished in a luxurious Egyptian villa, guarded by Nasser's police and consoled by a lonely voice of protest—that of Dean Rusk.[86]

The dip in U.S. prestige in Africa caused some grumbling in the African Bureau, particularly among those I have labeled liberal Messianists. There was a feeling—often quite vague—that not enough was being done to maintain good relations with Africa. A specific source of discontent was a White House reception for Michel Struelens (who had resumed his vocation as Tshombe's

84 Attwood, pp. 196–204.

85 Tshombe, p. 54.

86 CRISP, *Congo 1964*, pp. 484–490; *New York Times*, Oct. 9, 1964, p. 7.

personal representative to the United States). Struelens' way to the White House was prepared by his old friends, Senator Dodd, Harriman, and McGeorge Bundy of the President's staff.[87] The liberal Africanists complained, "This would never have occurred under JFK." They harbored many unhappy memories of the Katanga Lobby and wished to maintain some distance from Tshombe and his entourage. In late August the formation of a special interdepartmental task force on the Congo—under career man Palmer—decreased their day-to-day influence. This may well have been the intention of State Department higher-ups such as Harriman and Ball. In any case, it increased the sense of estrangement of some liberal Africanists. Although the latter's political opposition to the rebels was as strong as anyone's and precluded any meaningful negotiations, they suspected that *something* was not being done, e.g.: "My feeling was that we didn't exhaust every effort at negotiation—although I can't prove it."

The Stanleyville Airlift

Severely pressed by Western planes and mercenaries, the rebel leaders sought to bring into balance the security of whites residing in their areas. They were helped toward this course by their angry followers who did not always distinguish between the responsibility of Western governments and the responsibility of Western peoples. At first, the idea was to use the presence of whites as protection against bombardments and attacks. Later, the rebels threatened the lives of Belgian and American hostages in an attempt to persuade their governments to cease military aid to Tshombe.[88] This caused the United States to place some limitations on air attacks against population centers where whites resided. (In intra-Administration wrangling, the State Department bested the Defense Department.) [89] But American policy-makers were

87 On Harriman and Bundy, see *ibid.*, Aug. 31, 1964, p. 1.

88 CRISP, *Congo 1964*, pp. 376–397.

89 *Ibid.*, p. 383; Vandewalle, pp. 317–318. The bureaucratic conflict was described by two high officials in the State and Defense Departments.

unwilling to change their political goals—hence unwilling to significantly modify the military instrument—for the sake of the hostages. As a result, diplomatic efforts to free the hostages failed.[90] Most of the endangered whites were in the Stanleyville area, and their situation became extremely tenuous as the mercenary columns approached in November.[91] Approximately 300 Belgians and Americans were put under arrest in Stanleyville. It was feared that they would be slaughtered as the mercenaries entered the city. Kenyatta made a final attempt at mediation on behalf of the OAU, but it foundered on American refusal to consent to a cease-fire as a precondition for discussions on the hostages. Kenyatta thought this rebel demand reasonable and was distressed when it was rejected.[92]

On November 24, twelve C-130's dropped 545 Belgian paratroopers and their equipment on Stanleyville airport. They fought their way into town and began to evacuate the first of 1,600 foreign whites. Of 300 Belgian and American hostages being held at the Victoria Hotel, twenty-seven were killed by rebels when they saw the paratroopers approaching. Within four hours after landing the paratroopers were joined by the mercenary columns which helped them secure the city and collect the whites. The mercenaries and their ANC cohorts put on such a brutal display that the commanding officer of the paratroopers ordered his men to return to the airfield as soon as they were finished with their rescues. Two days later—on Thanksgiving—seven C-130's dropped Belgian paratroopers on the airfield at Paulis, 225 miles northeast of Stanleyville. The rebels fled, but not before executing twenty-two Belgians and one American in retaliation for the attack on Stanleyville.

90 Attwood, pp. 204–216; Reed, pp. 106–116, 228–230. In late October, Wayne Fredericks met with rebel representative Thomas Kanza in Nairobi. The latter insisted that the hostages could not be released unless Tshombe's planes were grounded. This offer was rejected. According to several sources, Fredericks investigated the possibility of bribing the rebels to release the hostages.

91 CRISP, *Congo 1964,* pp. 385–394; Reed, pp. 152–171, 192–240.

92 Attwood, pp. 209–216.

Approximately 350 whites were evacuated from the surrounding area. Operations "Red Dragon" and "Black Dragon" were now over. The paratroopers withdrew, leaving about 1,000 whites still in the rebel-held areas.[93] The overwhelming majority was not harmed by the rebels, but vengeance for the Stanleyville attack claimed the lives of around 200.[94]

All told, the parachute operations evacuated approximately 2,000 whites, including 58 Americans. But they also resulted in the execution of perhaps 300 whites, not to speak of a much larger number of physical and psychological casualties. Eight of the dead were Americans.[95]

Day-by-day accounts of the events leading to the airdrops are available elsewhere.[96] Here the author would like to emphasize—and bring to light—certain facts about the American role.

In policy-making circles a first and always important focus of concern was the five-man consular staff in Stanleyville. They had been imprisoned shortly after the rebels captured the city. Since August, the U.S. Embassy had been urging Washington to "send American troops to the rescue" of the confined diplomats. During September and October, before any other Americans had been arrested in Stanleyville, Harriman had met with General Earle Wheeler, chairman of the Joint Chiefs of Staff, and gotten Wheeler's aides to draw up plans for sending a small, airborne rescue force to the rebel capital. However, many State Department officials were reluctant to take such imperialistic-looking action, fearing a loss of American influence in Africa.

[93] Reed, pp. 241–269; Vandewalle, pp. 349–366, 382.

[94] CRISP, *Congo 1964,* p. xxxi; Vandewalle, pp. 122, 410–411; Reed, p. 273; Jean Kestergat, *Congo, Congo* (Paris, 1965), p. 183; Benoît Verhaegen, "Recension des ouvrages," *Etudes Africaines,* T.A. 123, Dec. 30, 1970, pp. 20 ff. (review of Vandewalle's book).

[95] Reed, p. 273. The author's figure of 8 American dead is probably more reliable than the official one of 4 in *Department of State Bulletin,* Feb. 8, 1965, p. 220.

[96] See especially CRISP, *Congo 1964,* pp. 376–411; Reed, *passim;* Vandewalle, pp. 267–428; *Le Soir,* Nov. 28 and Dec. 2, 1969 (articles by Major-General e.r. François Temmerman).

In November, concern for "white hostages" in the Eastern Congo mounted. As Tshombe's Western-supported, mercenary-led forces approached Stanleyville, rebel leaders threatened the lives of Belgian and American nationals behind their lines. In Stanleyville, 280 Belgians and 17 Americans (including the 5 diplomats) were arrested. Shortly thereafter, Spaak arrived in Washington for talks with Harriman and Rusk. Spaak and Harriman agreed on the need for a joint intervention at Stanleyville, using Belgian troops if diplomatic efforts to evacuate whites continued to be unsuccessful. Initially, other American policy-makers were "very cool" to the proposals.[97] The African Bureau knew there would be unfavorable reaction in the OAU and in Africa generally. The International Organizations Bureau, especially Adlai Stevenson and his deputy Charles Yost in New York, anticipated charges of imperialism at the United Nations. George Ball was cautious about America's increasing involvement in a "doubtful area of national interest." The President was particularly worried about the risk of American crewmen being shot during the operation. Could the costs outweigh the prospective gains?

Yet, in the end, Harriman and Spaak were persuasive. Something had to be done to rescue the American and Belgian hostages, deter others from using U.S. nationals (especially diplomats) as political levers, and encourage the Belgians to continue their aid to the Congo by avoiding a traumatic massacre. Clearly, "humanitarian" and "political" considerations were deeply entwined. That Belgian paratroopers would be up front during the proposed rescue would inevitably divert some attention from their American transporters and air cover. As one Defense Department official remarked, "The Belgians were like heaven-sent manna to get our people out."

But what about the approaching mercenary forces? Why couldn't they save the hostages? The mercenary-led columns counted less than 200 "reliable" (i.e., white) men.[98] Their very approach to Stanleyville might trigger massacres. Or, as they fought

97 Reed, pp. 106–107, 131–132, 185–187, 215.

98 *Ibid.*, p. 207.

their way into Stanleyville from the east or southeast, "the rebels could depart with the hostages on the road going due north to whatever city was up there, or due west toward Lisala." [99] On the other hand, a surprise landing at dawn by 545 French-speaking, respected (or feared) Belgians, many with past experience in the Congo, would seem to improve the chances for a rescue.[100]

The ground forces were, nonetheless, in the words of a top policy-maker, "an important element of the [Stanleyville] plan." Indeed, U.S. officials belatedly admit that the Stanleyville airlift was designed, in advance, to occur shortly before or simultaneously with the arrival of the mercenaries outside the city. This would facilitate the task of the paratroops in several ways. According to one key official, "For example, we believe [*sic*] that if the rebels were encircled their will to fight would have been greatly reduced and less force would have resulted with obviously fewer casualties." [101] In the words of another, "synchronization" ["that the mercenaries were on their way"] would "help the Belgian paratroopers to carry out the narrow purposes of the rescue—to rescue, not to occupy—with less force than would otherwise be required." [102] Furthermore, just as the mercenaries' arrival from the east or southeast carried a risk of the hostages being moved north and west, so the paratroopers landing on an airfield which controlled the road leading westward out of Stanleyville implied that the *simbas* might flee eastward with the hostages.[103] Obviously a squeeze play was required. The main purpose of the coordination then was to assure the safety of the maximum number of hostages with the minimum cost.

Further confirmation of the plan's nature was provided by a Belgian diplomat who was deeply involved in the preparations. According to him the idea was to get the paratroopers inside the city first, but to have the mercenaries enter shortly afterwards. The actual operation went "about like planned." [104]

[99] Letter to the author from a key American official, Nov. 7, 1968.

[100] Reed, p. 185. [101] Letter to the author, Nov. 7, 1968.

[102] Letter to the author, Nov. 20, 1968. [103] Reed, p. 231.

[104] An article based upon an official Belgian military study notes that synchronization was envisioned in a military planning conference of para-

In the somewhat roseate view of the American Embassy the appearance of both the paratroopers and the mercenaries would produce a rapid melting of *simba* resistance; hopefully it would also produce such demoralization that the entire rebellion would collapse and whites in outlying areas—who were not slated for rescue—would be safe.[105]

The strategic concept of the Stanleyville airlift necessarily implied a secondary objective: helping the mercenaries capture the city. This was seen as a "not unwelcome by-product" of the rescue operation. Perhaps the point should be made more strongly. One

---

troop leaders Nov. 20, but the date foreseen then was Nov. 25. *Le Soir,* Nov. 28, 1969. In this connection, Vandewalle cites a report of the Congolese military *Sûreté* in late October, probably written by Belgian and Israeli military advisers. Based on information provided by a European businessman who had managed to leave Stanleyville, it concluded: "The European population advocates an airborne attack on the airfield at Stanleyville with a simultaneous neutralization of Camp Ktele and its approaches. According to this opinion any thought of bombarding Stanleyville without immediate occupation would cost the lives of a great number of people who would be killed as hostages." Vandewalle, p. 256.

Most accounts of the rescue operation (e.g., Attwood's and Reed's) attribute synchronization to Thomas Kanza's appearance at the last minute in Nairobi to negotiate with American representative William Attwood on behalf of the rebel regime. His arrival would have caused a one-day postponement of the rescue, enabling the mercenary column to arrive at almost the same time as the paratroopers. However, interviews with U.S. and Belgian officials, along with Vandewalle's account, throw considerable doubt on this explanation. On Nov. 22, Col. Vandewalle was consulted by U.S. and Belgian officers about a planned parachute jump the next day. He remembers informing these officers that his troops would not arrive until Nov. 24, and that the paratroopers appeared too weak to accomplish the rescue alone. They were immediately converted to a one-day delay in order to achieve synchronization between the two attacking forces. (Only Col. Clayton Isaacson, commander of the C-130 force, insisted on a Nov. 23 jump, "before the political men went back on their decision. All these means hadn't been deployed for nothing.") The Belgian and American officers immediately intervened with their embassies to assure synchronization. *Ibid.,* pp. 315–316, 325–327.

Vandewalle's position was consistent with the overall plan for a coordinated operation, so it was probably responsible for any change of date. The highest U.S. planners deny that negotiations in Nairobi had any influence on the timing of the drop.

105 The account in CRISP, *Congo 1964,* pp. xxx–xxxi, is correct.

assignment of the paratroopers was to try and capture Gbenye. Of four companies that landed, one proceeded immediately to Gbenye's residence. He had left, but some of his officers were captured and his personal papers were seized.[106]

Coordination between the paratroops and the mercenary-led columns [107] reflected the close relation between hostage security and the force brought to bear against the rebellion. Inevitably, a certain copenetration of objectives occurred. On the mercenaries' side, this was manifested in the increasing number of rescue missions performed as they entered towns where whites were being held. And on the eve of the Stanleyville airlift, 17 or 18 Cuban exiles were added to Vandewalle's column with the mission of precipitating themselves in front as soon as Stanleyville was attained in order to free American *diplomats.* The U.S. Embassy was taking precautions lest the jump be called off at the last minute.[108] Here was further evidence that the presence of U.S. officials formed a major component of governmental concern for white hostages in Stanleyville.

In retrospect, some of the major assumptions behind the airlift were inaccurate. Complete surprise was not achieved.[109] The

[106] *Ibid.,* pp. 400–401.

The rescue motivation seems to have been predominant, although it was derived from an unshakable political will, surrounded by such political objectives as deterrence and maintaining the presence of an aid partner, and associated with the aforementioned secondary military objective. Vandewalle makes it clear that the paratroopers were not seen as *militarily* necessary for the conquest of Stanleyville, although their political contribution was crucial. Vandewalle, pp. 308, 314–315. See also *New York Times,* Nov. 26, 1964, p. 16. Cf. the opposing thesis of Paul F. Semonin, "Killing them Definitively," *Nation,* Jan. 31, 1966, pp. 129–132. In this article, Semonin did invaluable pioneering work on the political context of the airlift.

[107] When the jump finally occurred it was of course closely coordinated with the mercenary column's movements. See Michael Hoare (the mercenary leader) in *Le Figaro Littéraire,* Dec. 17–23, 1964, p. 9; Hoare, *Congo Mercenary,* p. 118; Reed, p. 261; Kestergat, pp. 160–161.

[108] Kestergat, p. 162; Vandewalle, p. 313.

[109] Newsmen discovered the movement of Belgian paratroopers to Britain's Ascension Island in the Atlantic. Some U.S. officials anticipated a

simbas put up considerable resistance, and there were perhaps 100 casualties among the 300 hostages interned in Stanleyville. The rebellion did not collapse. In fact, strong resistance continued within the city for several weeks. Vengeance was taken upon nearly 300 whites at Paulis and in the outlying areas.[110] It is quite possible—but not certain—that the parachute attack caused more white casualties than would have occurred had the mercenary columns continued their advance unaided. On the one side, there is the fact that very few whites were killed by the rebels *before* Stanleyville, even though the mercenaries had ravaged much of the Eastern Congo. An estimated 30 to 35 persons were slain, generally after *air* attacks.[111] There is also some evidence that it was the parachute jump, and not the arrival of the mercenaries, which precipitated acts of vengeance after Stanleyville.[112] For instance, at Kindu and in the Maniema generally, the advent of the ANC and its mercenary spearheads in early November did not result in massacres of Europeans despite formal orders to that effect by Gbenye and Olenga. On the other side, the rebels had long and loudly threatened death for the Stanleyville "prisoners of war" unless the ground attack was halted.[113] Of some interest are Tshombe's written reflections on the consequences of the airlift:

> I think today that there might have been fewer killings of Europeans without the paratroops' attack; it was that, and not the offensive of the Congolese army, that gave the signal for the massacre of Europeans. But of course this is nothing but an opinion which cannot be proved or disproved.[114]

---

possible leak, but a more direct route to the Congo was excluded due to the impossibility of obtaining overflight rights.

110 Markowitz and Weiss, p. 217; Reed, p. 273; Vandewalle, pp. 359, 361, 370–392.

111 *New York Times,* Nov. 25, 1964, p. 1; Reed, *op. cit.,* p. 233; *New York Times,* Sept. 17, 1964, p. 5; Oct 26, 1964, p. 3; Nov. 6, 1964, p. 6; CRISP, *Congo 1964,* pp. 377–378; Vandewalle, pp 121–122.

112 CRISP, *Congo 1964,* p. 410.

113 Verhaegen, *Rébellions, II,* pp. 653–654, 384–394.

114 Tshombe, pp. 40–41. Cf. Vandewalle, pp. 410–412, 417.

American officials (even the Africanists) underestimated the political reaction in Africa to the airlift.[115] Before Stanleyville, contingency plans were also elaborated for smaller rescues in Paulis, Bunia, and Watsa. The last two were canceled, against the recommendation of the Embassy. News of the Stanleyville operation had produced protests and violent demonstrations in a number of African states, especially Sudan, Congo-Brazzaville, Burundi, the United Arab Republic, Algeria, and Tanzania, but also in relatively "moderate Kenya" where Kenyatta said he was "revolted" by the intervention. Only three African leaders—Tsiranana of Madagascar, Wachuku of Nigeria, and Thiam of Senegal—publicly dissociated themselves from these protests. The upshot was that the Bunia-Watsa plan (a jump on the airfield at Bunia, then a drive via commandeered vehicles to Watsu 200 miles to the north) was abandoned. The Belgians were even more anxious to get out than the Americans, although both seem to have arrived at the same conclusion. Another factor influencing them was poor intelligence regarding the whereabouts of the remaining whites.[116]

Taking into account the various miscalculations, American officials still insist the Stanleyville airlift was successful. As I have indicated, no *conclusive* refutation of this view is possible if one accepts the basic goals of the policy-makers: counterrevolution and the safety of American nationals and other whites. (A lesser objective—good African relations—was damaged, but only temporarily.) The Stanleyville airlift must be judged within the overall context of American policy. Indeed, it was a fitting symbol of that policy as it had developed over the previous four years. In July 1960, instability in the Congo caused the Belgians to intervene militarily in order to protect their "humanitarian" and political interests. In November 1964, the Americans joined them.

[115] For instance, Adlai Stevenson was stunned. Attwood, pp. 227, 232.

[116] CRISP, *Congo 1964,* pp. 491–492, 409; Reed, pp. 271–272. Some details were provided in author interviews.

PART III

EVALUATION

CHAPTER VIII

A Critique of the Basic Assumptions of American Congo Policy

The International Communist Threat: Moderate Republican and Liberal Democratic Versions

All three U.S. Administrations viewed the Soviets—and, more remotely, the Chinese—as having the desire and potential to exert massive influence over the Congo and its neighbors. Such a development, it was thought, would jeopardize Western access to strategic raw materials and upset the world balance of political power.

The Moderate Republican exposition emphasized the wildness and instability of the new states and their consequent openness to external subversion. In the Congo this gave rise to interpretations of political behavior and allegations of Soviet influence that can be directly investigated—and challenged.

American officials tended to reduce Lumumba's stubborn anti-colonialism to personal psychopathology. They confused a disorderly, but fiercely independent, nationalism with absence of political capacity and purposiveness. When the Prime Minister reacted to King Baudouin's patronizing Independence Day speech; when his government turned to the U.S., and then to the U.N., the Afro-Asians, and the Soviets in its effort to remove Belgian forces from its cities; when Lumumba denounced Belgian "aggression" in front of an American Under Secretary of State after learning of a paratroop attack on Congo army barracks; when he threatened to dispense with the U.N. on account of its lack of action in

Katanga—Ambassador Timberlake and his superiors discerned a "personally unstable," "erratic," "unpredictable," "self-contradictory," mentally ill individual. Most students of the Congo are aware of Lumumba's personal idiosyncracies and weaknesses, but they do not make these factors bear such a large part of the burden of historical explanation. Lumumba's behavior is primarily traced to his passion for Congolese sovereignty and unity:

> As Premier of the Congo he could understandably only see the three urgent problems facing him in the few fatal weeks that followed independence—to put down the revolt of the *Force Publique;* to get the Belgians out; and to put an end to Katanga's secession.[1]
>
> Almost opportunistic in his means, Lumumba was fundamentally doctrinaire in his ends. Yet in so being, his tactics were always consistent within his overall strategy. To the outside world he appeared ambivalent and impulsive; in his own mind, however, Lumumba never deviated from his objectives.[2]

Certainly Lumumba's mercurial temperament, blind self-confidence, and inexperience made him more obdurate when the going got rough. But even here there was an important admixture of political judgment. As Legum asks,

> What alternatives were open to Lumumba? Fold his arms and hope that sooner or later negotiations might succeed; and meanwhile? Face the fragmentation of his government's authority and power, as well as his own.[3]

By failing to understand the political force of nationalism, the Moderate Republican anti-Communist faction exaggerated Lumumba's personal weaknesses and his vulnerability to external domination.

Related to this was the Americans' fear of "Communist" advisers in Lumumba's entourage. Since Lumumba was so unstable, it was thought that his closest assistants might be able to accumulate

[1] In Lumumba, p. xv.
[2] Morgan, "Politics in the Pursuit of Power," p. 167.
[3] Lumumba, p. xvii.

power. And since nationalism was not appreciated, a fairly heterogeneous group of leftists could seem to be imbued with a common and externally oriented purpose. Consider Serge Michel, a Marxist, but one who had openly and publicly condemned the Soviet's suppression of the Hungarian revolt, and a man who seems to have been a moderating and anti-Soviet influence in Lumumba's councils. According to Hoskyns:

> The nearest thing to "Communist" advice which Lumumba received at this time seems to have come from the Guinea diplomats in Leopoldville, and there is considerable evidence to suggest that they were responsible for some of his more intransigent statements. Michel, far from endorsing their advice, bitterly opposed it, and in a report on the subject which he wrote for the GPRA he accused the Guineans of playing the Russian game and stated that their efforts served to condemn Lumumba "more than is own mistakes." [4]

Another reputed "Communist" infiltrator was Mme. Andrée Blouin, Lumumba's chief of protocol. There is little doubt that she encouraged Lumumba's military opposition to U.N. policy, that she sometimes protected him from visitors with more moderate views, and that she was willing to appeal to Communist powers. But there is no convincing evidence that she was, as some of her Congolese and American opponents charged, "an agent of international Communism." Professor Herbert Weiss was closely acquainted with her activities as an aide of Gizenga in the period immediately preceding Independence. He portrays her as a militant African nationalist and strongly implies that the charges against her were invented by Gizenga's political opponents:

> For her, Gizenga was the leader [of the Parti Solidaire Africain] and she expected him to be followed in the manner of a Sekou Touré or a Kwame Nkrumah. This promptly resulted in some of the other leaders looking upon her as an opponent. . . .
>
> The attacks on Blouin were in part the result of a general decline in cohesion among the leaders. As she was in a spectacular and vul-

[4] Hoskyns, *The Congo Since Independence*, pp. 188–189.

nerable position and almost everyone felt inhibited about attacking Gizenga himself, she thus became "the king's evil councillor" and in a sense a scapegoat.[5]

Andrée Blouin's political contribution to the election campaign of Spring 1960 does not seem to mark her as a Soviet agent. She "introduced ideas that had proved eminently successful in Guinea, for instance, the organization of women, *investissement humain* (voluntary work), militancy against traditional chiefs, and something approaching total discipline." [6] Her autobiography indicates that her political *prise de conscience* occurred during the Independence struggle in Guinea, that it was very much bound up with her *prise de conscience* as a black African, that she was particularly interested in women's rights, and that she was on good terms with a number of African leaders in former French Equatorial Africa.[7] Herbert Weiss, who interviewed her and observed her behavior during the crisis, writes:

> My impression as to her political position was that she was more of a left wing political adventurer than a disciplined member of any group whatsoever. I know that she got into hot water with the Guineans and I am almost certain the same thing occurred later with regard to the Algerians. She lived in Algiers for some time after her stay in the Congo. Thereafter she seems to have gone to Switzerland. . . . She got into hot water with the Guineans at a time when a Communist agent who was disciplined would not have done so. In fact, as I recall, she planted the Guinean flag in front of her house in Leopoldville and a group of Guinean soldiers were sent to the house to pull it down.[8]

In her month-and-a-half as Lumumba's chief of protocol, she was certainly "flamboyant and very much in view and did talk a rather radical, neutralist language, and also seemed friendly to some of

[5] Weiss, pp. 178–179.

[6] *Ibid.*

[7] *La Wallonie,* a Belgian weekly, published the autobiography in a series of issues from October 21–22, 1961, through Feb. 3–4, 1962. On Mme. Blouin's political development, the articles from Nov. 25–26 are most important.

[8] Letter to the author, July 17, 1970.

the Soviet bloc diplomats, and certainly unfriendly to Western ones." That she did not have any serious policy-making influence is attested to by several observers: Weiss, Jane Rouch, Kashamura, Blouin herself.[9]

Misconceptions begat further misconceptions which had the effect of strengthening the original error. Ambasador Timberlake held "Communist" advisers responsible for Minister of Information Kashamura's inflammatory, antiwhite programming on the national radio. But it would seem that Kashamura's own personality is a sufficient explanation of his behavior. After Lumumba was deposed, Gizenga appointed Kashamura to head the government of Kivu Province. There, his encouragement of antiwhite and anti-opposition brutality shocked and dismayed his Lumumbist colleagues—who were receiving Soviet support—and he was never again an important force in Lumumbist politics.[10]

The official contention that Lumumba's behavior could be explained "in no other way" than by reference to a palace conspiracy is demonstrably false. His policies were rationally related to the militant nationalism which was his basic political formula. His "Communist" advisers like Michel and Blouin furnished conflicting recommendations. Many of those who were close to him during August 1960 were Congolese nationalists.[11] Although Mme. Blouin appears to have discouraged Western access to the Prime Minister, Lumumba was in constant touch with Nkrumah, who urged him not to accept Soviet technicians lest that "provoke a supply of counter-technicians to rebel forces."[12] Even when Lumumba accepted Soviet assistance, African diplomats in Leopoldville hoped that the probable failure of the offensive in Kasai and Katanga would "bring Lumumba round to the idea of compromise and negotia-

[9] Quotes are from *ibid.* See aslo Jane Rouch, *En cage avec Lumumba* (Paris, 1961), pp. 70, 132, 160; Anicet Kashamura, *De Lumumba aux colonels* (Paris, 1966), p. 65; Mme. Blouin in *La Wallonie,* Jan. 27–28, 1962.

[10] Verhaegen, *Congo 1961,* pp. 210–212; Hoskyns, *The Congo Since Independence,* pp. 378, 500.

[11] Hoskyns, *The Congo Since Independence,* p. 188.

[12] Nkrumah, *Challenge of the Congo,* pp. 33–34.

tion." And in fact, after the initial military reverses in Kasai, African diplomats found Lumumba "more ready to listen and more willing to treat with the United Nations." [13] This is hardly consistent with the theory of occult influence.

But the Eisenhower Administration regarded Lumumba's acceptance of Soviet military aid as the last of a series of actions tending to prove "Communist influence." The consequences of this judgment frustrated African hopes for some sort of accommodation between Lumumba's objectives and those of the U.N. There remains only the consensus of powerless scholars and independent observers: "The extent to which [Lumumba's] regime was dependent either on Communist advice or support was certainly exaggerated [by Western governments]." [14]

Liberal anti-Communism had more sympathy for, and a better understanding of, nationalism. It emphasized the "progressive" yearnings that lay beneath the untidy surface of Third World politics—the new nationalists were more rational than they seemed and had some capacity to resist external blandishments. In ferreting out Communist influence, the liberals were aware of the distinctions between "Soviet Communist," "Marxist," and "Leftist." Yet since the new leaders were struggling to control essentially weak states, it was felt that those who allied themselves with Soviet power risked domination. Subversion was simply a more difficult, tortuous, long-run, perhaps incomplete process than the conservative anti-Communist had envisioned. *The liberal variant indicated what would happen in the Congo if a Lumumbist was in power long enough.* Such a hypothetical formulation cannot be refuted by an accumulation of discrete facts. It will be necessary to present an alternative theory of "Lumumbism," and to introduce the comparative dimension.

The personal and political development of Patrice Lumumba—and that section of the political elite which supported him—was

[13] Hoskyns, *The Congo Since Independence*, pp. 193–195.
[14] *Ibid.*, p. 196; see also Legum in Lumumba, pp. vii–xxix.

conditioned by the discovery that equality and dignity could never be achieved within a framework of foreign political control.[15] Lumumba's thinking evolved, during the late fifties, from enthusiastic assimilationism to militant nationalism. The MNC-L program envisioned a period of wide-ranging national self-assertion, albeit limited by the colonial legacy of economic and administrative structures: Africanization, national unity, single party democracy, a presidential system, economic planning, human investment, revision of the statute of certain foreign companies (but not nationalization), search for new markets and protection of infant industries for the treatment of raw materials, nationalization of Lovanium University, "positive neutralism" in foreign policy. . . .[16] More than its pretty bourgeois populism (aid to the middle class, cooperatives, human investment, Lumumba's unsuccessful efforts to obtain a pre-Independence amnesty and stem the tide of pay raises for privileged politicians),[17] the MNC-L's nationalism constituted its dynamism and gave it such an intransigent allure. Even after the battle for Independence had been won, in January 1960, Lumumba's main issues revolved around the integrity of the national system and not what economic and social forms the new state would take.[18]

For Lumumba, "positive neutralism" was not a temporary expedient or a reflex adoption of a familiar political incantation; it was an integral part of his whole political approach. As he explained in a radio speech following one of his appeals to the Soviet Union in July 1960:

15 In analyzing the Lumumbists, the following secondary sources have helped to illuminate the primary material: Sartre's preface in Van Lierde; Merlier, *Le Congo,* pp. 185–213; Verhaegen, "Lutte des classes au Congo"; Lumumba; and Morgan.

16 Gérard-Libois and Verhaegen, *Congo 1960,* pp. 565–590; see also *ibid.,* pp. 28, 52, 174–176, 272, 277–280, 297–298, 346–347, 592–608.

17 *Ibid.,* pp. 329–330, 647. The propaganda of rural Messianic movements promised that on Independence Day the prisons would be opened. Lumumba's effort to realize this shows his sensitivity to the rural masses.

18 Thus, the major issues in the Spring of 1960 were Africanization, a presidential system, and the presence of Belgian forces.

We have said that if there were no means of obtaining satisfaction immediately, we were going to appeal to Soviet and Afro-Asian troops. We will never be Communists and we are not Communists, contrary to the campaign of destruction and obstruction that the enemies of our independence have led across the country. We are just Africans. We don't want to undergo any external influence, we want nothing from either doctrines of Western importation, or Russian, or American. The Congo remains the Congo. . . . *We don't want to get out of one dictatorship to fall under another dictatorship.* [Emphasis added.] [19]

If Lumumba called in Soviet planes, it was because his nationalist passion overstepped the bounds of political realism. By bringing in the Soviets to redress the balance against the Belgians and the Western-dominated United Nations, he practiced positive neutralism to the hilt—and guaranteed his own downfall. In his last public statements, Lumumba broaches an economic interpretation of Western policy, but he also reasserts the program of June 1960, including positive neutralism.[20]

In economic terms, it is useful to view Lumumbist nationalism as the political expression of an administrative bourgeoisie which depends upon Western technicians and investments for a large portion of its means, and which cannot anticipate an adequate substitute from "the East," i.e., a more or less complete changeover involving 10,000 technicians and billions of dollars. In this respect, the choice in the Congo has never been between a Western-dominated regime and an Eastern-dominated one, but rather between political forces which were in different degrees dependent upon Western favor. The Lumumbist half-challenge to the West was simply an effort to increase the Congo's leverage by varying its international sponsors and inaugurating a period of national self-assertion. In the absence of modern radical organizations which could support a program of socialist austerity, and which could mobilize the masses, the Lumumbists could not surpass the

[19] Van Lierde, p. 257.

[20] *Ibid.*, pp. 395–397; Gérard-Libois and Verhaegen, *Congo 1960,* pp. 833–834, 842–845.

limitations of their class and historical conditioning. Nothing shows this more clearly than Lumumba's performance in 1960.

Under the most trying conditions, Lumumba continued to act on the basis of his repeated assertion that "the Congo needs the European presence, foreign capital, and technicians." In spite of his pre-Independence difficulties with the Belgians, he offered the Foreign Affairs Ministry to two politicians generally considered favorable to the West, Kasavubu and Bomboko, and made an Independence Eve appeal for young Belgian technicians and teachers and also investors. On July 19, with thousands of Belgian troops occupying his country, Lumumba told a Stanleyville audience that he was for rapid Africanization of the civil service with Europeans staying on as advisers to the top officials. At the same time he appealed for order, especially respect for Europeans. In a radio speech of the 22nd, he denounced the "capitalists" who sustained Tshombe and announced his forthcoming visit to the U.S., where he envisioned contacts in many circles regarding the problems of industrialization. He had just signed an economic agreement with a Wall Street adventurer (Detwiler), and he was to seek economic and technical assistance, including military training for officers, in Washington, Ottawa, and London. Although he returned to the Congo disillusioned with Detwiler and disappointed by his inability to procure bilateral assistance outside the framework of the United Nations, he praised America's *"compréhension"* and noted "very constructive conversations with the American government which has assured me of all necessary aid for the Congo." He went on to speak of his contacts with American financial circles and of the U.S. Independence Day gift of 300 scholarships. In the same Leopoldville press conference, he distinguished between the Belgian government and people, said the Congo would welcome loyal technical assistants from the United States, Russia, France, Belgium, Ghana, Guinea—everywhere. He noted there were still Belgians in his government. On August 22nd he recalled Belgian magistrates and teachers for the fall. Indeed, Lumumba's last spoken message was full of the traditional assurances to European investors and technicians, even though it accused European economic interests of having sabotaged his government.[21]

The Lumumbists' partial dependence on the West had a psychological aspect as well. Like other African leaders, they had been *évolués,* i.e., they had internalized many Belgian and Western values. De Vos has Lumumba telling his European friends in 1959 that "we are formed in your image," and offers some confirming evidence in Lumumba's early mistrust of Communism. In 1956, during a sojourn in Belgium, Lumumba made contact with all political parties, but shied away from the Communists because "it has often been explained to him that they are dangerous and, in fact, they appear to him too well informed on his personal situation in the Congo." Although he was eventually to accept instrumental aid from Communist countries, Lumumba seems to have retained his distrust of Communism. In New York during July 1960, he declared, "In Africa everything that is progressive, that tends toward progress, is characterized as Communist, destructive." And in Leopoldville he insisted, "We will never be Communists and we are not Communists . . . we are simply Africans." [22] His speeches are full of homages to the American and French revolutions, to the American system of democracy.[23] Drawn to the very powers he had to challenge, Lumumba *insisted* on their respect. Thus in his speech recounting the results of his trip to the United States, he placed great emphasis on the warmth and dignity of his American reception, that he was treated as a chief of state—replete with 19-gun salute—that he was lodged over the protests of Belgium in Blair House, where "noted guests of the White House" stay:

The Head of the Congo Government, who is presented as anti-white, a destroyer, has been received on an equal footing by all the chiefs of

[21] Gérard-Libois and Verhaegen, *Congo 1960,* p. 272; Van Lierde, pp. 196, 246, 257–259; Gérard-Libois and Verhaegen, *Congo 1960,* pp. 635, 649, 588–591, 608; Van Lierde, pp. 395–397.

[22] De Vos, pp. 108, 50; Van Lierde, pp. 271, 257.

[23] Van Lierde, pp. 259, 271, 395, provide characteristic examples.

state of the Western countries [that he had just visited, namely, the U.S., Canada, and Britain].[24]

For along with their militance and national pride, the MNC-L leaders shared the Congolese elite's thirst for:

equality, assimilation, what Sartre has very justly called the "semi-Africanization" of cadres. That is why the Congolese bourgeoisie did not at all desire the departure of the whites, since it was precisely their presence which gave prestige to the professional and social hierarchy in which they burned to be integrated.[25]

In pursuing his policy of positive neutralism, Lumumba identified closely with Ghana and Guinea and with Pan-Africanist ideology.[26] His ideas of a presidential system and human investment seem to have been largely inspired by the Ghanaian and Guinean examples.[27] He was particularly close to Nkrumah, and they had secretly agreed, on August 8, 1960, to establish a confederation "with the approval of the governments and peoples of their respective states." [28] He clearly preferred African political and military assistance to the greatest extent possible. Having just emerged from the struggle for formal independence, a struggle which had received the support of existing African states, it was natural that he would anticipate a mutuality of continental interests. When the United Nations failed to serve his conception of national interest he toured six African countries, "first to try to persuade them to bring maximum pressure on Hammarskjold to deal with the Katanga situation and second, if this failed, to get their promise to give him military aid outside the United Nations to end Katanga secession." He also organized a summit conference of independent African states in Leopoldville August 25–30, 1960, to consider these questions further. He constantly sought to strengthen the African role in the U.N. operation. When, as a last resort, he turned to the Soviet Union for limited military assistance, he still

24 Gérard-Libois and Verhaegen, *Congo 1960,* pp. 590–591.
25 Verhaegen, "Lutte des classes au Congo," p. 35.
26 Van Lierde, pp. 235, 248; De Vos, pp. 69–70, 218–219.
27 Gérard-Libois and Verhaegen, *Congo 1960,* pp. 566–567, 585, 588.
28 Nkrumah, *Challenge of the Congo,* pp. 29–32.

kept in touch with representatives of the African states who were trying to mediate between Lumumba and Hammarskjold. They hoped to persuade the U.N. of the seriousness of the Katanga situation and also to convince Lumumba that the attack on Katanga was unlikely to be successful and was "prejudicing the neutrality of the Congo." Upon discovering their reaction, Lumumba was "more ready to listen and more willing to treat with the United Nations." [29]

In his preface to *La Pensée politique de Patrice Lumumba,* Sartre asks why "big capital and banking were dead set against a government whose leader never stopped repeating that he would not touch existing investments and would solicit new ones." He concludes that Lumumba had a certain openness to the aspirations of the masses—his class's illusion of universality had become his "personal passion"—so the capitalists and *évolués* feared "the radicalization of Lumumba by the masses." [30] But the performance of Lumumba's collaborators and successors in the Eastern rebellion seems to belie this possibility, as well as any drastic change in foreign policy. Before, during and after the rebellion they maintained the MNC-L ideology and program, including positive neutralism.[31] As late as November 1962 the MNC-L sent President Kennedy a telegram thanking him for American aid and warning of a government threat to close parliament.[32] Subsequent anti-Americanism in the rebellion seems largely situational. The Eastern rebellion leaders dabbled with Tshombe before his return from exile,[33] pleaded with Brussels for Belgian support,[34] and told a CRISP interviewer in 1966, "We are for positive neutralism and

[29] Hoskyns, *The Congo Since Independence,* pp. 165, 194–195.

[30] Van Lierde, pp. iii, iv, xlii–xliii.

[31] Ideology before the Rebellion appears in Beys, Gendebien, and Verhaegen, *Congo 1963,* pp. 210–230; *Courrier Africain,* Feb. 18, 1967, pp. 3–17, contains interviews with the CNL leaders in 1966.

[32] Gérard-Libois and Verhaegen, *Congo 1962,* pp. 78–79.

[33] CRISP, *Congo 1964,* pp. 137–138.

[34] *Courrier Africain,* Feb. 18, 1967, pp. 33–37, reproduces Gbenye's proposals at the moment of his quiet visit with Spaak in Aug. 1964.

nonalignment but with a priority of friendship for Belgium."[35] During the rebellion, the CNL established its closest diplomatic relations with about 10 African states.[36]

The Gizenga branch of the PSA seems to have had a more radical *style* and somewhat greater openness to "Eastern" influences than the MNC-L (As suggested earlier, this may reflect the special economic structure in Kwilu, or it may result from the party leaders' syndical and Belgian Socialist past).[37] In 1959 the PSA position was quite as *"petit-bourgeois"* as the other pro-Lumumba parties.[38] But its program did contain a reference to "the creation of collective peasant communities" which disturbed some of the moderate members (they would have preferred the word "co-operative").[39] Gizenga's travels from mid-December 1959–March 2, 1960, included stopovers in West Germany, Eastern Europe, Moscow, Paris, and Guinea. Apparently, he spent most of his time in Eastern Europe and Guinea. This was one of several missions abroad undertaken by members of the ABAKO-PSA cartel in 1959. Other delegations were sent to Brazzaville, West Africa, and Egypt, "in order to acquaint African leaders with the position of the cartel and to sound them out about the possibilities of forming a provisional government in exile."[40] Upon his return, Gizenga reiterated his policy of positive neutralism and respect for Belgian interests.[41] However, in view of his subsequent behavior it would

35 *Ibid.*, p. 17.

36 CRISP, *Congo 1964*, pp. 348 ff.

37 The Bapende and Bambunda palm cutters had a history of revolt against the great plantations. See above, pp. 20–21. Many PSA leaders had participated in *Action Socialiste*, the Belgian Socialist Party study group before Independence. Union influence was also important. Gizenga had been the head of a small, *independent* (cf. Adoula) union of teachers in Catholic schools. Weiss, pp. 79, 81–82, 93.

38 Herbert Weiss and Benoît Verhaegen (eds.), *Parti Solidaire Africain: Documents 1959–1960* (Brussels, 1963), pp. 15–18.

39 Weiss, *Political Protest in the Congo*, p. 161. With regard to radical style, note PSA leader Gabriel Yumbu's description of university students as "neocolonialists" during the Belgo-Congolese Economic Roundtable in 1960. *Ibid.*, p. 158.

40 *Ibid.*, pp. 126–130, 160.

41 Weiss and Verhaegen, *Parti Solidaire Africain*, pp. 263–272.

appear that he was impressed by his trip to Eastern Europe. In July, he was less than circumspect in his praise for Russian policy in Africa.[42] And when Lumumba was overthrown, Gizenga wrote to Peking requesting—among other things—volunteers, fighter planes, tanks, money and rice.[43] During 1961 a small but significant number of PSA-Gizenga leaders sojurned in China.[44] One of them, Felix-José Mukulubundu, returned to Stanleyville in late 1961 and became "officer-adviser on ideological life" in the Gizengist army. He drafted an oath of loyalty to the "worker and peasant government" and the "national and popular army." [45] A few of the China visitors were involved later in the Mulelist revolt, the only authentically radical movement the Congo has known.[46] Certain policies of the Gizengist regimes in Stanleyville have been regarded as manifestations of a radical will, especially the maintenance of soldier councils in the Army's Third Group (these had been set up during the mutiny),[47] Africanization of the private sector,[48] and concentration on violent revolution in Katanga rather than on the humdrum cares of daily administration.[49]

Yet Gizenga's ideology, and *praxis* in Stanleyville, were within the essential bounds of Lumumbism. Too much should not be read into certain militant-sounding sections of the PSA program. As a long-time associate of Gizenga explained, "the more radical vocabulary" could be the result of a leader having read speeches by Nehru and Nkrumah or having picked up a Czechoslovakian commercial brochure at his office in a trade ministry. More important,

> In economics we used the word collectivization and were convinced that a foreign-controlled economy was not good and would not respond to the aspirations of the masses whose support we asked; but economic

[42] Gérard-Libois and Verhaegen, *Congo 1960,* p. 635.

[43] Fritz Schatten, *Communism in Africa* (New York, 1966), p. 211.

[44] Verhaegen, *Rébellions,* II, 72; *Rébellions,* I, 176–178; 68–71.

[45] Verhaegen, *Rébellions,* II, 184.

[46] See above, n. 44.

[47] Described briefly in Benoît Verhaegen, "L'Armée Nationale Congolaise," *Etudes Congolaises,* X (July–Aug., 1967), 11.

[48] Sartre in Van Lierde, pp. xl–xli.

[49] Verhaegen, *Rébellions,* II, 188–189.

problems were not discussed in depth and would be only after we had power. Even when he went to Stanleyville Gizenga always avoided the economic problem since it could provoke premature disunity.

Concerning Gizenga's program of May 1961, Merlier justly writes:

[it] takes up again the program of Lumumba: neutralism, respect for private property, no nationalizations, development of the middle class with the help of small rural industries. . . .[50]

The author recently studied the organization and functioning of public institutions in Stanleyville during the Gizenga period. He found no evidence of radicalization in the organization of administration, attitudes toward foreign technicians, or in the educational process.[51] Although there was considerable violence and insecurity in the Eastern Congo in 1961, it was not directed by Gizenga who, to the contrary, tried to assure administrative and economic continuity.[52] The soldier councils were a legacy of the mutiny, not an innovation. One of Gizenga's closest collaborators in Stanleyville admits that the lack of a strategy for political mobilization of the masses was a great weakness of the dissident regime. The only Africanization in the private sector was the *provisional* transfer of abandoned plantations to African management. If an anti-Katanga obsession is to be the criterion for radicalism, then Lumumba was easily the most radical of all the Congolese leaders.

Gizenga was certainly more interested than many others in bringing in an Eastern counterweight, but this did not mean he was willing to abandon positive neutralism. In the absence of Kasavubu and Lumumba, in July 1960, he presided at a cabinet meeting which weighed an appeal to foreign forces. When Foreign Minister Bomboko suggested American troops, Gizenga took the initiative

50 Merlier, *Le Congo,* p. 337.

51 Authors' questionnaires were administered in several institutions during May 1970. Complementary material from provincial archives and interviews is found in Pius Imbata, "Organisation et fonctionnement des services administratifs en Province Orientale sous le régime Gizenga 1960–1961," (unpublished mémoire for Licence, Université Libre du Congo, July 1971), *passim.*

52 Merlier, *Le Congo,* pp. 335–337; Verhaegen, *Rébellions,* II, 135–190.

in contacting the US Ambassador. After Timberlake had joined the discussion, Gizenga and two other ministers signed a formal request for 3,000 American troops.[53] A day earlier, he appears to have been engaged in conversations with Belgian officials looking toward a clearing operation at the port of Matadi (Gizenga feared a food riot in Leopoldville where supplies were scarce). When Belgian forces subsequently attacked Matadi, Gizenga was accused by the *moderate* faction of PSA of having prepared the intervention.[54] During the summer of 1960, the foreigners closest to Gizenga were Madame Blouin and the Guineans, neither of whom can be considered as a surrogate for Moscow or Peking.

From Stanleyville, Gizenga reiterated his nonalignment and positive neutralism. Shortly after Lumumba's death he made this appeal to the U.S.,

> We welcome with a certain optimism the change of government which has just taken place in the United States of America. We form the most ardent wishes that Mr. John Kennedy, the new President of the United States of America, will understand that the West will be saved insofar as Africa will be entirely liberated and kept out of the Cold War and competition between the blocs.[55]

In a series of press interviews in 1961, he said he would accept aid from all countries if it were granted without strings. Recalling his earlier appeal for American military aid, he observed that those who had refused help had pushed Lumumba and him toward the Russians—and had then accused them of Communism. He disclaimed foreign assistance for his Stanleyville regime (in fact, he received very little), reiterating the concept of an open door for external aid.[56] Like Lumumba, Gizenga identified strongly with African and Third World anticolonialism. In Stanleyville his main supporters were some of the Casablanca powers, especially the

[53] Ganshof van der Meersch, pp. 426, 469.

[54] Gérard-Libois and Verhaegen, *Congo 1960,* pp. 478–484. Gizenga's role was clarified by Verhaegen in a conversation with the author.

[55] Verhaegen, *Congo 1961,* pp. 153–154.

[56] *Ibid.,* pp. 152–154, 159–160, 176–180.

United Arab Republic.[57] During March 1961 he expelled five Communist journalists.[58] While in the Adoula government he attended the Belgrade Conference of Non-Aligned States, with Adoula, and associated himself with the neutralist line of Nasser and Nehru.[59]

In our search for possible vehicles of outside Communist domination, we come at last to Mulele and his small group of Chinese-trained assistants. So little is known about this group's radical commitment that one must be satisfied with just a few observations:

(1) Their limited base (Kwilu) meant that they would not dominate a potential Lumumbist government.

(2) Past experience of anti-Western, Communist revolutions in small countries outside the periphery of Soviet military power indicates strong nationalist influences, e.g., Castro, Ho Chi Minh. The Mulelists' orientation toward China, their related self-reliance in revolutionary action, and the refractory nature of Congolese society would no doubt heighten the tendency toward nationalist adaption. Whether basic American interests would be jeopardized by a hypothetical Mulelist national government—e.g., through construction of hostile military bases, withdrawal of crucial natural resources—would seem to depend on the reaction of the West to the revolution.

(3) According to two of his closest associates, Mulele's political position was distinguished from that of other Lumumbists by two main characteristics: strategic sophistication and greater skepticism about Western policies. A colleague from prerebellion days recalled,

> Regarding strategy he always weighed the elements of force in a situation, saw repressive responses to moral appeals and the need to prepare oneself. He was not satisfied with Gizenga's attempt to win through parliamentary justifications. He saw the need to wage war.

[57] *Ibid.*, pp. 186–187; Hoskyns, *The Congo Since Independence*, pp. 299, 310–312.

[58] *Wall Street Journal*, March 8, 1961, p. 14; *Christian Science Monitor*, Mar. 1, 1961, p. 2.

[59] Verhaegen, *Congo 1961*, pp. 177–178, 438.

He was not so close-minded to "Communist countries" as others, carrying skepticism about Belgian teachings further. For example, he would say that for Congolese there was an "iron curtain" in Belgium.

By 1964 Mulele was radical enough to spark the Kwilu rebellion. But he did not think of himself as being committed to a foreign power's way of looking at politics. According to a close collaborator in the *maquis,* he advocated a particularly *national* brand of Communism:

> With regard to Russian and Chinese Communism, Mulele was well acquainted with the ideological divergences of the two great powers of world Communism and discussed them with his partisans, but he had a very personal attitude. According to him the Soviet system had succeeded but it was valid only in the Soviet context. The Chinese, to the contrary, had not yet succeeded, but the system doubtlessly also contained interesting elements. Concerning the Congo and Africa, it was necessary to observe the Soviet and Chinese systems but not to copy them slavishly, given that for the Chinese system the results were not yet known and for the Soviet system it was a question of a finished system having resolved its own problems. Thus an attitude of observation and prudence regarding these two systems and the Sino-Soviet ideological conflict.[60]

In a prescient, but overly indirect criticism of U.S.-Congo policy in August 1960, Senator Mike Mansfield cautioned against "a certain eagerness to project into Africa the many ramifications of the Cold War and other power rivalries which now plague the rest of the world." He went on,

> The field is wide open for that game at the moment. Africa is in transition and its leadership has only limited experience. But transitions are not forever and those who have learned the way to national independence are equipped to learn other matters. Most important, I believe the emerging African peoples have had enough of the roles of pawns moved on the chessboards of others. They will not meekly

[60] CRISP, *Congo 1965* (Brussels, 1966), p. 107.

assume that role again and they will react against those who seek to return them to it.[61]

On September 15, 1960, Averell Harriman held an interesting press conference in Leopoldville. Touring Africa on behalf of the Democratic presidential candidate, he had obtained an interview with Lumumba. The deposed Prime Minister had said, Harriman related, that he was not a Communist and that he viewed Communist imperialism as a danger, just as colonialism was. According to the American diplomat, Lumumba thought he could use the Russians and claimed 80 percent of the people were behind him. However, Harriman doubted that Lumumba could successfully outmaneuver the Russians.[62]

An analysis of the Cold War in the Third World also suggests the inadequacy of liberal anti-Communist perspectives. The most conspicuous Soviet "successes" have been products of extraordinary situations: wartime occupation (North Korea) or some combination of indigenous Communist strength and American economic and military intervention on behalf of a discredited status quo (Cuba and Vietnam). These conditions did not obtain in the Congo, and they do not presently exist in other parts of the Third World. Furthermore, under conditions of nuclear stalemate, quasi-detente, and polycentrism, even the special cases appear increasingly as net drains on Soviet power. And they do not always exclude good relations with the U.S. (viz., the recurrent overtures of the Cuban government for a rapprochement).

Soviet prospects in the Congo may *look* a little brighter if one takes into account some additional Afro-Asian nations which have earned the nebulous Western classification, "Soviet-influenced," especially the United Arab Republic, Syria, Algeria, Iraq, and Guinea. However, it remains to be shown that the Soviets have materially improved their international position through their relations with these countries. Again, there is much evidence that the

61 *Congressional Record,* Aug. 29, 1960, pp. 18122–18125.

62 *Libre Belgique,* Sept. 16, 1960, p. 5.

clients constitute a net burden on their patron, the Soviet Union, and that they do not rule out good relations with America.

In the Middle East, there have been significant Communist parties, recurrent Western military interventions, and a long record of American assistance to Israel. Yet fervent nationalist leaders like Nasser have maintained a foreign policy of "positive neutralism" (including the promotion of local revolutions), even while absorbing large amounts of Soviet aid. Theodore Draper has commented,

> The new nationalism of the new nations is sometimes about all that holds them together, and the only virtue they have to sell. As a result, no nationalism is as obsessive and single-minded as the latest one. The great powers which seek to use them must do so through playing on a species of primitive self-interest that is far more difficult to control than that of the old-style client states or the new variety of satellite states. The Soviet Union, for example, wooed Nasser's Egypt more by serving Egypt's nationalistic interests than by getting Egypt to serve its own. But Egypt is neither an old-fashioned client state nor a newfangled satellite. It represents a rather new-style "give-me" nationalism; Gamal Abdel Nasser has been one of the world's great practitioners of the new golden rule that it is better—for the great powers—to give than to receive.[63]

According to John Badeau, a noted Middle East scholar and Ambassador to the United Arab Republic in the Kennedy Administration,

> Despite the growth and variety of Soviet activity in the area, a Russian takeover of any Middle Eastern state has not yet occurred. It is noteworthy that after a decade of Soviet influence no Arab country can properly be called a Soviet satellite, nor has any permitted a Communist party to exist, or irrevocably lost a significant measure of its freedom of action to the Soviets. . . .
>
> No Arab government has been consistently hostile to the United States (except when the Arab-Israel issue is in balance) or has al-

[63] Theodore Draper, *Israel and World Politics* (New York, 1968), pp. 128–129.

ways pursued policies at variance with American interests. Even those states which have caused the deepest misgivings have at times taken stands helpful to the American position. President Nasser raised the first Arab voice publicly and vigorously to protest the Soviet resumption of nuclear testing when he spoke before the conference of nonaligned states at Belgrade in 1961. He ceased supplying arms to the Congo rebels when it became apparent that they were losing the struggle and his relations with the United States were in jeopardy. Soviet attempts to obtain acceptance for the existence of Communist parties in the revolutionary Arab states have been consistently rebuffed, despite the presence of large Soviet-aid programs.[64]

Badeau believes that nonalignment has expressed itself in "pendular oscillation between East and West rather than in maintaining a fixed position between the two." He shows that this oscillation does not refer to such tangibles as military bases, defense pacts, resource concessions, political systems, or the Arab nationalists' definition of vital interests in foreign policy. For the giver, he says, the return on foreign aid is largely diplomatic and rhetorical.[65] (Benefiting from the largest Soviet-aid program in the Third World, for example, President Nasser kindly endorsed the Soviet invasion of Czechoslovakia.) "Prestige" is not unimportant in world affairs, *because it may be a means toward more substantial political objectives*. But two decades of experience in the Middle East indicate there is almost no connection between prestige gains and power gains.

From the point of view of selfish national interest, Soviet aid to Middle Eastern "progressives" may well be a misallocation of resources. A larger increment to national power might result from spending on internal needs—the expansion of Soviet productive and military potential and providing an answer to the revolution of rising expectations among Soviet consumers. The Arab-Israeli war of June 1967, highlighted the risks involved in unilateral aid to fundamentally uncontrollable new nationalisms. These risks

64 John S. Badeau, *The American Approach to the Arab World* (New York, 1968), pp. 23, 103.

65 *Ibid.*

were not only financial or relative to prestige; they involved the peace of the world and the national security of the Soviet Union.[66]

Guinea provides another instance in which particularly unfavorable experiences with the West led to a large Soviet aid presence, but not to Soviet control. Victimized by a Western diplomatic and aid boycott, President Touré accepted a $100-million Soviet-bloc aid package, established a very strong trade relationship with bloc countries, and welcomed about 1,500 Communist technicians. Nevertheless, American businessmen with investments in Guinea retained their "faith in Touré's good will and common sense." [67] In 1961, a new American Ambassador found Touré eager to tap Western resources for economic development. In addition, the very presence of a large number of Soviet officials and programs fed a nationalist resentment: the assertion of Soviet political and cultural values and a poorly planned and executed aid program did much to diminish Guinean hospitality. Touré felt perfectly free to accept American aid and establish friendlier relations with the U.S. In a revealing passage, the former American Ambassador—William Attwood—illuminated the client-patron relationship in new nations:

> In the spring of 1962 the [Guinean] government promulgated a new investment law that explicitly encouraged private capital, declared its intention of joining the International Monetary Fund and signed an Investment Guarantee Agreement with the United States. Each of these steps was taken over the objection of the Communist advisers who still occupied desks in government ministries; that they *were* taken was evidence that the advisers weren't actually in charge, as we once suspected.[68]

[66] Other sources which were particularly useful on the Middle East included: Georgiana Stevens (ed.), *The United States and the Middle East* (Englewood Cliffs, N.J., 1964); "The Arab and Israeli War," symposium in *Foreign Affairs,* XLVI (Jan. 1968), 304–336; Philip E. Moseley, "The Kremlin and the Third World," *Foreign Affairs,* XLVI (Oct., 1967), 64–77; Walter Laqueur, "Russia Enters the Middle East," *Foreign Affairs,* XLVII (Jan., 1969), 296–308.

[67] Attwood, pp. 14–15.

[68] *Ibid.,* pp. 75–76. In addition to Attwood's book, my analysis draws from: Zbigniew Brzezinski, *Africa and the Communist World* (Stanford,

If these limits on Soviet power exist in areas where there are significant Communist parties and recurrent Western military interventions (the Middle East) or where the emergence into nationhood was greeted by a traumatic "free world" quarantine (as in Guinea), then it is practically impossible to imagine the Congo slipping into the "Soviet camp."

Themselves reluctant to assume unilateral military and economic burdens (and risks) in an area of low strategic priority, American policy-makers often had inflated estimates of Soviet intentions. In July 1960, the Eisenhower Administration was so fearful of Soviet military intervention that an attack carrier was stationed off the Congo's coast. Even such an apologist for American policy as Ernest Lefever has written of this period: "The real Communist danger was the subversive exploitation of civil strife and chaos, and not in a direct military confrontation as implied in some American statements." [69] In February 1961, the Kennedy Administration also conjured up the specter of Soviet intervention, and ordered contingency plans drawn up for limited war. Yet, a few months earlier, the Russians had clearly indicated that support for their Congolese favorites would be overwhelmingly verbal.[70] Moscow had failed to act when Lumumba was ousted, jailed, and finally murdered. At the U.N., Khrushchev had declared that the Lumumba regime was the "only lawful" government in the Congo that "enjoys the confidence of the Congolese people." But he had also "avoided any specific commitment that would imply direct Soviet involvement in the Congo conflict, because 'the Congolese people themselves will be able to deal with the difficulties in restoring order.' " [71]

1963), *passim;* and Beard Richard Stokke, *Soviet and Eastern European Trade and Aid in Africa* (New York, 1967), pp. 176–187.

[69] Lefever, *Uncertain Mandate,* p. 77 .

[70] Apparently, this was recognized quite soon by those Congolese who sought to rely partly on Soviet aid. An "important" leader of the CNL told a CRISP interviewer in 1966 that "the experience of 1960" showed Eastern aid could not assure the future of the Congo. *Courrier Africain,* Feb. 18, 1967, p. 16.

[71] Lefever, *Uncertain Mandate,* p. 100.

Actually, Gizenga was to receive only a tiny amount of military and financial assistance from Russia. The Soviets even waited until July 1961, before accrediting a diplomatic mission in Stanleyville. Gizenga's dissatisfaction with this policy appears to have influenced his decision to expel the five Communist journalists in March 1961.[72]

The director of the CIA himself admitted that Soviet ambition was "overrated" in the Congo. Shortly after his retirement in 1962, Allen W. Dulles participated in a television interview with Eric Sevareid. In the course of the discussion he remarked:

> Now, I think that it is true that the Communists practice on us and on other countries toward which they're directing their attack, they try on us what I would call the overload theory. They will start a lot of petty annoyances in various parts of the world, without knowing whether they are going to seriously push them ahead, in order to divert our attention, maybe, from the major points of their attack.

Sevareid asked, "Could you give any concrete examples of what has turned out to be minor or major?" And Dulles replied,

> Well, I think we overrated the Soviet danger, let's say, in the Congo. They went in there with a great fanfare. They supported Gizenga. They established a Lumumba Institute in Moscow, and it looked as though they were going to make a serious attempt at take-over in the Belgian Congo. Well, it didn't work out that way at all. Now, maybe, they intended to do it, but they beat a pretty hasty retreat.[73]

Several factors account for the minimal Soviet input in the Congo. Sub-Saharan Africa has a low priority in great-power competition. Moreover, the nuclear "balance of terror" has minimized the risk of a direct confrontation between the U.S. and the Soviet Union in the Third World. Still, this has not prevented the Soviets from establishing large military aid programs in Egypt, Syria, Algeria, Laos, or North Vietnam. In the Congo, the Soviets

[72] *Ibid.*

[73] "CBS Reports," Apr. 26, 1962: "The Hot and Cold Wars of Allen Dulles." Transcript obtained from CBS Television, pp. 19–20.

faced the situation of "extended and vulnerable lines of communication, with no certainty that all the intervening countries whose territory would have to be crossed would have granted permission for the passage of Soviet arms and men."[74] Thus the logistical situation enhanced the influence of the African states that preferred to work within the U.N. (however slow-moving and Western-influenced) rather than open up their continent to unfettered Cold War rivalry.

In addition, the Soviets were aware of a particularly unfriendly terrain in Africa:

> Moscow recognized fairly early that African Communism suffered from a lack of native leadership and cadres: every one of the handful of African revolutionaries trained in Moscow had left the movement. Africa, moreover, seemed to be politically volatile and immature beyond the limits of Communist toleration: time and again, some ephemeral "Marxist" group would dub itself a Communist party, only to have its leaders and its total membership (sometimes identical) defect without remorse or second thoughts. . . .
>
> No African fellow traveler has ever remained a stable and dependable ally of the U.S.S.R.: for Moscow the only safe Lumumba was a dead Lumumba.[75]

In September 1960, Russell Warren Howe reported that Soviet diplomats were skeptical even of alleged Congolese Communists:

> The Russians are aware you cannot trust an African to be a Communist first and an African second as you can trust a Togliatti, a Thorez or a Browder to be a Communist before all else.
>
> "These Congolese Marxists could slip through our fingers like water. They're not worth the full treatment," a Communist diplomat remarked to this correspondent recently.[76]

Even before Lumumba's overthrow, the Soviets were somewhat impressed by the limits of their power in Africa. Perhaps the Soviet Union first learned about the uncontrollable Third World

[74] Helmudt Sonnenfeldt, "The Soviet Union and China, in Kitchen, p. 28.
[75] Brzezinski, pp. 23, 33. [76] *Washington Post,* Sept. 1, 1960, p. A-28.

nationalists in Africa—just as she absorbed her first hard lessons in polycentrism in Asia.

For all these reasons, one must respect Richard Lowenthal's judgment that:

> It seems likely that from the beginning both the Soviets and the Chinese Communists (who had even less capacity) saw the importance of the Congo not as a possible base for establishing a stronghold of their power but as a field for continent-wide propagandist exploitation of the conflicts that were bound to arise in this vast territory, with its singular combination of wealth in raw materials and poverty in trained African cadres.[77]

Moderate Conservatism and Liberalism in the Congo

Domestic ideologies not only shaped the content of anti-Communism; they also contributed independently to American policy. Having internationalized the Congo crisis largely for security reasons, the Eisenhower Administration went on to foster those Congolese politicians whose views on racial, economic, and social questions seemed to approximate the views of conservative Eastern businessmen. It was U.S. toleration of conservative-looking secessions that paved the way for Lumumba's appeal to the Soviet bloc and Washington's invocation of the chaos-to-Communism syndrome.

In the subsequent Democratic Administrations anti-Communism was not only *pursued through,* but also *augmented by,* a distinctively liberal vision of African development. Strong support was given to Adoula, whose outlook on race relations, economic policy, and the pace of social change appealed to liberal elites. Opposition to Tshombe and the Lumumbists was, in part, based on the rejection of "conservative" and "radical" approaches to African "modernization." Indeed, as the group of *liberal Africanists* accumulated experience in African politics and Washington infighting, their expressions of anti-Communism appeared increasingly as a

[77] Brzezinski, p. 178.

rationalization of more basic objectives. With the collapse of America's "liberal" protégés in 1964, the threat of "Communist subversion" provoked further American intervention.

It is within this broad perspective of alternative models of development that the argument between "pro-Europeans" and "pro-Africanists" is best understood. It is true that this controversy had some independent basis in the vested interests of middle- and lower-level bureaucrats in the Bureaus of African and West European Affairs and the Pentagon. But, at the policy-making level, it was clearly subsidiary to basic ideological preferences—liberal Messianism, or conservatism. Actually, there was never much evidence for assertions that Congo policy had great significance for the future of America's European or African relations. Thus, Kennedy's turn toward the Africanists was but a minor wave amidst the squalls wracking NATO. More substantial issues—centering in Europe—would determine the future of the European alliance. As Nielsen remarks concerning a related matter (U.S. policy and the Portuguese colonies in Africa):

> The alliance has developed serious weaknesses in recent years, but these do not relate primarily to differences over colonial policy. They turn on more central issues of strategy, burden-sharing, and nuclear weapons control.[78]

In Africa, the Kennedy Administration showed that it was possible to establish decent relations with Ghana, Guinea, and the United Arab Republic, while disagreeing sharply with them over the Congo and other issues. In 1964, when American policy collided with that of the Organization of African Unity, culminating in an emotional confrontation over the Stanleyville "rescue," the U.S. still "came out of it all relatively unscathed. The storm did pass." [79] African leaders had a hard-headed appreciation of national priorities and international realities.

78 Waldemar Nielsen, *African Battleline: American Policy Choices in Southern Africa* (New York, 1965), p. 30.

79 Attwood, p. 236.

The moderate conservatives' approach to the Congo envisioned a formally independent government which, in fact, responded to Belgian tutelage. Such a system would ensure the continuation of an appropriate atmosphere for corporate profit-making (foreign, including some minority American shares) and other expatriate pursuits. The American government input would be mainly technical assistance.

In practice, this approach was abortive because it underestimated nationalist political forces, forces so strong that it would take a full-blown colonialism or at least considerable outside intervention, to repress them. Thus, while the Western powers managed to maintain friendly cliques in Leopoldville and Elizabethville during late 1960, they were not able to establish conservative *government* in the Congo. The largest, most nationally oriented, political grouping rejected Western tutelage and organized an independent regime at Stanleyville. Other nationalist elements were dismayed by Mobutu's cautious policy toward Tshombe and his narrow political base. The ineffective Leopoldville regime could not hold the lid on numerous centrifugal forces. By January 1961, Belgian lives and property were secure *only* in South Katanga, the pro-Western client regime in Leopoldville was imperiled, and the U.N. prop was faltering. Having become more deeply involved in the Congo than it had ever expected, the United States was forced to reconsider its policy—or face even larger burdens.

The liberals proposed a "moderate nationalist" solution. Tutelage would be replaced by "mutually beneficial" collaboration between a nationalist regime and the West. Obvious taints on sovereignty, such as Katangan secession, would have to go. Absolute protection of Belgian interests was foregone, but it was understood that economic and social change should be gradual, not "disruptive" or "dislocating." American economic aid would promote a "take-off" into self-sustained economic growth. Under these conditions, American business enterprise and political principles would gradually penetrate the Congo. American investment and trade would rise; democratic institutions would (hopefully) take root.

These hypotheses also failed the test of experience. Adoula was an intelligent anti-Communist union leader and politician. But he lacked a significant political base and was unable to create one. Interestingly, the Belgians considered appointing him *formateur* (former of the government) before Independence, but rejected the idea because Adoula "although 'without question one of the best brains in the country' had no electoral support and in any case kept himself in the background."[80] Although American support of the U.N. in Katanga temporarily bolstered Adoula's nationalist legitimacy, it only postponed the final reckoning. By 1962, the Lumumbists were effectively excluded from political power and the regime was greatly dependent upon the Army and the security apparatus. When Adoula fell, the liberal dream for the Congo had already turned into a nightmare. The government had invited substantial foreign forces to put down an internal revolution. At least half the country escaped the rule of Leopoldville (even in that limited sense in which modern governments "rule" the new nations). Antiwhite and anti-Western sentiment was more widespread and virulent than ever before. Economic development was at a standstill largely because of the ineffectiveness of the "liberal" politicians (e.g., without a political counterweight, the civil service, especially the army, held the budget in thrall). American investors shunned the Congo; and the vestiges of representative government, parliament, and parties, were fast disappearing. Through the application of inappropriate domestic categories, the liberal policy-making elite ironically ended up supporting the conservatives' favorites—Tshombe and Mobutu—supplying them with substantial and embarrassing amounts of military tutelage.

An Overall Judgment

American policy in the Congo from 1960 to 1964 did not meet the principal criteria for success advanced by U.S. officials. It did not strengthen national security, since the international Communist

[80] Belgian Resident Minister Ganshof van der Meersch, quoted in Hoskyns, *The Congo Since Independence,* p. 76.

threat was illusory. It did not realize liberal hopes for Africa. Actually, it seems that Stevenson and some of Kennedy's White House assistants were disillusioned by the Congo experience. This is not to say that the liberals had *no* successes. By helping to end Katanga secession, the U.S. (and U.N.) made a serious contribution to maintaining the territorial integrity of the Congo. Although this policy was, in great part, a means toward larger ends—which were not achieved—it did represent an important accomplishment for liberal officials. Significantly, it involved the resolution of a largely *external* problem.

The conservatives seem to have fared better. This was not because their perception of Congolese political reality was superior to that of the liberals; in fact it was less adequate. Support for the pro-Western forces in the Congo required a military-political intervention that went far beyond conservative anticipations. Ironically, it was the liberals' crusading zeal which would justify the force necessary to realize the conservatives' goals. In both cases, the contradictions between ends wished and means utilized reflected the contradictions between the environments of policy-makers and those of the Congolese.

In the end, American policy kept one group in power and helped destroy its leading opponents. It was a success if measured by the sole criterion of power to get one's way. But in the light of the broadest and most deeply felt objectives of the policy-makers, it was at least beside the point and at most a tragic error.

To make a complete assessment of the U.S. impact on Congo political development one must transcend the categories of success established by U.S. officials. Granted that American concepts of alternative Congo regimes were naive, did the very attempt to apply these notions eliminate regimes that *were* open to the Congolese? [81] Did it contribute to the emergence of a particular structure for the modern state?

[81] Aristide R. Zolberg, "A View from the Congo," *World Politics,* XIX (Oct., 1966), 137–149, applies David Easton's concepts of political "community," "regime," and "authorities" to the Congo.

Unfortunately, the problem of the international environment's effect on the emergent Congo regime has received little systematic consideration from overspecialized academics and nontheoretically inclined participant-raconteurs. The one serious effort to raise this issue was made by Hoskyns in *The Congo Since Independence: January 1960–December 1961*. However, this book covers a relatively short period, and it was written too soon to reflect the results of increasing academic preoccupation with the internal political structures of the Congo. This bring up another obstacle to interpretation: there is still a large research gap in Congo studies, and in African studies generally. We do not know enough about the range of political alternatives in the Congo (and similar states) to judge whether a certain regime was inevitable or received crucial assistance from the international system. In addition, we lack important information concerning the phenomenon to be explained: the present regime. As Professor Zolberg has observed regarding African political studies, we are especially deficient in our knowledge of the "development of political groups and cleavages, of their relationship to the nonpolitical environment, and hence, in general, of the characteristic structures and processes which constitute the legacy which the new African states inherited," "the 'output' of the political system, or at least the government . . . programs of action in different spheres," how "Africans perceive the political world," particularly the "intermediate elites and the population at large," "what occurs at the more intimate and more particular level of the local community," and "the relationship between tradition and modernity in contemporary African states." [82]

Recognizing these limitations, the author believes that existing research provides a basis for identifying variables, internal and external, which seem to account for the main features of the emergent Leopoldville regime of 1960–1964. However, the relative weight of national and international components cannot be determined at this time. The effort here is simply to formulate

[82] Zolberg, *Creating Political Order*, pp. 151–155.

more clearly a problem which is central to any overall critique of American intervention in the Third World.

The Congo regime of 1960–1964 had the following general characteristics: severe and increasing factionalism in the government and party system, transformation of parties from embryonic mass organizations to caucuses of political elites, shift of effective power toward strategic military and administrative elites, alienation of the masses—particularly in the rural areas, collapse of Western democratic institutions, and "limited, but endemic, civil war in many parts of the country." [83]

Roots of this kind of regime are easy to locate in the history of the Congo before Independence. At the beginning of colonization, the Congo contained, like other European acquisitions in Africa, a "number of more or less disparate societies, each with a distinct political system, and with widely different intersocietal relationships." [84] Under Belgian colonialism,

> the social and economic changes introduced by the development of a money economy, while providing the conditions necessary to the rise of nationalist sentiment, also created situations that led to fundamental divisions among, and within, the Congolese societies.[85]

Uneven development policies, uneven responses of traditional systems to modernizing influences, and a divisive colonial educational system added to the difficulties of national integration. Belgium's refusal to permit political and labor organizations until shortly before Independence resulted in poorly integrated national and even local parties, an incohesive and inexperienced political elite, and masses who seem to have been less involved in party

[83] Jean-Claude Willame, "The Military Intervenes," in Kitchen, p. 165. The description of the Congo regime is largely based on Young, *Politics in the Congo;* Weiss, *Political Protest in the Congo;* Hoskyns, *The Congo Since Independence;* and Lemarchand, *Political Awakening;* as well as numerous sources cited throughout this work.

[84] Zolberg, "The Structure of Political Conflict," p. 7.

[85] Lemarchand, *Political Awakening,* p. 120.

activity and less realistic about the meaning of Independence than elsewhere in Africa.[86]

Congo specialists are inclined to trace the main features of the 1960–1964 regime to this background. Thus, Congo political history unfolds with the fatalism of a Greek tragedy. Even the individual events precipitating the dialectic of fragmentation, alienation, and so on—such as the army mutiny, the exodus of Belgian administrators and absorption of Congolese party cadres into the bureaucracy, the Katanga and South Kasai secessions, the constitutional crisis of September, 1960—appear largely embedded in the political legacy of 1960.

Yet there are some facts which point to a more complex interpretation, one which takes into account the international environment of 1960–1964. First, the performance of the second, post-1965 Mobutu regime suggests that the Congo's capacity for centralized government may have been greater than its actual performance in the early sixties.

Second, it is rarely emphasized that the U.N. and its principal supporter, the U.S., tolerated Belgian-supported secession for nearly two years, and that this had extremely serious consequences for the Congo's political development. Katangan secession stimulated centrifugal forces in several important provinces. It was the issue on which the governing elite's cohesion foundered in 1960. Later, it helped split the leading nationalist party and destroy the Lovanium coalition. It led toward the downfall of probably "the one political leader who was capable of thinking and acting nationally and who had sufficient personality to appeal to the people over the heads of local and tribal leaders." [87] It created enormous economic burdens and pathologies for a Central Government which desperately needed every ounce of distributive capacity in order to solidify its legitimacy. Consider also the support Lu-

[86] *Ibid.* See also Young, *Politics in the Congo;* and Weiss, *Political Protest in the Congo.*

[87] Hoskyns, *The Congo Since Independence,* p. 380.

mumba's government would have gained had the U.S. and U.N. helped it dispose of European meddlers in those first, crucial months. At one point, Hoskyns remarks,

> The secessionist aims of CONAKAT had very little support in the rest of the country; a swift, sharp campaign against the party's leaders and their European advisers would considerably increase the prestige of the new government.[88]

Thus American tolerance of European-backed secession may have weakened the forces for a minimally effective national government and a greater degree of mass orientation to modern, national politics.

Third, repeated American intervention excluded from power the largest, most important segment of the political elite, the only group that was able to achieve enough cohesion to form a government in July 1960. These were the elements most influenced by the "mass party" model of African political development, and most sympathetic to the aspirations of the masses for a better life. With its "rural radicalism" and its unfinished elite (nonuniversity trained and not ushered onto the throne of power by a colonial apprenticeship), the Congo may have had a better chance to realize the mass party model than most African countries. In any case, one need not be an optimist regarding the prospects for democracy and social justice in Africa to call attention to international policies which probably hampered even limited steps in these directions in the Congo.[89]

[88] *Ibid.*, p. 81.

[89] For some stimulating but pessimistic analyses of Africa's prospects, see Zolberg, *Creating Political Order;* Samir Amin, *Le Développement du capitalisme en Côte d'Ivoire* (Paris: Editions de Minuit, 1967), esp. Conclusion; Yves Benôt, *Idéologies des indépendances africain* (Paris: François Maspero, 1969); Bob Fitch and Mary Oppenheimer, *Ghana: End of an Illusion* (New York: Monthly Review Press, 1966); Giovanni Arrighi and John S. Saul, "Socialism and Economic Development in Tropical Africa," *Journal of Modern African Studies,* VI (Spring, 1968), 141–169; and "Nationalism and Revolution in Sub-Saharan Africa," in Ralph Milliband and John Saville (eds.), *Socialist Register 1969,* pp. 131–188.

CHAPTER IX

Explanations and Conclusions

The Roots of American Policy

Why were basic assumptions in American policies at such variance with international realities? Comparative analysis of three Administrations has already suggested a relationship between perspectives on Congo political development and the social-historical backgrounds of a few key decision-makers.

This is not to say that there is a one-to-one cause-effect relation between elite backgrounds and American policies in the Congo. Under the heading "basic assumptions" in U.S. policy, we have treated certain ideologies of African and Third World development. But policies also include the ways in which these ideologies are implemented. The modes of application depend upon many factors besides officials' ideologies. Thus, all three Administrations assigned Africa a relatively low strategic priority and preferred to work through the U.N. as much as possible. All took some care to orchestrate America's Congo interests with her European ones. All were aware that the strategic and material importance of the Congo implied that fewer chances should be taken than in a relatively minor country such as Guinea.[1] In addition to essentially strategic considerations, modes of application were influenced

[1] See above, p. 136, n. 49. The case of Guinea also shows how a series of special circumstances may produce a policy which could not be anticipated from elite perspectives on African development. Ambassador Attwood's description of the special circumstances, however, indicates just how unusual Guinea was, and how much the exception proves the rule. See above, pp. 136, 278.

by international events and reactions. The Congo became an object of intense concern when the behavior of Lumumba and the Soviets *activated* the policy-makers' "from-chaos-to-Communism" complex. The liberal Africanists' views acquired added *urgency* when the Afro-Asian nations upped their pressure on Katanga, when Gizenga withdrew from Adoula's government, when an opposition cartel threatened Adoula, when Tshombe proved so very stubborn in negotiations with the Central Government. On the other hand, the Europeanists were weakened by political changes in Belgium, Rhodesia, and North Katanga. In 1964, the form, extent, and auspices of U.S. intervention were largely determined by the calculations of the Binza group and Tshombe. Lastly, we have seen how domestic pressure groups and bureaucratic interests had an impact on American policies.

If ideological guides to the Congo did not determine the outcome of U.S. foreign policy in a one-to-one way, they did produce distinctive policy *emphases,* once it was determined that the Congo was an important country and that its political character fell within the parameters of U.S. policy concerns. This is not surprising since ideological considerations have some influence on strategic evaluations and the will to exploit events is frequently as important as the events themselves.[2] In sum, while there is no question of attaining 100 percent policy predictability, comparative analysis has highlighted relationships between the *general thrust* of U.S. policy and the perspectives on African development held by decision-makers with certain backgrounds.

These men were members of the upper class—or their recruits—and they manned strategic posts in the Executive branch (particularly in the State Department and White House, but also in the Defense Department and CIA). Congress played but a minor role in the development of Congo policy, Senator Dodd's pesky, but abortive, campaign representing the lone important initiative. Even such intelligent specialists as Senators Fulbright and Humphrey appear to have relied upon the Executive for crucial facts and

[2] For examples, see above, Chapters IV and V.

interpretations. Public opinion was largely inactive. The few concerned groups—rightists, missionaries, interested businessmen—did not have a decisive effect. And the Executive branch did its best to cut off their sources of information and publicize its own case.

The main lines of Executive action cannot be explained by reference to "latent public opinion." The American people may oppose Communist expansion, but they leave it to the President to determine whether a particular situation contains this threat, and what actions should be taken to neutralize it. Public opinion on foreign policy is characterized by extremely low levels of awareness, information, and emotional involvement.[3] Lipset has analyzed poll data in the following way:

> There is a very great difference in the reliability of response with respect to domestic and foreign policy. Domestically, the polls indicate that we are dealing with relatively stable attitudes, on issues such as the welfare state, race relations, etc. In addition, when new issues arise such as how to deal with inflation, unemployment or Medicare, people can react to them in terms of direct personal experience or liberal-conservative predispositions.
>
> Conversely, in the area of foreign policy, most Americans know very little, and are only indirectly involved. They have no way of checking on often conflicting reports from countries and regions under contention, nor on public sentiments elsewhere in the world. Consequently, the press and political leaders can have much more influence in determining public opinion on foreign issues than on domestic issues. Whether Tshombe is a villain or a hero, whether the downfall of Nkrumah is good or bad, is defined *for* the average American rather than *by* the average American.[4]

[3] V. O. Key, Jr., *Public Opinion and American Democracy* (New York, 1961), pp. 81, 134, 215, 258; Warren E. Miller and Donald E. Stokes, "Constituency Influence in Congress," *American Political Science Review,* LVII (Mar., 1963), 45–56; Gabriel Almond, *The American People and Foreign Policy* (rev. ed.; New York, 1960), pp. xx–xxvi, 69–86, 136–143; Michael Harrington, "For a Dynamic Majority," in *New Leader,* Mar. 27, 1967, pp. 19–20.

[4] Seymour Martin Lipset, "The President, The Polls, and Vietnam," *Transaction,* III (Sept.–Oct., 1966), 19–20.

Thus, Americans "agree on certain larger objectives, peace without the expansion (or contraction) of Communism, and find it necessary to trust the judgment of national leaders as to what is possible given these purposes." [5]

Two types of upper-class executive determined basic policies in the Congo. In analyzing the relation between social-historical settings and political concepts, the author has found Mannheim's "total" conception of ideology extremely useful:

the particular conception of ideology operates primarily with a psychology of interests, while the total conception uses a more formal functional analysis, without any reference to motivations, confining itself to an objective description of the structural differences in minds operating in different social settings. The former assumes that this or that interest is the cause of a given lie or deception. The latter presupposes simply that there is a correspondence between a given social situation and a given perspective, point of view, or apperception mass. In this case, while an analysis of constellations of interests may often be necessary it is not to establish causal connections but to characterize the total situation. Thus interest psychology tends to be displaced by an analysis of the correspondence between the situation to be known and the forms of knowledge.[6]

As shown in Chapter I, one group of policy-makers was upper class, predominantly business-experienced or business-oriented, and strongly ethnocentric. Its political background tended to be Republican, and its diplomatic one, European.

One other characteristic should be described. These officials were part of a "political generation" which had accepted the hastily drawn lesson of "two worlds" (or, in the Soviet Union, "two camps") from the brief period of monolithic Communist expansion after World War II.[7] Originally, a political generation

[5] *Ibid.*, p. 20.

[6] Karl Mannheim, *Ideology and Utopia: An Introduction to the Sociology of Knowledge* (New York, 1936), pp. 57–58.

[7] Lafeber, pp. 55–56; Richard Pfeffer (ed.), *No More Vietnams? The War and the Future of American Foreign Policy* (New York, 1968), pp. 8–9 (discussion by Arthur M. Schlesinger, Jr.).

may not overlap a particular age group. It is defined by "historically significant experiences" which predispose the subjects to certain attitudes and actions.[8] However, if new events and new, relatively innocent, minds interact to produce a new political generation, the older group may acquire an age-referent (e.g., "over 30"). Arthur Schlesinger, Jr., himself not entirely free of the limitations of the "Cold War" generation, has recognized its reality and contemporary relevance:

> America and Russia appeared for a moment in history after 1945 to be the world's two superpowers. At the same time, the phenomenon of Stalinism gave rise to an American anti-Communism which rightly saw Communism as a relatively unified world movement directed from a single center. For many people in the 1940's this necessary and correct anti-Communism hardened into a series of conditioned reflexes which continued to guide their thoughts after Communism itself was beginning to be transformed under the stress of nationalism.[9]

In Chapter I, it was noted that the policy-makers themselves explained their anti-Communism partly by reference to postwar historical experience. It is not excluded that class-rooted suspicions affected the interpretation of these experiences, viz., the history of U.S.-Soviet relations.

Generational characteristics produced the notion of an international Communist threat in the Third World. Corporate, caste, Republican, and European settings implied an inability to sympathize with or understand the demands of blacks for rapid, sometimes disruptive, social change. (In some cases, business interests in the Congo or its neighbors may have contributed to this perspective.) The resulting piece of ideology was the from-chaos-to-Communism complex.

Having projected American power into the Congo for security

[8] For an enlightening discussion—and application—of the concept of political generation, see Maurice Zeitlin, "Political Generations of the Cuban Working Class," in James Petras and Maurice Zeitlin (eds.), *Latin America: Reform or Revolution* (New York: Fawcett, 1968), pp. 264–288.

[9] Pfeffer, pp. 8–9.

reasons, these officials tried to work through like-minded (i.e., "responsible conservative") indigenous forces. This was a natural development. As Stalin remarked in the Spring of 1945, "Whoever occupies a territory also imposes on it his own social system."[10] It appears that without the paramount justification of national security, the moderate Republican elite would not have been eager to spread American influence and values. For conservative business types, the absence of significant American investment facilitated the acceptance of Belgian predominance.

As shown in Chapter IV, another group of decision-makers was also upper class, but more likely to choose "public service" careers over business ones. Most important, they were upper-class liberals who had spent much of their lives managing and rationalizing the post-New Deal accommodation between corporate privilege and the claims of the less-advantaged (including racial minorities). As prominent Democrats, their role was similar to that of the corporate lawyers who led the Progressive movement fifty years earlier. According to Richard Hofstadter, the Progressive leaders never wanted, for instance,

> a sharp change in the social structure, but rather the formation of a responsible elite which was to take charge of the popular impulse toward change, and direct it into moderate, and, as they would have said, "constructive channels," a leadership occupying, as Brandeis aptly put it, a position of independence between the wealthy (self-interested businessmen) and the people, prepared to curb the excesses of either.[11]

[10] Quoted in Lafeber, p. 15. For a similar statement by former Secretary of Commerce Henry Wallace, see John Spanier, *American Foreign Policy Since World War II* (2nd rev. ed.; New York, 1965), pp. 28–29.

[11] Richard Hofstadter, *The Age of Reform: From Bryan to F.D.R.* (New York, 1955), p. 163. For insightful discussions of contemporary upper-class liberalism, see Seymour Martin Lipset, *Political Man: The Social Bases of Politics* (Garden City, N.Y., 1963), pp. 318-322; E. Digby Baltzell, *The Protestant Establishment: Aristocracy and Caste in America* (New York, 1964), pp. 226–315; Baltzell, *Philadelphia Gentlemen*, pp. 39–42, 132, 139, 234, 393–394; G. William Domhoff, *Who Rules America?* (Englewood Cliffs, N.J., 1967), pp. 28–31.

The liberal decision-makers naturally gravitated toward diplomatic assignments which dealt with "underdeveloped countries."

These officials were also members of the Cold War generation. In addition, they were part of a more exclusive generation of (frequently upper-class) liberals who had constructed the New Deal and then seized the occasion of World War II to announce its coming globalization. One might label this the generation of the Atlantic Charter. Schlesinger has some suggestive thoughts on this subject too:

> the concept that the United States has a saving mission to the world . . . is an old idea, rekindled by Woodrow Wilson in 1917–1920 and enlarged by World War II into a kind of global New Dealism. Global New Dealism meant that we have an obligation to deal with poverty, repression and injustice "everywhere in the world." The concept led to many excellent post World War II undertakings such as UNRRA, the Marshall Plan, and economic development and technical assistance programs. The human carriers for this idea have a direct line of descent, extending from Woodrow Wilson through Franklin D. Roosevelt to Lyndon Johnson and Hubert Humphrey—two fervent young New Dealers of the 1930's and 1940's.[12]

It has been shown that the upper-class liberals involved in Congo policy were some of the principal architects of the concept of a global liberal mission.

Generational and class characteristics again led to suspicion of international Communism in the Third World. But now upper-class liberalism and experience in the new nations produced greater identification with and sympathy for African nationalist aspirations. The result was sophisticated anti-Communism.

The liberal elite naturally sought to realize anti-Communist goals through liberal means. However, generational experiences led them to make the export of American liberalism an end in itself. Instrumental anti-Communism blended into global New Dealism.

This analysis of significant political differences between Ad-

[12] Pfeffer, pp. 8–9.

ministrations suggests that specifically "bureaucratic" sources of foreign policy were secondary. We have noted the impact of the bureaucratic division of labor during the Katanga crisis, with the African, West European, and International Organizations Bureaus of the State Department, and the Azores-conscious Defense Department lining up in accordance with narrow vested interests. But even here, intra-Administration *political* differences seemed more fundamental. Thus the behavior and relative power of the African Bureau changed under different Administrations. Through key personnel switches—Gullion for Timberlake, Fredericks for Penfield, Williams for Satterthwaite—Kennedy and Bowles shaped the bureau into a more liberal and influential participant in policy-making. When President Johnson decided to take a more moderate stance, he gave some of the bureau's Congo business to Averell Harriman, and later conferred some responsibility on an interdepartmental task force. The International Organizations Bureau was more liberal and activist under Cleveland and Stevenson than it had been under Francis Wilcox and Henry Cabot Lodge. And the European Bureau had less influence on African policy under Democrats than it did under Republicans.

Extrabureaucratic forces also determined how interorganizational squabbles would be resolved. The perspectives of Presidents and their senior advisers were crucial elements of such major decisions as: keeping an open mind on the Katanga gambit in 1960, using force to end the Katanga secession in 1962, and overriding African sensitivities in repressing the rebellion of 1964. Such influential decision-makers as Eisenhower, Herter, Dillon, Kennedy, Bowles, Williams, Ball, Johnson, and Harriman were leaders of political and private institutions first, with corresponding interests and ideologies, and public bureaucrats second. Their basis of recruitment was political rather than bureaucratic. As the *Pentagon Papers* suggest, top political advisers have often disregarded or deformed uncongenial information from below. One should be wary of any explanation of U.S. policy which fails to account for significant changes and ignores vital aspects of decision-making.

While bureaucratic influences were not decisive, they were undoubtedly important. The professional diplomats' inability to transcend customary categories of anti-Communism and (to a lesser extent) Europeanism may have reflected some well-known pathologies of the State Department bureaucracy—disproportionate recruitment from the upper class, especially in the past; on-the-job, rather than theoretical, training; importance of pleasing older superiors for advancement; the lingering after-effects of past purges which penalized the unconventional.[13] Moreover, the Defense Department and the CIA generally illustrated the bureaucratic transformation of instrumental values into terminal values.[14] Their expressions of anti-Communism were particularly strong, and they constantly pushed their favorite techniques to the fore. Finally, we have seen the tendency to develop ego-investment in certain policies, particularly at the working level of bureaucracies.[15]

Withal, if bureaucratic bias hindered the emergency of new perspectives in American foreign policy, it is also true that the political elite—which had its own store of political-diplomatic knowledge—frequently opposed change. When they didn't oppose it (as in the case of the liberal elites), they were able to substantially modify bureaucratic behavior, introduce new blood into the bureaucracy, and create new bureaucratic interests in line with policy preferences.

The Congo and U.S. Foreign Policy

In some respects, the Congo was an unusual case of American intervention in the Third World. Involvement and freedom of action were limited by the low strategic priority assigned to Africa, the relative paucity of U.S. business interests in the Congo and neighboring states, and the African political interests of the NATO allies.

On the other hand, this study has identified, as the major determinants of Congo policy, certain basic assumptions about Third

[13] *Ibid.*, pp. 20, 44–45, 47, 68–69; Smith Simpson, *Anatomy of the State Department* (Boston, 1967).

[14] Cf. Pfeffer, pp. 51–96, 102–103.

[15] Cf. *ibid.*, pp. 49, 53–54.

World politics and "the international Communist threat." America's behavior in the Congo from 1960–1964 should therefore approximate the range of policies pursued in the Third World during that period. There is substantial evidence that this is, in fact, the case. The characteristic patterns of Moderate Republican and Liberal Democratic anti-Communism are visible in recent American policies in Latin America, the Middle East, Asia, and Africa. Contrast, for example, the Eisenhower Administration's policies in the Dominican Republic, Laos, Egypt, and Ghana, with those of the Kennedy and (to a lesser extent) Johnson Administrations.

The Congo provides a fairly typical example of American power vis-à-vis "left" (occasionally Communist) nationalist forces in the Third World. Currently, these movements are encountering strong resistance from "moderate," often more privileged, groups; they also suffer from a dearth of military capacity. (Vietnam is an exception.) Under the circumstances, limited applications of America's overwhelming political, paramilitary, and military power are adequate to repress "pro-Communist" elements in these small states. Such actions may be based on a distorted concept of national security and may fail to transform their objects into images of America, but they are still quite deadly (viz., Iran, 1953; Guatemala, 1954; Lebanon, 1958; British Guiana, 1961; South Vietnam from 1954–1961; Dominican Republic, 1965; Bolivia, 1971; etc.).

Finally, the roots of Congo policy suggest that some fashionable explanations of American intervention in the Third World are inadequate. With regard to the role of economic interests, several points can be made. The United States helped crush the Katangan secession over the protests of some interested businessmen with good political connections; there seem to have been few business interests on the side of the course eventually taken. It is not clear that America's economic stake in the Congo was sufficient to provoke a sizeable politico-military intervention. Extensive interviews with policy-makers and informed individuals indicate that, at least in Africa, broad social-historical perspectives were more relevant than economic expansion (unless, of course, every one is either lying or deluding himself). Insofar as U.S. decision-makers may wish to foster American business in the Third World, they are forced to make political judgments regarding resistance to this goal.[16] These political judgments are strongly related to social-historical settings.

The author has not here evaluated economic theories of the origins of the Cold War. Nor has he explored all the ramifications of America's private and public "aid" to underdeveloped areas.[17] Rather, he has suggested an explanation of why the Cold War was projected into the Congo, why a relatively modest economic interest was joined by a relatively large political one, and why the latter assumed various forms. As a particularly important "case," the Congo should furnish leads toward the understanding of American intervention in the Third World during the sixties and seventies.

It may be objected that the narrow scope of a case study tends to obscure the real roots of ideology. Thus by adjusting the lens for a wider view, one might come to see liberal and conservative anti-Communism as reflections of America's economic stake in the whole Third World. Their conceptual richness would, essentially, "rationalize" far-flung material positions. Their application in the Congo would not be a result of that country's economic importance, but of the *momentum* created by interests elsewhere. At best, this study would have indicated why different means were employed by different Administrations in the Congo crisis.

16 This seems to be admitted by the Marxist writer, Harry Magdoff, *The Age of Imperialism* (New York: Monthly Review Press, 1969), pp. 14–15.

17 For relevant critiques, see especially Paul A. Baran, *The Political Economy of Growth* (New York: Monthly Review Press, 1957); André Gunder Frank, *Capitalism and Underdevelopment in Latin America* (New York: Monthly Review Press, 1969); Green and Seidman, esp. Part III; Michael Harrington, *American Power in the Twentieth Century* (New York, 1967); Arrighi and Saul, "Socialism and Economic Development"; and "Nationalism and Revolution in Sub-Saharan Africa," in Milliband and Saville.

An adequate evaluation of this argument would require a full-length study of postwar U.S. diplomacy in underdeveloped areas. Nevertheless, the author may be permitted some preliminary criticisms. First, in a great many countries in Asia and Africa, it is by no means obvious that American economic interests are sufficiently important to occasion costly interventions. That such significant cases as the Congo and Indochina are frequently attributed to "momentum" should raise questions about the adequacy of this explanation. Second, it would seem odd that the irrational spreading effect was not contained by the very concrete interests which favored the Katanga gambit. Third, and most fundamental, the tendency to reduce ideology to a cover for specific material objects smacks of "vulgar Marxism." In his classic sociological analysis, Marx presented ideology as a full-bodied expression of social relations. Particularly in the *Communist Manifesto* and the historical essays, he undertook a conceptual analysis of bourgeois ideology to show how it was rooted in the basic life-conditions of a specific class. His famous portraits of the French peasantry and lumpenproletariat are in the same vein. It goes without saying that ideology must constantly be compared with behavior and referred to its social matrix. But this is a far cry from the conception of ideology as conscious or half-conscious lie or as "mere" rationalization.[18]

The weakness of bureaucratic explanations has been discussed above. Accounts which stress "American character" or "the American style," or which try to apply cumbrous psychological uniformities (e.g. "the arrogance of power") neglect the crucial social-historical referents. The neglect impedes politically meaningful analysis of American foreign policy, because patterns of behavior are not related to group or class pressures. A similar criticism can be made of theoretical models of international relations

[18] For a sophisticated Marxist's attempt to distinguish economic and political policies, see Tom Kemp, *Theories of Imperialism* (London: Dobson, 1967), esp. Chapters II, VI, VIII, and IX.

which focus on the structure and "rules" of the inter-State system but avoid analysis of internal social structures. This study has tried to show that contrary to a long-cherished American belief, "politics" and partisanship by no means stop at the water's edge."

Bibliography

Books

Alexander, Major General H. T. *African Tightrope*. New York: Frederick A. Praeger, 1965.

Almond, Gabriel. *The American People and Foreign Policy*. Rev. ed. New York: Frederick A. Praeger, 1960.

Alperovitz, Gar. *Atomic Diplomacy: Hiroshima and Potsdam*. New York: Vintage, 1967.

Attwood, William. *The Reds and the Blacks*. New York: Harper and Row, 1967.

Alvarez, Luis Lopez. *Lumumba ou l'Afrique Frustrée*. Paris: Editions Cujas, 1964.

Badeau, John S. *The American Approach to the Arab World*. New York: Harper and Row, 1968.

Ball, George W. *The Discipline of Power*. Boston: Little, Brown, 1968.

Baltzell, E. Digby. *Philadelphia Gentlemen, The Making of a National Upper Class*. Glencoe, Ill.: The Free Press, 1958.

——. *The Protestant Establishment: Aristocracy and Caste in America*. New York: Random House, 1964.

Barber, William J. *The Economy of Central Africa: A Case Study of Economic Development in a Dualistic Society*. London: Oxford University Press, 1961.

Beys, Jorge, Paul-Henry Gendebien, and Benoît Verhaegen. *Congo 1963*. Brussels: CRISP, 1964.

Bowles, Chester. *Africa's Challenge to America*. Los Angeles: University of California Press, 1956.

——. *Ambassador's Report*. New York: Harper and Brothers, 1954.

——. *The Conscience of a Liberal: Selected Writings and Speeches*. New York: Harper and Row, 1962.

——. *Promises to Keep: My Years in Public Life, 1941–1969.* New York: Harper and Row, 1971.

——. *Tomorrow Without Fear.* New York: Simon and Schuster, 1946.

Brzezinski, Zbigniew. *Africa and the Communist World.* Stanford: Stanford University Press, 1963.

Burns, Arthur Lee, and Nina Heathcote. *Peacekeeping by U.N. Forces.* New York: Frederick A. Praeger, 1963.

Carter, Gwendolyn M. (ed.). *Politics in Africa: 7 Cases.* New York: Harcourt, Brace and World, 1966.

Centre de Recherche et d'Information Socio-Politiques (CRISP). *Congo 1959.* Brussels: CRISP, 1960.

——. *Congo 1964. Political Documents of a Developing Nation.* Princeton: Princeton University Press, 1966.

——. *Congo 1965.* Brussels: CRISP, 1966.

——. *Morphologie des groupes financières.* Brussels: CRISP, 1966.

Cleveland, Harlan. *The Obligations of Power.* New York: Harper and Row, 1966.

Current Biography Yearbook, 1953, 1958–1963. Ed. Candee, Marjorie Dent, and Charles Maritz. New York: H. W. Wilson Co., 1954, 1959–1964.

Davis, Kenneth S. *The Politics of Honor: A Biography of Adlai E. Stevenson.* New York: G. P. Putnam's Sons, 1967.

De Vos, Pierre. *Vie et mort de Lumumba.* Paris: Calmann-Lévy, 1961.

Domhoff, G. William. *Who Rules America?* Englewood Cliffs, N.J.: Spectrum, 1967.

Draper, Theodore. *Israel and World Politics.* New York: Viking, 1968.

Eisenhower, Dwight D. *Waging Peace 1956–1961.* New York: Doubleday, 1965.

Epstein, Howard M. (ed.). *Revolt in the Congo.* New York: Facts on File, Inc., 1964.

Ferkiss, Victor C. *Africa's Search for Identity.* New York: George Braziller, 1966.

Gamme, Pierre. *Le Diamant dans le monde.* Brussels: Office de Publicité, S.C., 1947.

Ganshof van der Meersch, W. J. *Fin de la souveraineté belge au Congo.* Brussels: Institut Royal des Relations Internationales, 1963.

Gavshon, Arthur L. *The Mysterious Death of Dag Hammarskjold.* New York: Walker and Co., 1962.

Gendebien, Paul-Henry. *L'Intervention des Nations Unies au Congo 1960–1964.* Paris: Mouton et Cie., 1967.

Gérard-Libois, Jules. *Le Rôle de la Belgique dans l'Opération des*

Nations Unies au Congo 1960–1964. Travaux Africains nos. 68–71. Brussels: CRISP, 1966.

——. *Sécession au Katanga*. Brussels: CRISP, 1963. (*Katanga Secession*. Tr. Rebecca Young. Madison: University of Wisconsin Press, 1966.)

Gérard-Libois, Jules, and Benoît Verhaegen. *Congo 1960*. Brussels: CRISP, 1961.

——. *Congo 1962*, Brussels: CRISP, 1963.

Geyelin, Philip. *Lyndon B. Johnson and the World*. New York: Frederick A. Praeger, 1966.

Gilis, Charles-André. *Kasavubu au coeur du drame congolais*. Brussels: Europe-Afrique, 1964.

Goldschmidt, Walter (ed.). *The United States and Africa*. New York: Frederick A. Praeger, 1963.

Gordon, King. *The United Nations in the Congo: A Quest for Peace*. New York: Carnegie Endowment for International Peace, 1962.

Green, Reginald H., and Ann Seidman. *Unity or Poverty? The Economics of Pan-Africanism*. Baltimore: Penguin, 1968.

Hance, William. *The Geography of Modern Africa*. New York: Columbia University Press, 1964.

Harrington, Michael. *American Power in the Twentieth Century*. New York: League for Industrial Democracy, 1967.

Heinz, G., and H. Donnay. *Lumumba Patrice: Les cinquantes derniers jours de sa vie*. Brussels: CRISP, 1966.

Hilsman, Roger. *To Move a Nation: The Politics of Foreign Policy in the Administration of John F. Kennedy*. Garden City, N.Y.: Doubleday, 1967.

Hilsman, Roger, and Robert C. Good (eds.). *Foreign Policy in the Sixties*. Baltimore: Johns Hopkins Press, 1965.

Hoare, Mike. *Congo Mercenary*. London: R. Hale, 1967.

Hofstadter, Richard. *The Age of Reform: From Bryan to F.D.R.* New York: Alfred A. Knopf, 1955.

Horowitz, David (ed.). *Corporations and the Cold War*. New York: Monthly Review Press, 1969.

Hoskyns, Catherine. *The Congo Since Independence: January 1960–December 1961*. London: Oxford University Press, 1965.

Houart, Pierre. *La Pénétration communiste au Congo*. Brussels: Centre de Documentation Internationale, 1960.

INFORCONGO. *L'Economie du Congo Belge et du Ruanda-Urundi*. Brussels: INFORCONGO, 1958.

Joye, Pierre, and Rosine Lewin. *Les Trusts au Congo.* Brussels: Société Populaire d'Editions, 1961.

Kalanda, A. Mabika. *La Remise en question.* Brussels: Remarques Africaines, 1967.

Kamarck, Andrew M. *The Economics of African Development.* New York: Frederick A. Praeger, 1967.

Kamitatu, Cléophas. *La Grande Mystification du Congo-Kinshasa.* Paris: François Maspero, 1971.

Kashamura, Anicet. *De Lumumba aux colonels.* Paris: Buchet/Chastel, 1966.

Kestergat, Jean. *Congo, Congo.* Paris: La Table Ronde, 1965.

Key, V. O. *Public Opinion and American Democracy.* New York: Alfred A. Knopf, 1961.

Kitchen, Helen (ed.). *Footnotes to the Congo Story: An "Africa Report" Anthology.* New York: Walker and Co., 1967.

Kraft, Joseph. *Profiles in Power: A Washington Insight.* New York: New American Library, 1966.

Lafeber, Walter. *America, Russia and the Cold War 1945–1966.* New York: John Wiley and Sons, 1967.

Lash, Joseph P. *Dag Hammarskjold: Custodian of the Brush Fire Peace.* Garden City, N.Y.: Doubleday, 1961.

Lefever, Ernest W. *Crisis in the Congo: A United Nations Force in Action.* Washington: The Brookings Institution, 1965.

——. *Uncertain Mandate: Politics of the U.N. Congo Operation.* Baltimore: Johns Hopkins Press, 1967.

Legum, Colin. *Congo Disaster.* Baltimore: Penguin, 1961.

Lemarchand, René. *Political Awakening in the Belgian Congo.* Berkeley and Los Angeles: University of California Press, 1964.

Lipset, Seymour Martin. *Political Man: The Social Bases of Politics.* Garden City, N.Y.: Anchor, 1963.

Lumumba, Patrice. *Congo My Country.* Translated by Graham Heath. Forword by Colin Legum. New York: Frederick A. Praeger, 1962.

Mannheim, Karl. *Ideology and Utopia: An Introduction to the Sociology of Knowledge.* New York: Harvest, 1936.

McKay, Vernon. *Africa in World Politics.* New York: Harper and Row, 1963.

——. *L'Afrique et les Américains.* Montrouge, France: Editions France-Empire, 1967.

Merlier, Michel. *Le Congo de la colonisation belge à l'indépendance.* Paris: François Maspero, 1962.

Merriam, Alan P. *Congo: Background of Conflict.* Evanston, Ill.: Northwestern University Press, 1961.

Michel, Serge. *Uhuru Lumumba.* Paris: Juillard, 1962.

Milliband, Ralph, and John Saville (eds.). *Socialist Register 1966.* New York: Monthly Review Press, 1966.

Murphy, Robert. *Diplomat Among Warriors.* Garden City, N.Y.: Doubleday, 1964.

Nielsen, Waldemar A. *African Battleline: American Policy Choices in Southern Africa.* New York: Harper and Row, 1965.

Nkrumah, Kwame. *Challenge of the Congo.* New York: International Publishers, 1967.

——. *Neocolonialism: The Last Stage of Imperialism.* New York: International Publishers, 1966.

O'Brien, Conor Cruise. *To Katanga and Back.* New York: Simon and Schuster, 1962.

——. *Writers and Politics.* New York: Pantheon, 1964.

Organisation de Coopération et de Développement Economique. *L'Industrie des metaux non-ferreux.* Paris: O.C.D.E., 1967.

Perlo, Victor. *The Empire of High Finance.* New York: International Publishers, 1957.

Pfeffer, Richard (ed.). *No More Vietnams? The War and the Future of American Foreign Policy.* New York: Harper Colophon, 1968.

Porter, John Sherman (ed.). *Moody's Bank and Finance Manual, 1960–1964.* New York: Moody's Investors Service, 1961–1965.

——. *Moody's Industrials Manual, 1960–1964.* New York: Moody's Investors Service, 1961–1965.

Reed, David. *111 Days* in Stanleyville. New York: Harper and Row, 1965.

Rouch, Jane. *En cage avec Lumumba.* Paris: L'Edition du Temps, 1961.

Schatten, Fritz. *Communism in Africa.* New York: Frederick A. Praeger, 1966.

Schlesinger, Jr., Arthur M. *A Thousand Days.* New York: Fawcett, 1967.

Scott, Ian. *Tumbled House: The Congo at Independence.* London: Oxford University Press, 1969.

Servan-Schreiber, J. J. *The American Challenge.* New York: Avon, 1969.

Simpson, Smith. *Anatomy of the State Department.* Boston: Houghton Mifflin, 1967.

Sorenson, Theodore. *Kennedy.* New York: Harper and Row, 1965.

Spaak, Paul-Henri. *Combats inachevés,* II. Paris: Fayard, 1969.

Spanier, John. *American Foreign Policy Since World War II.* 2d rev. ed. New York: Frederick A. Praeger, 1965.

Stevens, Georgiana (ed.). *The United States and the Middle East.* Englewood Cliffs, N.J.: Spectrum, 1964.

Stokke, Beard Richard. *Soviet and Eastern European Trade and Aid in Africa.* New York: Frederick A. Praeger, 1967.

Tshombe, Moise. *My Fifteen Months in Government.* Translated by Lewis Bernays. Plono, Texas: University of Plono Press, 1967.

Tully, Andrew. *C.I.A.—The Inside Story.* New York: W. Morrow, 1962.

United Nations Statistical Yearbook, 1962. New York, International Office of the U.N., 1963.

Urquhart, Brian. *Hammarskjold.* London: Bodley Head, 1973.

Vandewalle, Colonel e.r. Frédéric. *L'Ommegang: Odysée et reconquête de Stanleyville, 1964.* Brussels: F. Vandewalle-Le Livre Africain, 1970.

Van Lierde, Jean. *La Pensée politique de Patrice Lumumba.* Paris: Présence Africaine, 1963.

Verhaegen, Benoît. *Congo 1961.* Brussels: CRISP, 1962.

——. *Rébellions au Congo,* I. Brussels: CRISP, 1966.

——. *Rébellions au Congo,* II. Brussels: CRISP, 1969.

Von Horn, Major General Carl. *Soldiering for Peace.* New York: David McKay and Co., 1967.

Weiss, Herbert F. *Political Protest in the Congo: The Parti Solidaire Africain During the Independence Struggle.* Princeton: Princeton University Press, 1967.

Weiss, Herbert and Benoît Verhaegen. *Parti Solidaire Africain (PSA): Documents 1969–1970.* Brussels: CRISP, 1963.

Welensky, Sir Roy. *Welensky's 4,000 Days.* New York: Roy Publishers, 1964.

White, Theodore. *The Making of the President 1960.* New York: New American Library, Signet, 1962.

Who's Who in America, 1960–1965. Chicago: Marquis-Who's Who Inc., 1960–1965.

Wilcox, Francis O., and H. Field Haviland, Jr. (eds.). *The United States and the United Nations.* Baltimore: Johns Hopkins Press, 1961.

Willame, Jean-Claude. *Les Provinces du Congo: Structure et fonctionnement.* I: Kwilu-Luluabourg-NordKatanga-Ubangi. IV: Lomani-Kivu Central. Leopoldville: IRES Lovanium, 1964–1965.

Williams, William Appleman. *American-Russian Relations 1781–1947.* New York: Rinehart, 1952.

Young, Crawford. *Politics in the Congo: Decolonization and Independence.* Princeton: Princeton University Press, 1965.

Zolberg, Aristide R. *Creating Political Order: The Party States of West Africa.* Chicago: Rand McNally and Co., 1966.

Articles and Periodicals

Africa Today (Special Issue), XIII (Jan., 1966).

"The Arab and Israeli War," *Foreign Affairs,* XLVI (Jan., 1968), 304–336.

Arrighi, Giovanni and John S. Saul. "Socialism and Economic Development in Tropical Africa," *Journal of Modern African Studies,* VI (Spring, 1968), 141–169.

Blouin, Andrée. Series of biographical articles, *La Wallonie* (Liège), Oct. 21–22, 1961, through Feb. 3–4, 1962.

Business Week, 1960–1964.

Bustin, Edouard. "Confrontation in the Congo," *Current History,* LII (Mar., 1967), 70 ff.

——. "Confrontation in the Congo," *Current History,* LIV (Feb., 1968), 83 ff.

Christian Science Monitor, 1960–1964.

Cleveland, Harlan. "Memo for the New Secretary of State," *New York Times Magazine,* Dec. 11, 1960, pp. 11 ff.

Congressional Quarterly Almanac, Vol. XVIII, 87th Congress, 2nd Session, 1962.

Cordier, Andrew W. "Challenge in the Congo," *Think,* XXXI (July–Aug., 1965), 21–29.

Courrier Africain du CRISP, 1959–1967.

"The Engelhard Touch," *Forbes,* Aug. 1, 1965, pp. 20–24.

Fox, Renée C., Willy de Craemer, and Jean-Marie Ribeaucourt. "The Second Independence: A Case Study of the Kwilu Rebellion in the Congo," *Comparative Studies in Society and History,* VIII (Oct., 1965), 78–109.

Harrington, Michael. "For a Dynamic Majority," *New Leader,* Mar. 27, 1967, pp. 19–21.

Hatch, John. "Hostages, Mercenaries and the CIA.," *Nation,* Dec. 14, 1964, pp. 452–459.

Herman, Fernand. "La Situation économique et financière du Congo en 1962," *Etudes Congolaises,* IV (Mar., 1963), 1–27.

——. "La Situation économique et financière du Congo en 1963," *Etudes Congolaises,* VI (Apr., 1964), 1–36.

Hoare, Michael. Article in *Le Figaro Littéraire,* Dec. 17–23, 1964, p. 9.

Hoskyns, Catherine. "The Congo as the U.N. Leaves," *World Today,* XX (June, 1964), 231–234.

"How to Do Business Successfully in Africa," *Business Abroad,* XCIII (Dec. 1968), 25–26.

Howard, Charles P. "Katanga and the Congo Betrayal," *Freedomways,* II (Spring 1962), 136–48.

International Commerce (formerly *Foreign Commerce Weekly*), 1959–1967.

Iron Age, 1960–1962.

Jeune Afrique (formerly *Afrique Action*), 1960–1964.

Kateb, George. "Kennedy as Statesman," *Commentary,* XLI (June, 1966), 54–60.

Kraft, Joseph. "George Ball—An Operator on the Potomac Comes to the East River," *New York Times Magazine,* July 21, 1968, 5 ff.

——. "School for Statesmen," *Harper's,* XXCVII (July, 1958), 64–68.

Lacroix, J. L. "Inga," *Etudes Congolaises,* X (Jan., 1967), 1–17.

Laqueur, Walter. "Russia Enters the Middle East," *Foreign Affairs,* XLVII (Jan., 1969), 296–308.

Le Clerq, Hugues. "Analyse générale de l'inflation congolaise," *Cahiers Economiques et Sociaux,* I (Oct., 1962), 3–40.

"Les Mercenaries dans l'histoire du Congo (1960–1967)," *Courrier Africain,* Nos. 74–75, Feb. 26, 1968.

Libre Belgique (Brussels), Jan. 1960–Mar. 1961.

Lipset, Seymour Martin. "The President, The Polls, and Vietnam," *Transaction.* III (Sept.–Oct., 1966), 19–24.

Markowitz, Marvin D., and Herbert F. Weiss. "Rebellion in the Congo," *Current History,* XLVIII (Apr., 1965), 213–218.

Meet the Press, Dec. 3, 1961.

Merlier, Michel. "L'Economie congolaise de 1960 à 1965," *Le Mois en Afrique,* No. 4 (Apr. 1966), pp. 22–36.

Miller, Warren E., and Donald E. Stokes. "Constituency Influence in Congress," *American Political Science Review,* LVII (Mar. 1963), 45–56.

Moseley, Philip E. "The Kremlin and the Third World," *Foreign Affairs,* XLVI (Oct., 1967), 64–77.

Muleas, John P. "Christian Herter-Heir Unapparent," *New Republic,* Feb. 6, 1956, pp. 8–10.

New York Herald Tribune, 1960–1961.

New York Times, 1960–1964.

Nzongola, George N. "Les Classes sociales et la révolution anti-coloniale au Congo-Kinshasa: le rôle de la coloniale bourgeoisie," *Cahiers Economiques et Sociaux,* VIII (Sept., 1970), 371–388.

O'Brien, Conor Cruise. "The United Nations and the Congo," *Studies on the Left.* VI (May–June, 1966), 3–27.

Ostrander, F. Taylor. "U.S. Private Investment in Africa," *Africa Report,* XIV (Jan., 1969), 38–40.

"Partners in Apartheid, United States Policy on South Africa," *Africa Today,* Vol. XI (Mar., 1964).

"Poids socio-politique des ressortissants de l'Equateur à Kinshasa," *Courrier Africain,* No. 84, Nov. 8, 1968.

Rudin, Harry R. "Political Rivalry in the Congo," *Current History,* L (Mar., 1966), 159 ff.

Ryelandt, Bernard. "Evolution des prix à Leopoldville," *Cahiers Economiques et Sociaux,* I (Oct., 1962), 57–65.

Semonin, Paul F. "Killing them Definitively," *Nation,* Jan. 31, 1966, pp. 129–132.

——. "Proxy Fight in the Congo," *Nation,* Mar. 6, 1967, pp. 303–306.

Smith, Richard Austin. "The Rockefeller Brothers—II," *Fortune,* LI (Mar., 1955), 116 ff.

Stevenson, Adlai E. "The New Africa," *Harper's,* CCXX (May, 1960), 48–54.

Stolle, Jane. "Gamble in the Congo," *Nation,* Feb. 18, 1961, 131–132.

Survey of Current Business, XL (Sept., 1960).

Temmerman, Major General e.r. François. Articles in *Le Soir,* Nov. 28 and Dec. 2, 1969.

Time, 1960–1964.

Turner, Thomas. "L'Ethnie tetela et le MNC-Lumumba," *Etudes Congolaises,* XII (Oct.–Dec., 1969), 36–57.

Verhaegen, Benoît. "L'Armée Nationale congolaise," *Etudes Congolaises,* X (July–Aug., 1967), 1–29.

——. "Les Associations congolaises à Léopoldville et dans le Bas-Congo avant 1960," *Cahiers Economiques et Sociaux,* VIII (Sept., 1970), 389–416.

——. "La Décolonisation au Maniema 1958–1959: Notes en marge de Rébellions au Congo-Maniema," *Etudes Africaines,* Nos. 114–115, 1970.

——. "Lutte des classes au Congo," *Révolution,* X (July–Aug., 1964), 31–38.

——. "Recension des ouvrages," *Etudes Africaines,* No. 123, Dec. 30, 1970.

Wall Street Journal, 1960–1964.

Washington Post, 1960–1964.

Wolfe, Alvin. "Economies in Bondage: The Mining Industry," *Africa Today,* XIV (Jan., 1967), 16–20.

——. "The African Mineral Industry: Evolution of a Supernational Level of Integration," *Social Problems,* XI (Fall, 1963), 153–64.

Young, Crawford. "Congo-Kinshasa Situation Report," *Africa Report,* XII (Oct., 1967), 12–18.

Ziegler, Jean. "Le Katanga Lobby aux Etats-Unis," *Courrier Africain,* Mar. 21, 1963.

Zolberg, Aristide. "A View from the Congo," *World Politics,* XIX, (Oct., 1966), 137–149.

——. "The Structure of Political Conflict in the New States of Tropical Africa," *American Political Science Review,* LXII (Mar., 1968), 70–87.

Public Documents

United Nations. *Annual Report* of the Secretary-General on the Work of the Organization, June 16, 1962–June 15, 1963, A/5501.

United Nations. Security Council. *Official Records.* Supplement for Oct., Nov., Dec. 1960, S/4557—. Supplement for Jan., Feb., Mar. 1963, S/5240. Supplement for Apr., May, June 1963, S/5240. Addenda Supplement for Apr., May, June 1964, S/5784.

United States Bureau of the Census. *Statistical Abstract of the United States 1966.* Washington: U.S. Government Printing Office, 1966.

United States Bureau of Mines. *Minerals Yearbook,* 1960. Washington: U.S. Government Printing Office, 1961.

United States Congress, Senate. Committee on Foreign Relations. *Study Mission to Africa,* Nov.–Dec. 1960. Committee Print, Feb. 12, 1961.

——. Committee on Foreign Relations. *United States in the United Nations 1960: A Turning Point.* Committee Print. 3 Vols. 87th Congress, 1st Session, 1961.

——. Committee on the Judiciary. *Visa Procedures of Department of State.* Hearings before the Subcommittee to Investigate the Administration of the Internal Security Act and Other Internal Security Laws. Committee Print. 87th Congress, 2nd Session, 1962.

United States, *Congressional Record,* 1960–1964. Vols. CVI–CX.

United States Department of Commerce. *Africa. A Growth Market for*

U.S. Business. Washington, U.S. Government Printing Office, 1968.

——. *"Overseas Business Reports,* Basic Data on the Economy of the Democratic Republic of the Congo (Kinshasa)," OBR 68–6, Apr. 1968.

United States Department of State. *Bulletin,* 1960–1964.

——. *U.S. Participation in the U.N. 1961,* Department of State Publication No. 74-13. Washington: U.S. Government Printing Office, Aug. 1962.

Unpublished Materials

Cleveland, Harlan. "The Theory and Practice of Foreign Aid." Paper prepared for the Special Studies Project of the Rockefeller Brothers Fund, Syracuse, Maxwell School, 1963.

"Compte Rendu de la réunion tenue au Cabinet de Monsieur Finant, Président du Governement Provincial (Province Orientale)," Stanleyville, Sept. 24, 1960. Archives de la Province Orientale, Kisangani. Mimeographed.

Farrell Lines. "Africa News Digest," New York, 1960–1964. Mimeographed.

Herter, Christian. "Problems of Foreign Aid," Speech to the Economic Club of Detroit (Michigan) Mar. 22, 1948.

Hobson, Christopher, et al. "Information on U.S. Involvement in South Africa," Chicago, 1965, Mimeographed.

Imbata, Pius. "Organisation et fonctionnement des services administratifs en Province Orientale sous le régime Gizenga 1960–1961," Mémoire, Université Libre du Congo, July 1971.

Kaplan, Stephen. "Images of the Congo: The Problems and Importance of News Reporting During a Third World Crisis." Master's Thesis, University of Chicago, 1968.

LeMelle, Tilden. "Role of Large and Small Powers in the Congo Crisis," Denver 1963. (Typewritten paper)

Morgan, Mary C. "Politics in the Pursuit of Power: The Foreign Policy of Patrice Lumumba." Honors Thesis, Smith College, 1967.

National Association of Secondary Materials Industries. "Metals Report," New York, June 22 and July 13, 1960. Mimeographed.

Ostrander, F. Taylor. "The Corporate Structure of Rhodesian Copperbelt Mining Enterprise." New York, Aug. 31, 1962. Mimeographed.

——. "The Place of Minerals in Economic Development." A talk presented to the Council of Economics at the 92nd Annual Meeting of the American Institute of Mining, Metallurgical and Petroleum Engineers, Dallas, Texas, Feb. 27, 1963. Mimeographed.

"Report on the Conference on African Resources," sponsored by New York University and Africa Fair Inc., New York, Mar. 27–29, 1961. Mimeographed.

Timberlake, Clare Hayes. "First Years of Independence in the Congo: Events and Issues." Master's Thesis, Department of International Affairs, George Washington University, 1963.

Other Sources

Annual Reports of the Council on Foreign Relations, 1959–1965.

Annual Reports of Corporations with Interests in the Congo, 1959–1964.

Dillon, Read and Co., *The Belgian Congo: Fifteen Year 5¼% External Loan Bonds of 1958*. Prospectus. New York: Apr. 15, 1958.

"The Hot and Cold Wars of Allen Dulles," CBS Reports, Apr. 26, 1962 (typewritten transcript).

List of Officers of African-American Institute, 1959–1965.

Personal interviews with policy-makers and informed individuals.

Portions of files of American Committee for Aid to Katanga Freedom Fighters (Letters, telegrams, news releases).

Index

Adams, Paul, 230
Adoula, Cyrille, 21, 21n., 22n., 105, 105n., 106, 106n., 109, 127, 149-151, 153-154, 158-159, 161-164, 167, 169-170, 170n., 178-180, 182-183, 183n., 184-186, 199-208, 212-213, 226-227, 230-231, 231n., 232-234, 236, 243, 282, 285, 292
African-American Institute (AAI), 173, 174n., 176
Afro-Asians, 43, 69, 257; interests in Congo, 26-27; Lovanium Conference activity, 149; Lumumba considers troop appeal to, 65, 74, 78-79, 264; positions toward the U.N. Operation, 65, 77-78, 101-104, 106-107, 107n., 115, 136, 139-140, 142-145, 153-154, 157-159, 163-165, 167, 292; support for Stanleyville regime, 146, 148
Aiken, Senator, 140
Algeria, 26, 117, 221-222, 254, 275, 280; Provisional Government of (GPRA), 82, 259
Alliance des Bakongo (ABAKO), 19, 72, 85-86, 185, 232, 269
Alvarez, Luis Lopez, 95
American Committee for Aid to Katanga Freedom Fighters, 168-169, 171-172; *see also* Katanga Lobby
American Eur-African Development Corporation, 34
American Federation of Labor–Congress of Industrial Organizations (AFL–CIO), 105, 105n.
American Metal Climax (AMAX), 33, 35, 50, 76, 126, 172-174, 178
American South African Investment, 35
Anaconda Copper, 225
Anglo-American Company, 33, 129n.
Angola, 26, 31-33, 73, 134, 228, 231
Armée Nationale Congolaise (ANC), 22, 139, 141-142, 209; alleged Soviet aid offers to, 185-186; exploitative behavior, 203, 285; invasion of Kasai, 84, 88; and Lovanium Conference, 147, 151; Mobutu's role in, 96, 100, 108, 109n.; mutiny of, 55-58, 68-69, 257; and 1964 rebellions, 220, 226-228, 237-243, 246-253; Third Group of (Stanleyville), 270; Western military aid to, 211-214, 226-230, 233, 237-243, 246-253
Armée Populaire de Libération (APL), 217, 220
Association des Baluba du Katanga (BALUBAKAT), 19, 68, 152
Atlantic Council of the United States, 145
Attwood, William, 136n., 244-245, 251n., 278, 291n.
Azores, 166, 298

Badeau, John, 276
Bakongo, 16, 19

Ball, George, 132-134, 136, 163, 165-166, 174, 183, 186, 186n., 193, 205n., 223, 246, 249, 298
Baluba: of Kasai, 16, 22, 66; of Katanga, 68, 70; *see also* Association des Baluba du Katanga
Bangala, 16
Bank of America, 38n., 39n.
Banque du Congo, 36
Bapende-Bambundu, 202, 216
Batetela–Bakusu, 18, 202
Battle Line, 171
Baudouin, King, 47, 55, 257
Bayeke, 19-20, 66, 70
Beichman, Arnold, 61, 86
Belgian-American Banking Corporation, 34, 172
Belgium, 25, 31, 44, 53-54, 199, 208, 257, 265-266, 268-269, 289, 292; aid to Katangan secession, 68-72, 74, 92, 139; aid to South Kasai secession, 102; colonial system, 15-16, 22, 196-197, 288; decolonization by, 16-17, 20, 21; interests in Congo, 23-25, 46, 63; intervention in mutiny, 56-66, 272; military aid to Congo Government, 211-214, 220, 227-228, 237-253; and overthrow of Lumumba, 86, 88, 94, 98-99, 102; positions toward the U.N. Operation, 62-63, 140-141, 144-145, 147, 152-194; and return of Tshombe, 233-235
Belgo-America Development Corporation, 175-176
Binza group, 109, 138, 230-232, 235-236, 292
Bisukiro, Marcel, 20
Blacks, U.S., 44, 117, 122, 175
Block National Démocratique (BND), 162
Blouin, Andrée, 82-83, 259-261, 272
Bohlen, Charles, 105
Bolikango, Jean, 21, 21n., 149
Bolivia, 300
Bomboko, Justin, 58, 88-89, 95, 100, 109, 127, 162, 200, 230-231, 231n., 233, 243, 265, 271
Bosch, J. van den, 58
Bowles, Chester, 117, 120, 122-123, 125-126, 130, 133-134, 138, 142, 145, 174, 193, 205n., 225, 298
British Guiana, 136n., 300
Brown Brothers Harriman, 225
Buckley, William, 168
Bunche, Ralph, 57, 60n., 61, 78
Bundy, McGeorge, 246
Burden, William, 50
Burundi, 134, 217, 254
Byrd, Harry F., 171

Canada, 213
Canup, William, 145, 156
Cardoso, Mario, 87
Casablanca Conference, 115
Central Africa, 26-27, 31, 53, 80, 83, 159, 163, 185
Central African Federation, *see* Rhodesia and Nyasaland, Federation of Centre de Regroupement Africain (CEREA), 19-20, 21n.
Cerro de Posco, 50
Ceylon, 63, 142
Chase Manhattan Bank, 37, 176-177
Chile, 30
Church, Senator, 140, 159
Citizens Committee for NATO, 45
Cleveland, Harlan, 117, 117n., 121, 125, 125n., 128, 130, 134, 174, 179, 191, 195, 209-210, 212n., 298
Cobalt, 23, 28, 28n., 29, 29n., 180
College of Commissioners, 88, 95, 100, 102, 104, 108
Columbium-tantalite, 28n., 29; *see also* Tantalum
Commerce and Industry Association of New York, 39
Committee of National Liberation (CNL), 201, 217, 219-220, 231-233, 236-237, 269, 279n.
Committee of One Million, 168, 172
Communist threat in Congo, 52-53, 55, 59-60, 62, 66, 75, 79, 79n., 80-84, 87, 121, 133-136, 159, 160n., 163-164, 166, 169, 184-186, 191, 204, 208, 220-221, 222-225; evaluation of, 257-283, 295, 297

Compagnie des Chemins de Fer du Congo Supérieur aux Grands Lacs Africains (CFL), 219
Compagnie Générale d'Automobiles et d'Aviation au Congo (CEGEAC), 37
Confédération des Associations Tribales du Katanga (CONAKAT), 20, 66-68, 71-72, 152, 180, 290
Conference of Independent African States, 27
Conference of Non-Aligned States (1961), 273; (1964), 245
Conference on African Resources, 36
Congo parliament, 53, 92, 95, 102, 104-105, 139, 145-152, 156, 184-185, 200-201, 208; Chamber of Representatives, 19, 65, 179, 185, 200; Senate, 64
Congo-Brazzaville, 36, 72-73, 127, 134, 150, 217, 254
Conseils des Sages, 218-219
Copper, 23-24, 28, 28n., 29-30, 180, 219
Copperbelt, 25, 28-29, 33, 39, 50, 67, 76, 76n., 126
Cordier, Andrew, 60n., 89-90, 90n., 91, 92n., 102
Corning Glass International, 47, 173
Council on Foreign Relations, 50, 174, 177
Creel, Dana S., 176-177
Croquez, 88
Cushing, Benjamin Hilton, 242
Cuba, 27, 134, 275; exiles from (CIA), 229, 229n., 239-240, 252; missile crisis, 184; U.S. invasion of, 193
Czechoslovakia, 55, 98, 134, 149

d'Aspremont-Lynden, Harold, 71
David, Jean, 93n., 94-95
Davister, Pierre, 232, 234
Dayal Rajeshwar, 102-104, 106, 111, 146-147
De Gaulle, Charles, 26, 43, 72
Democratic Advisory Council, 117, 117n.
Denis, 88
De Schryver, 58
Detwiler, Edgar, 265
Devlin, Lawrence, 95-96, 96n., 97n., 109, 138, 145
De Vos, Pierre, 21n., 266
Dewey, Thomas, 48
Diamond Company of Angola, 23, 34
Diamonds, 23, 28-29, 30n., 34, 127-128
Dillon, Douglas, 34, 37, 45, 48-50, 53, 76, 78
Dillon group, 34-35
Dillon, Read and Co., 34-35, 35n., 38, 49
Dirksen, Senator, 159, 169
Dodd, Thomas, 149, 159-161, 161n., 169, 169n., 171, 175, 175n., 181, 225, 246, 292
Dodds, William A., 226, 227n.
Dominican Republic, 300
Donnay, H., 137
Draper, Theodore, 276
Drexel and Co., 49-50
Dulles, Allen W., 280
Dulles, John Foster, 30n., 48
Dungan, Ralph, 182
Dylan, Bob, 23

East Africa, 26-27, 31
Eastern Europe, 52, 55, 162, 269-270
Eastland, Senator, 171
Ecuador, 63
Egypt, 52, 81, 141-142, 149, 162, 215, 221-222, 254, 269, 273, 275, 280, 283, 300
Eisenhower, Dwight D., 27, 43, 45-46, 49, 59, 61, 74, 116, 139, 177, 191, 214, 262, 279, 282, 298, 300
Engelhard, Charles, 33, 35, 50, 172-173
Engelhard Hanovia, 35
Equateur Province, 72, 96
Ethiopia, 162, 162n., 179, 214, 227, 243
European-African Development Corporation, 172-175
Eyskens, Prime Minister, 71

Farber, Herbert, 175-176
Farrell Lines, 39
Filatures et Tissages Africains (FILTISAF), 37
Fomin, André, 81, 83
Force Publique (Congo Colonial Army), 68, 70, 85, 95, 214, 258
Ford Foundation, 130
France, 44, 116, 131, 148; aid to Katanga secession, 72-73; interests in Congo, 25-26, 46; and overthrow of Lumumba, 86, 88; positions toward the U.N. Operation, 63, 140, 144, 165, 168, 181n., 212; and return of Tshombe, 233
Fredericks, Wayne, 130-131, 146, 158, 173, 223, 247n., 298
Fulbright, William, 140, 292

Gabon, 36
Ganshof van der Meersch, Walter, 54
Gardiner, Robert, 190n.
Gates, Thomas S., Jr., 49-50
Gbenye, Christophe, 15n., 162, 200-202, 207-208, 217, 219, 222, 252-253, 268n.
Gendebien, Paul-Henry, 87, 94, 190n.
General Motors, 34, 172
Gérard-Libois, Jules, 23
Ghana, 19-20, 37-38, 79n., 84, 93n., 106, 127, 149, 228, 267, 283, 300
Gizenga, Antoine, 20, 54, 58, 78, 82, 85, 110, 136, 141, 146, 148-150, 151n., 153-155, 159, 162, 164, 200-202, 207-209, 232, 236, 259-261, 292; political evaluation of, 269-273, 280
Godley, G. McMurtrie, 235-236
Goldwater, Senator, 171
Great Britain, 54, 148, 267; aid to Katanga secession, 72; interests in Congo, 25-26, 46; positions toward U.N. Operation, 63, 155, 157, 159, 164, 167-168, 179, 181, 187, 189-190
Greece, 52, 134
Greene, Michael J. L., 212
"Greene Plan," 212-213
Guatemala, 300
Guggenheim interests, 34, 36; *see also* Ryan–Guggenheim group
Guinea, 20, 43, 52, 79n., 81, 84, 127, 141, 259-260, 267, 269, 272, 275, 278-279, 283, 291
Gulf Oil, 38
Gullion, Edmund, 131, 158-159, 163, 170, 178-179, 182, 190, 206-208, 212, 226, 235, 298

Hagerty, James, 59
Halberstam, David, 207
Hammarskjold, Dag, 60, 60n., 62, 77, 77n., 78-80, 83, 87, 90n., 91-92, 101-102, 104-105, 107, 107n., 110-111, 141-143, 147, 153-157, 157n., 158-159, 164, 268
Harriman, E. H., 225
Harriman, Edward H., 223
Harriman, W. Averell, 134, 136n., 161, 222-225, 228, 228n., 237-238, 243, 246, 248-249, 275, 298
Heinz, G., 137
Heinzerling, Lynn, 83
Herter, Christian, 45, 48-49, 51n., 57, 59-60, 66, 79n., 84, 111
Herter, Christian, Jr., 48, 51n.
Hickenlooper, Senator, 171
Hightower, John, 105
Hilsman, Roger, 186, 193
Hochshild, Harold R., and family, 126, 173-174
Hofstadter, Richard, 296
Home, Lord, 148
Hoover, Herbert, 45, 48, 171
Hoskyns, Catherine, 78, 82, 92, 108, 259, 287, 290
Howard, Charles, 94
Howe, Russell Warren, 81, 281
Humphrey, Senator, 153n., 159-160, 292, 297

Ileo, Joseph, 21, 21n., 91-92, 95, 95n., 105
India, 115, 145-146, 153n., 179, 183, 189-190
Indochina, 117, 131; *see also* Laos and Vietnam
Indonesia, 135
Inforcongo, 96

Inga Dam, 37-38, 50
International Basic Economy Corporation, 37
International Business Machines (IBM), 38
International Confederation of Free Trade Unions (ICFTU), 105, 205
International Court of Justice, 177-178
International Monetary Fund, 53, 208, 278
Iran, 52, 300
Iraq, 275
Ironsi, Major General, 226-227, 227n.
Isaacson, Clayton, 251n.
Israel, 19, 58, 212-213, 251n., 276
Italy, 25, 63

Jagan, Cheddi, 136, 136n.
Janssens, General, 56, 214
Jayle, 88
John Birch Society, 172
Johnson, Lyndon B., 128, 211, 225, 238n., 249, 297-298, 300
Johnston, Eric, 38n., 39n.

Kalonji, Albert, 22, 86, 207
Kamitatu, Cléophas, 92
Kandolo, Damien, 109, 230-231
Kanza, Thomas, 245, 247n., 251n.
Kariba Dam, 29
Kasai Province, 23, 61, 84, 127, 261; South Kasai, 25, 28-29, 32, 34, 207, 289; State of South Kasai, 72, 80, 86, 88, 138
Kasavubu, Joseph, 17, 19, 22, 54, 57-58, 61, 64, 72n., 84, 87-90, 90n., 91, 91n., 92-93, 93n., 94-95, 95n., 96-101, 104-106, 106n., 107-108, 127, 142-143, 145, 148-149, 185, 200, 230-234, 236, 265, 271
Kashamura, Anicet, 82, 85, 260
Kasongo, Joseph, 93n.
Katanga Calling, 103
Katanga Information Services, 103, 175
Katanga Lobby, 177, 193, 246; *see also* American Committee for Aid to Katanga Freedom Fighters
Katanga Province, 18-20, 23-34, 46, 50, 58, 60-61, 66-80, 84, 86, 92-93, 100-101, 103, 110, 130, 137, 139-140, 143-144, 148-149, 152-194, 203-205, 211, 230-231, 234n., 238, 258, 261, 267, 284-286, 289-290, 292, 298, 302
Kaysen, Carl, 182
Keating, Senator, 159
Kellogg Company, 130
Kennecott Copper Company, 34, 36
Kennedy, Edward, 106n.
Kennedy Foundation, 116
Kennedy, John F., 49, 11, 116-117, 122, 122n., 125n., 127, 130-135, 135n., 141, 143, 158, 161, 161n., 163, 168, 170, 175, 177, 181, 181n., 183-184, 187, 191-194, 211, 214, 246, 265, 272, 276, 279, 283, 298, 300
Kennedy, Robert, 136n.
Kenya, 254
Kettani, General, 96, 98, 98n.
Khiary, Mahmoud, 149-151, 154, 156, 157n., 170
Khrushchev, Nikita, 27, 61, 64-65, 134-135, 279
Kiewewa, A., 232
Kimbanguism, 197
Kirk, Alan G., 178
Kitawala, 197-198
Kivu Province, 18-19, 205n., 217, 229n., 230, 261
Kraft, Joseph, 224, 224n.
Krock, Arthur, 176
Kwilu Province, 198, 202, 208, 215, 217-218, 226, 228n., 236, 269, 273-274

Ladenberg, Thalman and Co., 37n.
Lallemand, Roger, 232
Laos, 134-135, 225, 280, 300
Lausche, Senator, 171
Lavallee, Jerome, 150n.
Lazard Frères, 33, 33n., 37n., 172, 178
Lefever, Ernest, 77, 279
Legum, Colin, 80, 258
Leopoldville Province, 24, 72

Liberia, 31, 142, 243-244
Lie, Trygve, 125
Liebman, Marvin, 168-169, 171
Lihau, Marcel, 88
Linner, Sture, 147, 156
Lipset, Seymour, 293-294
Lodge, Henry Cabot, 63, 65, 177, 298
Loi Fondomentale, 17, 88, 102, 170, 178
London Metal Exchange, 30
Lovanium Conference, 145-151, 151n., 154, 163, 201, 204-205, 289
Lowenthal, Richard, 282
Lower Congo, 24, 38, 58, 198
Lulua, 16, 18
Lumumba, Patrice, 17-20, 22, 23n., 46-47, 53-58, 61-62, 64-66, 68-69, 71, 73-74, 74n., 75, 77-93, 93n., 94, 94n., 95-98, 100-102, 104-105, 105n., 106-117, 108, 110, 136-138, 138n., 139-143, 146, 199, 201-202, 215, 237, 275, 279-282, 292; political evaluation of, 257-272
Lumumbists, 93-94, 105n., 110, 115, 139-140, 143, 150-151, 153, 180, 184-185, 198-202, 204, 207, 217, 220, 234, 237, 261-262, 264, 266, 273, 282, 285
Lunda, 19-20, 66, 70
Lundula, Victor, 92, 162

McCloy, John, 176-177
McCone, John, 238n.
McGhee, George, 133, 133n., 160, 166, 174-175, 181-182, 193
McKay, Vernon, 173
Macmillan, Harold, 168
McNamara, Robert, 128n., 194, 238n.
Malagasy (Madagascar), 72n., 243, 254
Malaysia, 52
Mali, 134
Malik, Charles, 121
Malley, Simon, 238n.
Manganese, 28, 28n.
Maniema, 18, 202, 202n., 220, 253
Mannheim, Karl, 294
Mansfield, Mike, 274-275
Mao Tse-tung, 215-216
Marx, Karl, 302
Menghessa, Iyassu, 214
Mennen Company, 122
Merlier, Michel, 271
Meyer, Charles, 176
Michel, Serge, 82-83, 259, 261
Middle East, 276-279
Missionaries, 69, 216, 219, 226; Belgian, 23, 196; U.S., 61, 109, 172, 293
Mobil Oil, 34, 48, 173-174
Mobutu, Joseph, 88, 94-97, 97n., 98-101, 103-105, 106n., 107, 107n., 108-109, 109n., 110, 137n., 139n., 141-142, 145, 147, 150-151, 180, 188, 200, 208, 214, 227, 230-231, 231n., 232-233, 237, 243, 284-285, 289
Mongo, 16, 18-19
Monnet, Jean, 132
Morgan Guaranty Trust, 35-36, 38, 49-50, 172-174
Morgan interests, 49
Morocco, 98
Morse, Wayne, 45
Mouvement National Congolais (MNC), 18; –Kalonji (MNC–K), 18, 86; –Lumumba (MNC–L), 18-20, 96, 151n., 217-218, 232, 263, 267-268
Mozambique, 26, 134
Mpolo, M., 85
Mulele, Pierre, 20, 202, 215-217, 219-220, 236, 270; political evaluation of, 273-274
Munongo, Godefroid, 66, 141, 237, 243
Murphy, Robert, 45, 47, 49-50, 53, 75, 132, 173, 175

Nasser, Gamal Abdel, 245, 273, 276, 277
National Review, 168-169, 171, 176
Ndele, Albert, 97, 109, 230-231
Nehru, J., 270, 273
Nendaka, Victor, 97, 97n., 109, 147, 230-231, 233, 237, 243
Newmont Mining, 32n., 33, 35-36, 172

Ngalula, Joseph, 86
Ngombe, 16
Nickerson, Albert, 174
Nielsen, Waldemar, 283
Nigeria, 37, 162, 162n., 226-228, 243-244, 254
Nixon, Richard, 171
Nkrumah, Kwame, 79n., 136, 136n., 259, 261, 267, 270, 293
North Atlantic Treaty Organization (NATO), 30, 43-44, 61, 74, 76, 118, 168, 212, 283
North Korea, 275
Norway, 213
Nyembo, A., 58

O'Brien, Conor Cruise, 89n., 108, 149, 154-156
Office de Cités Africains, 34
Olenga, N., 253
Oppenheimer, Harry, 33
Organization of African Unity (OAU), 227, 238, 241, 243-244, 247, 249, 283
Orientale Province, 18, 271n.
Ostrander, F. Taylor, 173-174

Palmer, Joseph, II, 243, 246
Parti Solidaire Africain (PSA), 19-20, 259, 269-270
Parti de l'Unité Nationale (PUNA), 85-86
Penfield, James, 51, 76, 131, 298
People's Republic of China, 215, 221-222, 238n., 257, 270, 272-274
Peru, 50
Philippines, 52
Poland, 63
Portugal, 26, 165, 168, 228, 283

Rassemblement des Démocrates du Congo (RADECO), 210, 210n., 231
Rattan, Donald, 242
Raudstein, Knut, 242, 242n.
Reston, James, 79, 82n.
Reynolds Aluminum, 38, 127
Reynolds, J. Louis, 38, 127
Reynolds Metals, 126
Rhodesia and Nyasaland, Federation of, 25-33, 39, 46, 50, 66, 72-73, 126, 148, 157, 188, 240-243, 292
Rhodesian Selection Trust, 33
Rockefeller brothers, 34, 36, 176; David, 37, 50, 177; Laurance, 37
Rockefeller Brothers Fund, 37, 121, 129, 177
Roosevelt, Franklin D., 125, 297
Rouch, Jane, 261
Rural radicalism, 195-199, 204, 215-221
Rusk, Dean, 133, 133n., 146, 158, 168, 183n., 194, 228, 238n., 249
Ryan, Allan A., 33
Ryan-Guggenheim, group, 33-34, 36, 172; *see also* Guggenheim interests

Sabena Airlines, 70, 80
Sartre, Jean-Paul, 20, 268
Satterthwaite, Joseph, 43, 76, 130, 298
Schlesinger, Arthur, Jr., 116, 193-194, 224, 295, 297
Scott, Ian, 44n., 146
Sendwe, J., 149
Senegal, 214, 243-244, 254
Senghor, Leopold, 164
Sevareid, Eric, 280
Sharpeville incident, 32
Shields, W. C., 39
Sierra Leone, 127
Simba, 217-220, 240, 251, 253
Sinclair, Colonel, 97
Slim, Mongi, 62-63, 77n.
Société Aluminum and Electric International, 38
Société Congolaise de Banque (SOCOBANQUE), 38
Société Congolaise pour la Production, la Manufacture et le Commerce d'Ananas (ANACONGO), 37
Société pour la Fabrication au Congo de Bôites Métalliques et de Tous Articles en Tôle Émaillée (COBEGA), 37
Société Générale de Belgique, 23-24, 34, 38, 72n., 127, 175-176

Société Internationale Forestrière et Minière du Congo (FORMINIERE), 33-34, 72n.
Société de Recherches et d'Exploitation de Bauxites au Congo (BAUXICONGO), 37
Sorenson, Theodore, 128n.
Soumialot, Gaston, 202, 217, 219, 219n.
Southern Africa, 26-27, 31-36, 39, 50, 68, 118, 172, 174, 185
Southwest Africa, 33, 35
Soviet Union, 52-53, 55, 59, 60, 80, 82, 116, 121-122, 124, 133-135, 140-141, 162, 166, 168, 180, 184-185, 201, 222, 224, 292, 295; aid to Lumumba, 74n., 79, 81, 83-85, 88, 91; aid to 1964 rebellion, 221, 221n.; diplomats expelled by Mobutu, 98; interests in Congo, 27, 279-282; and Lovanium Conference, 149; positions toward the U.N. Operation, 63, 77-78, 143-144, 165, 186, 212; reaction to mutiny and Belgian intervention, 61-62, 64-65; threat to Congo and Third World evaluated, 257, 259, 261-264, 272, 274-282, 295
Spaak, Paul-Henri, 145, 147, 154, 170n., 187, 187n., 188, 188n., 219, 228, 233, 237-238, 243, 249, 268n.
Spofford, Charles, 174, 174n.
Staebler, Neil, 130-131
Stalin, Joseph, 296
Stanford, Neal, 83, 86
Stanleyville regime (1961-1962), 110, 110n., 115, 141-143, 145-150, 154-155, 162, 164, 272, 284
Stevenson, Adlai, 85n., 117, 120, 122-123, 123-130, 132, 134, 138, 140, 143-144, 164, 173-174, 178, 192, 205n., 249, 254n., 286, 298
Struelens, Michel, 103, 150, 154n., 159-161, 161n., 175, 175n., 183, 207, 245-246
Sudan, 141-142, 221, 254
Syria, 275, 280

Taft, Robert, 49
Taiwan, 135
Tanganyika Concessions Ltd. (TANKS), 23, 26, 33, 37
Tantalum, 29; *see also* Columbium-tantalite
Tanzania, 221, 254
Tempelsman, Leon and Maurice, 127, 128, 128n, 176
Texaco, 38n.
Thant Plan, 180-181, 192-193
Thant, U, 164-167, 170-171, 182-183, 183n., 184, 189-190, 213, 226-227
Thiam, 254
Thomas, Colonel, 242
Thurmond, Senator, 159, 171
Timberlake, Clare, 51, 51n., 52n., 57-59, 80-82, 89, 91, 94, 98, 103-104, 106, 131, 137, 139-140, 142, 145-146, 258, 261, 272, 298
Tin, 28
Touré, Sekou, 116, 136, 136n., 259, 278
Truman, Harry S., 133, 177, 224
Tshombe, Moise, 58, 66, 69, 71, 74-78, 94, 103, 118, 141-142, 145-148, 150-159, 161, 163-170, 170n,. 171-172, 178-182, 184-185, 187-191, 201, 225, 228, 230-231, 231n., 232-234, 234n., 235-239, 243-246, 249, 253, 268, 282, 284-285, 292-293
Tsiranana, 254
Tully, Andrew, 89, 97n., 137
Tunisia, 62-63, 227

Uganda, 221
Unilever, 26
Union Minière du Haut Katanga, 24, 33, 47, 129n., 149, 178, 188, 190-191, 219
Union of South Africa, 26, 31-36, 38, 73, 166n., 237, 240-243
United Arab Republic (UAR), *see* Egypt
U.S. Central Intelligence Agency (CIA), 66, 86, 88-89, 94-96, 96n., 97, 97n., 98-99, 107n., 108-109, 130, 137, 137n., 138, 145, 149, 174, 174n., 185, 201, 208, 210,

U.S. C.I.A. (*cont.*)
210n., 226, 229, 229n., 230-231, 239-240, 242, 280, 292, 299
U.S. Congress, 60, 161, 177-178, 183-184, 207, 212, 225, 292; House Foreign Affairs Committee, 140, 177; Senate Foreign Relations Committee, 140, 159, 177; Africa Subcommittee of Senate Foreign Relations Committee, 117, 159
U.S. Defense Department (Pentagon), 108, 130, 139, 142, 166, 166n., 183-184, 226-227, 230, 246, 283, 292, 298-299
U.S. Health, Education and Welfare Department (HEW), 122, 122n.
U.S. State Department, 44, 47, 49, 53, 57, 65, 76, 78, 80, 90n., 103-104, 110, 130, 132, 136, 136n., 137-138, 148-150, 158-161, 163-164, 166, 169, 174, 180, 181n., 183, 187n., 189-190, 207, 212, 241, 243, 246, 248, 283, 292, 298-299; Agency for International Development (AID), 173-174, 205, 205n.; Bureau of African Affairs, 43, 45, 51, 54, 76, 105, 146, 153, 159-160, 166, 172, 176, 182-183, 186, 221n., 223, 225, 227, 235, 243, 245, 249, 283, 298; Bureau of Intelligence and Research, 160, 186, 193; Bureau of International Organizations (U.N. Bureau), 115, 130, 159, 166, 183, 207, 249; Bureau of West European Affairs (European Bureau), 45, 76-77, 131, 139, 166, 184, 298; International Cooperation Administration (ICA), 53
U.S. National Security Council (NSC), 166, 183
U.S. and Foreign Securities, 34-35, 50
USS WASP, 60-61
United Nations, 26-27, 46, 57-62, 64, 66, 72, 74-75, 78-80, 82, 84, 101, 107-108, 116, 125-126, 129, 134, 139, 141-145, 147-150, 152-194, 199, 211-214, 226, 231, 234n., 257, 262, 264, 267-268, 281, 289-291; Appeal for Children, 126; Civilian Operation in the Congo, 94-95; Conciliation Commission, 115; "Congo Club," 87n.; Consultative Committee (Congo Advisory Committee), 87, 187, 213; Educational, Scientific, and Cultural Organization (UNESCO), 125; Force (UNF), 64, 70, 74-75, 77n., 79, 84, 91, 111, 136, 145, 153, 155, 157-158, 165, 187, 189, 199, 205, 207, 212, 226, 229n.; General Assembly, 43, 60n., 101, 103-104, 107, 109-110, 110n., 111n., 144, 165, 177; Operation in the Congo (ONUC), 99, 101-102, 104, 111, 162, 177, 179, 189, 226; and overthrow of Lumumba, in Secretariat, 85-99; Secretariat, 87-88, 98, 101-102, 104, 115, 154, 165, 167, 190, 226; Secretary-General, *see* Hammarskjold, Dag, *and* Thant, U; Security Council, 60n., 62-65, 74, 77, 110n., 136, 138, 142-144, 162, 164-165, 187, 207, 229n.
Uranium, 23, 28, 47

Van Bilsen, A. J., 88, 90
Van den Haag, Ernest, 172
Van der Meersch, John, 34, 173, 175
Vandewalle, Frédéric, 228n., 238-241, 251n., 252, 252n.
Verhaegen, Benoît, 88, 201, 205n., 220, 239n., 272n.
Vietnam, 142n., 162, 194, 223, 225, 275, 280, 300, 302; *see also* Indochina
Von Horn, Carl, 89n., 91

Wachuku, 254
Wadsworth, James J., 104-105, 107, 111
Watts, John, 50
Weiss, Herbert, 259-261
Welensky, Roy, 73, 148-149, 167, 187
West Africa, 20, 31, 269

West Germany, 25
Wheeler, Earle, 248
White House staff, 168-169, 173, 182, 192-193, 286, 292
Whitney, J. H., Company, 34
Wieschoff, Heinz, 60n., 87
Wiesel, Sam, 242n.
Wilcox, Francis, 298
Williams, Frank, 242n.
Williams, G. Mennen, 117, 122, 122n., 125, 125n., 130-131, 134, 138, 140-141, 146, 153, 160, 179, 205n., 223, 243, 298
Wilson, Woodrow, 297
World Bank, 53, 128n.

Yarborough, Senator, 159
Yergan, Max, 168, 171
Yost, Charles, 249
Youlou, Fulbert, 72-73, 86, 88, 94
Young Americans for Freedom, 168, 172
Young, Crawford, 197, 221-222
Yugoslavia, 52

Zhukov, G. K., 81
Zola, E., 232
Zolberg, Aristide, 287

American Foreign Policy
in the Congo, 1960–1964

Designed by R. E. Rosenbaum.
Composed by Vail-Ballou Press, Inc.,
in 10 point linotype Times Roman, 3 points leaded,
with display lines in monotype Perpetua.
Printed letterpress from type by Vail-Ballou Press.
Bound by Vail-Ballou Press
in Columbia book cloth
and stamped in All Purpose foil.